A dual Premiership player an... **Bachar Houli** has created w... Road and the MCG. Houli's ... bedrock of his career – from yo... Club in Melbourne's western .... and captaining the Vic Metro Under-16 team, to the 2006 AFL draft that saw him join Essendon, and on to becoming one of Richmond's best players of the AFL era. His honours and achievements include: 2008 NAB Rising Star nominee; 2011 Fred Swift Medal; 2019 All-Australian; 2019 Yiooken Award; 2020 Victorian representative – State of Origin for Bushfire Relief match.

Off the field, Bachar is the AFL's first devout Muslim player. He has helped bring to life a number of initiatives that have generated great community impact: the Bachar Houli Cup, an inter-Islamic schools football competition; the Bachar Houli Academy, a football talent program established to nurture young Islamic footballers aspiring to follow in his footsteps as a player and person; and the Bachar Houli Foundation, that aims to support social cohesion and build young leaders within the Muslim community.

Walkley Award-winning broadcaster, author, academic and musician **Waleed Aly** is co-host of network TEN's *The Project* and co-presenter of ABC RN's *The Minefield*. Among his accolades and achievements are: being named as one of *The Bulletin* magazine's 'Smart 100' in 2007; participating in the Prime Minister's 2020 Summit in 2008; Victoria's Local Hero in the 2011 Australian of the Year Awards for his work in fostering cross-cultural understanding in the community; the 2016 Gold Logie Award for the Most Popular Australian TV Personality and Silver Logie Award for Best Presenter; the 2017 Silver Logie for Best Presenter; and delivering the 2016 Andrew Olle Media Lecture. He lectures in politics at Monash University, working in its Global Terrorism Research Centre. Waleed is a regular panellist on the ABC's Sunday morning sports show *Offsiders*, a columnist with *The Age* and the *Sydney Morning Herald*, and a regular contributor to the *New York Times*.

BACHAR HOULI

with WALEED ALY

FAITH, FOOTBALL & FAMILY

PENGUIN BOOKS

PENGUIN BOOKS

UK | USA | Canada | Ireland | Australia
India | New Zealand | South Africa | China

Penguin Books is part of the Penguin Random House group of companies
whose addresses can be found at global.penguinrandomhouse.com.

Penguin
Random House
Australia

First published by Ebury Press, 2020
This edition published by Penguin Books, 2021

Text copyright © Bachar Houli and Waleed Aly, 2020

The moral right of the authors has been asserted.

Cover design by James Rendall © Penguin Random House Australia
Front cover photograph by Julian Kingma
Text design by Midland Typesetters, Australia
Typeset in 12.5/18 pt Bembo by Midland Typesetters, Australia
Every effort has been made to trace creators and copyright holders of the
photographic material included in this book. The publisher welcomes
hearing from anyone not correctly acknowledged.

Printed and bound in Australia by Griffin Press, part of Ovato, an accredited
ISO ANZ/NZS 14001 Environmental Management Systems printer

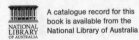

A catalogue record for this
book is available from the
National Library of Australia

ISBN 978 0 14379 643 5

penguin.com.au

MIX
Paper from
responsible sources
FSC® C009448

For my family and community who have ridden every bump.
For those who are different, who know that being different
isn't a roadblock but an advantage.
For my heroes who are striving for that great off-field
premiership of unity and solidarity in our society.

This is for you.

CONTENTS

FOREWORD

BACHAR HOULI MADE HIS first speaking appearance at a school as an Essendon player in his first week on the job. A young man at the back of the class began talking disruptively. Bachar called him to the front and made him apologise to his classmates. But Bachar wasn't finished. 'Now promise me you'll go home tonight and tell your mum and dad you love them,' he said.

I first heard this story from an AFL employee in early 2007, just before Bachar made his debut. It had become quietly famous in those parts because no one had seen anything quite like it before. Who was this guy? Which 18-year-old kid who has barely even attended a training session as an AFL player, let alone played a game, does something like this? I loved the story then for exactly the same reason I love it now: it captures Bachar in miniature.

First, it's so fantastically Lebanese. Family looms large in

Lebanese culture, and love and respect for parents are probably the crowning feature. Even the most misbehaving child will submit to this idea. People might go astray in many ways, but someone who is rude to or neglectful of his or her parents is truly lost. So when Bachar chose to conclude this moment like this, he wasn't doing something off-beat or beside the point. He was turning to what, for him, was the obvious and natural full stop. He was reminding the boy of one of the most foundational, anchoring principles he could think of – directing him to remember who he was, to consult his moral compass and reorientate himself.

But there was also a lightness to it, because Bachar had changed the subject to something on which he presumed everyone agreed. Bachar didn't even bother to ask whether or not the boy loved his parents – that was assumed, because anything else was unthinkable. The only necessary reminder was for the boy to tell them. I imagine him saying it in the way a parent might say, after reprimanding their young child, 'Now, go on outside and play.' It's even a touch playful – I think of Bachar rustling the boy's hair as he speaks.

It's inevitable that family is a major theme in this book. It's not deliberately this way; it just pours forth when Bachar starts talking about his life. To talk to him even briefly is to understand that family is among the things he values most. To talk to him at length is to discover how profoundly it infuses every aspect of his story. It's at the heart of his decision to take up football as a kid, and his progression to the highest level of the game. It's central to his deepest relationships in football, with people like Damien Hardwick, Ivan Maric and Trent Cotchin.

It's the thing that allowed him to meet, and then court, Rouba, who became his wife.

Wherever you look in Bachar's story there's an aunty, or an uncle, or a friend who might as well be. There's a sibling, or a cousin, or a Lebanese neighbour whose relationship with Bachar is thoroughly fraternal. You might think these people are all similar. They're not. They are diverse in age, in temperament, in their attitudes towards life. This is probably the key to understanding Bachar. He knows who he is and what he believes, but he's comfortable around people who are thoroughly different, because he spent his childhood forming thick, life-defining bonds with them. And he's mature beyond his years because he has spent his life with older people. When Bachar addressed that school group in his first week as an AFL player, he was 18 on paper, but more like 28 in spirit. That was why he exuded an easy authority.

But probably the most remarkable aspect of the classroom encounter is that he's there at all. He'd have been forgiven, at that age, for being consumed with figuring out how to survive his first few training sessions, and yet he was making himself available for community work. But then, Bachar walked into an environment that made his whole career a form of community work. He must be the most hyped number 42 draft pick in AFL history. Even before his debut, his media file would comfortably have matched that of Bryce Gibbs or Tom Hawkins, the highest-profile draftees from his year. There was no doubt Bachar could play; his press was more a function of social curiosity, as he was the first practising Muslim selected to play at the highest level. There is an argument that the attention was overblown. At one level, that is unquestionable. But wasn't that true of almost every news story with a Muslim protagonist at the time?

Bachar was drafted in 2006, little over a year after the London Tube bombings, which introduced the notion of homegrown terrorism to the public imagination. Four months later, the Operation Pendennis raids in Melbourne and Sydney franked that fear, part of the biggest counter-terrorism investigation in Australian history, which led eventually to eighteen terrorism convictions. This was a time of heightened, frenzied, public anxiety about multiculturalism, and especially about young Muslim men. Bachar had simply walked into that zeitgeist. In a troubled time, he was an ambassador by circumstance, irrespective of choice. He knew that before he was even drafted.

I remember the Friday night in May 2007 when Bachar made his AFL debut against North Melbourne. I remember feeling, as I walked into what was then called the Telstra Dome, that something momentous was happening. I remember being nervous, like I had something major at stake. And I suppose, like so many Australian Muslims, I did. The AFL is a unique stage in Australian society. Muslims had been cast as villains on so many public stages for so long. This felt like a rare opportunity for one of us to be cast as a hero. I remember seeing Bachar line up next to Michael Firrito, who seemed twice his size in every direction, and thinking he just looked so out of place. But he wasn't. And that was the whole point.

For the most part, Bachar entered the game with a sense of genuine goodwill surrounding him. The Bomber Shop at Windy Hill had sold out of Bachar Houli badges. So did the stand at the Telstra Dome on the night of the game. Even *The Footy Show* claimed to have adopted him the night before, as they announced Bachar's debut selection. It wasn't all smooth sailing, of course. The topic was out of Sam Newman's comfort zone, who looked up wide-eyed at the cheering studio audience and asked if they were Muslims, as if he were sniffing out a fifth column. Only Trevor Marmalade seemed at ease when he quipped that Essendon would win the toss and kick towards Mecca. But it was a start.

Bachar marked and goaled with the first kick of his career, and the crowd let out a prolonged roar. He was mobbed by teammates; the feeling among those near me suggested a rare brand of excitement. An errant handpass in the last quarter did not draw anger, but sympathy. He followed up with a strong tackle and was applauded warmly. And me? I rode every moment of Bachar's game. I called for him to run into open space, I tensed as he held that mark, I pumped my fists as he kicked that goal. That was me out there.

Thirteen years later, I'm speaking with Damien Hardwick, the man who has coached Bachar at Richmond to two premierships and All-Australian selection, and who personally selected Bachar to play under him for Victoria. 'Dustin Martin's won two Norm Smiths,' Hardwick tells me. 'But ever since I've been at the footy club, Bachar Houli's been our best-performed finals player. Period.' It's an arresting thing to hear when commentators are seriously debating whether Dusty is the best finals player ever, but Hardwick says it with total ease, fully aware of how counterintuitive it sounds, and fully confident in his declaration. He even has an explanation, rooted in the fact that Bachar's just so used to carrying the weight of expectation. 'I feel Bachar always plays with that,' he says. 'I just always feel like he's playing for a greater purpose.'

Islam is central to that, both as a creed that shapes Bachar's values and behaviour, and as an identity marker that makes him a representative of so many. Football's an aspect of his life, but it's not the sum of it. Islam clearly sits above, providing purpose and perspective, and his story cannot be told without it. At every stage, through success and failure, injury and health, during Ramadan and outside of it, Bachar describes his approach in Islamic language, drawing on Islamic concepts, constantly asking himself what it is that Islamic teachings about character demand of him. And that's what gives his football a greater purpose: to introduce his teammates, his coaches and even the fans to Islam in a way they so rarely get to see it, and to model for those in his community a way of being a proud Muslim who doesn't compromise himself but who is also proudly Australian. I think Bachar's instinctively a teacher. Once you know him, that classroom is exactly where you'd expect him to spend his first week as an AFL player.

That's how he's blazed trails. He's taught AFL clubs to incorporate things like fasting and Islam's prescribed daily prayers into their training and match-day schedules as needed. He's even taught a few of his coaches that Islam makes him a better footballer, not a compromised one. What Bachar can't really say, and may not even know, is that he's made life a little bit easier for Muslims in all kinds of community football clubs, who might now have a way of being open about Ramadan with their coaches, or finding a place to pray when one of the prayer times arrives. And Bachar's opened up countless conversations with teammates and coaches that have made them genuinely respectful, fascinated by what he believes and does in a way they never could have been, had their window into Islam been media coverage alone. In turn, he's made countless conversations between Muslims and their colleagues in all walks of life that tiny bit easier because he's broken the ice for them by being so clear about who he is.

We're lucky he was the first. It might have been someone less talented, someone clubs saw as too much trouble and simply discarded. It might have been someone less confident, too timid to mention those moments when football and Islamic practice intersect, leaving the next Muslim AFL player to explain why they're raising issues their predecessor didn't. It might have been someone less trusted and trustworthy, suspected of using a religious practice such as, say, fasting as a way of taking shortcuts with training. Or it might have been someone whose approach to Islam is less traditional, engendering an expectation that every other Muslim should be willing to make compromises. But it was destined to be Bachar. He ended up exactly where he should be, where he needed to be.

Sometimes it takes someone of extraordinary talent to allow their people the chance to be ordinary.

Waleed Aly
July 2020

1

STANDING UP

IT'S 15 MINUTES INTO the third quarter of the 2017 Preliminary Final. We're about a goal in front. I run off the ground, but instead of going to the bench I run straight down into the changerooms. I have something to do.

I've never played in a game like this. It is unquestionably the biggest of my career, and it's a game that will probably never be repeated. I've never seen the MCG like this before. It's not just that there are more than 94,000 people here. We're playing Greater Western Sydney, a new club with few supporters, so we have practically the whole place to ourselves. That already makes the day unique, but the fact Richmond is enduring a 37-year premiership drought, and hasn't even made a Grand Final for 35 years, puts it over the top. In fact, the Tigers have only played in two other Preliminary Finals in that time, and on both occasions got completely smashed. This time we are favourites.

The Tiger Army is always famously loud, but on this day they let out the pent-up frustration and pain of more than three decades. It is a unique moment. Even if we play GWS in the same game in coming years, and even if we draw the same crowd, it can never be the same. Not for another 35 years, at least.

But this game is also unusual for another reason: the timing. It is a twilight game with a late start time of 4:45 pm; during the season, the twilight games would start at 3:20 pm. That might seem trivial, but for me it makes a huge difference. It means the game falls across the daily prayer times about as awkwardly as it possibly can.

It's well known that Muslims pray five times a day. The prayers are spaced across the day, each occurring in a specific period of time: before sunrise (called *fajr*); just after the sun has passed its highest point (called *dhuhr*); in the midafternoon, as the shadows are lengthening (called *asr*); at sunset (called *maghrib*); and finally once the twilight has gone (called *isha*).

Each of these is a window of time rather than a specific moment. So, for example, you can pray *dhuhr* any time from when it begins until the start time for the next prayer. That gives you a window of a few hours to do something that might take five minutes. Because of the way the prayers are spaced out, some windows of time are longer than others. *Dhuhr* has a big window, especially in the summer, when the days are long. But the sunset prayer, *maghrib*, is always really short.

That's a problem in this twilight Preliminary Final. Today, *maghrib* runs from about 6:15 pm to 7:40 pm. The timing couldn't be worse, really, because it was too early to pray at

2

half time, and it will be too late to pray after the game. So I have no option but to find some time during the game. And that time turns out to be 15 minutes into the third quarter. I figured that was better than trying to squeeze it in at three-quarter time, in case the coach needed to speak to me or I needed a rubdown or something. When you're on the bench, you're not really needed. It's your time.

I'd started the second half on the ground, knowing that *maghrib* would start around the time of my first rotation. As I approach the bench, I look towards the property steward. 'I'll be real quick,' I say, and then I run down the stairs, grab a towel, orient it towards Mecca, calm myself and begin. A few minutes later I re-emerge and we kick an avalanche of goals that ultimately decides the game and launches us into our first Grand Final for 35 years.

This was a significant moment for me. It came at a crucial point in the biggest game of my life, the kind where you could easily imagine that nothing matters more. And yet for me it was important to live my belief that there was some-thing that really did matter more. It meant a lot to me as a Muslim that I was able to remove myself from the chaos of the game and focus.

It might be hard for non-Muslims to understand that. Perhaps it begins to make sense once you understand just how important those compulsory prayers are in Islam. In fact, calling them 'prayers' probably obscures how central they are, because 'prayer' might sound like a voluntary thing people do before bedtime when they ask God for whatever they want. Muslims have that practice too, but in Arabic it's called *du'a*, which is often translated as 'invocation' or 'supplication'; the word is derived from an Arabic verb meaning 'to call out' to someone. The five daily prayers are called something else – *salat* – which carries a different meaning.

Unlike *du'a*, *salat* has prescribed words and movements that are exactly as the prophet Muhammad used. These are the prayers you might have seen on television, where big congregations gather behind an imam, who recites passages from the Qur'an, with the people bowing and prostrating in unison. It is much more a ritual than *du'a*, and is even preceded by a ritual ablution, called *wudu*, where we wash our hands, arms, faces and feet. This is not simply a way of being clean before you face God, but is also a psychological preparation for what is to come – a kind of transit lounge between one world and the next.

Salat is a rich word, because while it does mean 'prayer', it originates from a word that means 'contact' or 'connection', so it carries that meaning too. This captures the idea that *salat* is the foundation of a Muslim's connection with God. 'The closest a person is to his Lord is when he is in prostration,' said the Prophet. That's the reason that prayer takes place five times throughout the day at appointed times: it ensures that this connection is constantly being renewed, that we don't bury it beneath all the worldly aspects of life that tend to overwhelm and distract us.

And so, every few hours, I pause what I'm doing just briefly and take time to reflect. It's like a reset for the next part of my day. If there's a moment I want to stray, prayer is the thing that brings me back. It reminds me.

That's why *salat* has the status of being the second 'pillar' of Islam. In a famous statement by the Prophet, he lists the Five Pillars of Islam, apparently in order of their frequency. The first is the *shahadah* – the basic declaration of faith that there is one God and that Muhammad is His prophet. That, of course, exists at every moment. Then there's *salat*, which happens five times daily. After that come fasting during Ramadan and paying a compulsory proportion of one's wealth to charity, a duty called *zakat*, both of which happen annually. And last is the pilgrimage to Mecca, *hajj*, which Muslims are obliged to do once in their life. That's how important *salat* is. Without it, the whole structure of Islam falls down.

Fulfilling the duty of *salat* is simple enough when you're surrounded by mosques and the call to prayer rings out across the city throughout the day. It's easy in places where a society's rhythm is built around these regular pauses, and everyone understands how it works. But it can be a very different story when you're part of a minority Muslim community.

Every Muslim living in the West knows the feeling of trying to find somewhere to pray when a prayer time arrives and you're nowhere convenient – when you're out and about in the middle of the city, for instance, surrounded only by people, streets and laneways, or in the middle of a shopping centre, and time is fast ticking away. It creates a unique feeling of tension, impatience and discomfort, because you know that sooner or later you'll have to bite the bullet and pray somewhere where it will be difficult to explain what you're doing. You can delay it all you like, but the moment will arrive.

All Muslims have stories of praying in a stairwell, a carpark or the sick bay at work, or even in an empty elevator, just hoping that no one presses the button to call the lift. Parks are often a good option, though you might need to find some strategically placed shrubs or trees so you'll be concealed. Clothing store fitting rooms are often good, although it can be a bit strange when you're in prostration if there's a big gap between the bottom of the door and the floor. When I was about 14 I would use a secluded spot behind the clubrooms at my footy club. I've also prayed at the Royal Melbourne Show when it was teeming with people, and on the side of the freeway during peak hour.

There's a lot to consider. Where are you least likely to have someone walk in on you? And if they do, where will you look least suspicious? And what if you haven't done *wudu* yet? Where are you going to find a place to wash your feet? That's definitely the hardest bit. There's nothing more embarrassing than getting caught by someone with your foot in the sink.

Some people are more comfortable being seen praying in public than others. I'm probably more comfortable with it than most, but even so it's a sensitive thing, because in a place like Australia, with the public image of Muslims being what it is, you're potentially making yourself a target. People can be prejudiced or even scared when they see Muslims praying in public because they associate it with something sinister – and then who knows what might happen? That's why possibly the least comfortable place I've had to pray was in the waiting area at an airport. I could just tell people were thinking I was about to hijack the plane.

I'd always prayed as a kid, but by the time I was 14 or 15 I was taking *salat* really seriously. I went to Werribee Islamic College, so for me – unlike for a lot of other Muslim kids in Australia – figuring out how to pray at school never presented a problem. But as I went further in football, it became clear that I'd be interacting more and more with people who'd never even seen a Muslim pray. That forced me into a position where I needed to become more confident in my faith, more ready for the questions that would inevitably come my way. The turning point happened in 2004, when I was 16.

I was captaining the under-16 Vic Metro squad in Adelaide for the national carnival, and rooming with two teammates, Daniel Beckwith and James Arundale. Previously on these sorts of tours I'd roomed with my dad, who'd take the week off work to come with me. But this time that wasn't an option.

Daniel was a fairly quiet kid who was about my size, but James was a man-child – thickset, tall and very strong – who played the game hard. He was from the Dandenong Stingrays, so I figured he'd grown up in a pretty tough area. Above all, he was intimidating. And he was the kind of kid who was always the life of the party, who'd have the music blaring at the first available opportunity.

How was I going to pray in front of these guys? How would I even explain the basic concept to them? What possible explanation could I give for performing these strange movements which they'd probably only ever seen on some bad news story, except by connecting it to the concept of a god they probably didn't believe in? I don't think they even knew I was a Muslim, so I was coming from a long way back.

Our hotel room was an open space with our beds, with a bathroom attached. *Salat* has to be performed somewhere clean, so I could hardly use the toilet, and there were no other quiet or secluded areas I could use. The afternoon was rushing along, and it was time to pray. I was getting *that* feeling. Time was running out. And eventually I'd had enough. For my prayer to have any point, I knew, I needed to feel comfortable. I had to front-foot it and discuss with Daniel and James what I was about to do. So I did.

I was captain of the squad, and had been for a few years. Yet although I was never the most vocal, I had the respect of my teammates. That made the prospect of talking about my prayer with them slightly easier. But I'd also never done anything like this before. When I played club footy, my prayer ritual on match days consisted of going to that quiet spot behind the changerooms. During footy camps I'd run off into the bushes to pray. This was the first time I had no escape.

We sat on the edge of the sofa bed. Daniel was listening, but the conversation naturally went mostly in James's direction. First I explained the basics of Islam, and eventually I got to the point of explaining the daily prayers. I told James that when I pray I need quiet so I can focus, and I asked if he wouldn't mind turning the music down. Now I wasn't just letting him know what I was doing – I was asking him to be quiet!

'Do you mind us watching?' James asked.

I couldn't say no, so away we went. And I felt the pressure to put on a show. *Make it really sincere*, I told myself – which of course makes little sense, given that praying sincerely to God is the opposite of a performance for a roommate. *Should I make it a long one?* I wondered. *Or would that make things more uncomfortable? And once I'm finished, should I just sit in contemplation for a while, or should I get up straightaway and ask James what he reckons?*

In the end, I just did it. Luckily, the direction of Mecca was towards the door, not towards them. I'm not sure I had complete concentration in my prayer because I was so conscious of James and Daniel watching me.

Being watched doesn't bother me so much now, but at the time it brought home to me just how much in life seems to be about how people see us – how obsessed we are with others' perceptions. These days I want people to see what they don't know: that the practice of praying is an inherently humble, peaceful one; that it's defined by placing yourself at the lowest possible level in front of the One who is Highest. That's who I am. That's who we are. Our actions should emanate peace and submission. Prostration is an expression of the sincerity in a person's heart, and points to something greater. It's quite a thing to experience. I think that, on some level, open-hearted people pick that up.

'That was amazing!' James said when I had finished. 'That was so peaceful, what you just did. Do people know about what you do?'

'Nah,' I said. 'This is really the first time I've ever exposed what I do.'

'Why are you shy about this?' he went on. 'It's who you are! You should be proud of that. Why don't you start teaching people this stuff? I think it's important.'

James's reaction is probably still the best review I've had. The fact that it was coming from the mouth of a 16-year-old – and specifically a straight-down-the-line, tell-it-like-it-is, rough-as-guts 16-year-old – meant that it affected me profoundly. It was a genuine turning point in my life.

Suddenly I felt confident that I could handle this from now on. And I accepted that my life was forcing me to learn more about my religion and myself. If I was going to be open about being a Muslim, I decided, I'd have to be up to the task.

2

ODD MAN IN

By the time I got drafted, everyone knew me as a 'devout Muslim'. When I attended the draft camp in 2006, all the recruiters who interviewed me asked about my religion. I was fielding questions on how Ramadan worked, and what would happen when prayer times fell during games.

I understood why they were asking. These clubs were considering investing heavily in me as a player, and they needed to know their investment wouldn't be undermined by practices they weren't familiar with. So it was reasonable that they'd be concerned about how things like praying and fasting would affect my training standards or my game-day performance. It was really no different to the range of lifestyle questions that are still always part of these interviews, exploring how people approach school or life at home, so clubs can figure out how they might impact a person's football.

Even so, and even having fronted up to my Vic Metro teammates and taken ownership of these issues, it was still a pretty intimidating experience. Here were these grown men in positions of authority drilling me with questions that went to the heart of who I was. And here was I, an 18-year-old kid, proud of who he was but knowing his career lay in their hands, having to come up with answers that were true to myself but wouldn't cost me my dream. We were a very long way away from the 15-minute mark of the third quarter in the 2017 Preliminary Final.

'It's okay, I can pray after the game or whatever,' I would say. 'I can break my fast if I have to. It won't affect the game.' I'd answer very confidently, but when I look back now I think I could only have been half sure of myself.

I don't know how believable I was or how many doubts they were left with. It's possible that some clubs decided not to take a punt on me because of these things. All I know is that at least one club wasn't deterred, because finally, at pick 42 in the 2006 National Draft, Essendon read out my name. I'd made it — to the beginning, at least. And I'd made it on something like my own terms.

I'd landed at a great club. Essendon had around a dozen Indigenous players at the time, so I was in an environment that was used to handling diversity to some extent. A lot of that was down to Kevin Sheedy, who was a pioneer for inclusion, particularly with Indigenous players, and who had established a club culture that took these things seriously.

Sheeds genuinely believed that one of football's great strengths was its ability to bring people together who'd come to Australia from all over the world. He expected the club's players and staff to embrace others for who they were, and encouraged people from minority cultures to express their cultural heritage. One way I chose to do that was to bring in something Mum had cooked or maybe some Lebanese sweets every month or so. The coaches were always excited to receive them. It might not sound like much, but it created a bond between us.

I felt like Sheeds understood me. When he gave me my senior debut in 2007, he went to the trouble of explaining to the playing group why this was a significant moment for the Muslim community and the AFL. Sheeds loved storytelling, and mine was exactly the kind of story he loved. I'm not sure everyone at the club got why Sheeds cared so much about this stuff, but it certainly made a difference to me. My belief that Sheeds was a big supporter helped my football enormously.

When Sheeds left at the end of my first year, that encouraging culture within the club withered away. I brought in those Lebanese sweets a couple more times in 2008, but they weren't as warmly received. Eventually, I stopped.

While I would have liked for it to have lasted longer than one year, my time with Sheeds laid an invaluable foundation for me. As we approached Indigenous Round in my first season, for instance, we had a session where the Indigenous players were asked to address the playing group on their 'tribe' – where they came from and what they represented. I wasn't sure exactly why – maybe because, as a Lebanese Muslim, I was 'different' enough – but the coaches thought it would be good for me to contribute as well, so I was asked

13

to talk to the whole playing group about my way of life and what I believed in.

It was a different time to today, when football has many different multicultural programs and players have all become at least a little familiar with cultural diversity. Back in 2007, however, the AFL had never even held a Multicultural Round. Some players might never even have met a Muslim before, and might know nothing about Islam. Think of it as my James conversation multiplied by forty-odd teammates.

It was the first time I'd stood up in front of a large group to talk about something so personal and so important to me. That's not the easiest thing, but it helped enormously that it was happening in a context of people sharing their stories and learning about each other. People's hearts were already open, and they weren't in a judgemental mood.

I can't say the content I presented was especially earth-shattering. I spoke about the basics of Islam, focusing mostly on the Five Pillars of Islamic practice. The most significant thing to come out of it was that my teammates felt they now had permission to talk to me about my faith. The result was a stream of informal conversations around the club whenever we had some idle time. Sheeds wanted us to 'go and learn and find out' about different cultures, and my teammates did. I was happy to oblige them, as I felt it was my duty to answer questions if people had them, even if these weren't conversations I particularly wanted to instigate.

Naturally, some players showed more interest than others. I had regular conversations with Mark and Jason Johnson, Adam McPhee and Henry Slattery, and over time I ended up becoming closest to them. Very often they'd start asking questions while we were in the hot-and-cold tubs after training, when we were in a relaxed mood. You know, just your usual sauna conversation about religion.

The timing was probably good, too. By 2007 it felt like the War on Terror was in a bit of a lull. The London Tube bombings were nearly two years in the past, and the war in Iraq wasn't dominating the news as it once had. Things were still happening, but for me as a Muslim, life in Australia didn't feel anywhere near as intense as it had for most of the time since the September 11 attacks.

That timing probably influenced the kind of questions my teammates would ask. They didn't ask me much about politics, for example, but they were keen to learn about the day-to-day life of a practising Muslim. Of course, that meant the usual stuff on fasting and praying. Interestingly, I found that my teammates were more interested in knowing *why* I did these things, while the coaches tended to be more focused on *how*.

I really liked the players' approach. First, it showed that they had a genuine interest, and wanted to have a discussion with some depth. I could tell by the way they looked me in the eye that they were attentive, that they were leaning in. And when we left these conversations, we certainly had a greater respect for each other than we did before.

Second, I believe it's important for Muslims to have a sense of why we do what we do. Religion shouldn't be the mindless repetition of rituals – it should be actively lived, and that's best done when you have a clear sense of purpose. So I found myself talking about what makes prayer important, and what

I get out of it. Or I'd talk about how fasting can be spiritually rewarding – how it heightens your awareness of your own limitations and your dependence on God, and how it leads you to feel gratitude for what you have and empathy for those who have less.

Beyond that, my teammates were keenly interested in halal food, alcohol and sex. That shouldn't have been surprising, I guess, because, for young men particularly, those three things make up a huge part of life.

The food questions – 'Why don't you eat pork? What's halal meat?' – were probably least mind-blowing for them, although they seemed surprised to hear about the fact that the Old Testament has similar prescriptions, which is why there's so much similarity between Jews and Muslims on this. I suspect it was the first time they'd learned that the rules around halal slaughtering are carefully designed to inflict as little pain as possible on the animal, given the bad press halal meat receives because of some really dubious practices around the world. The Islamic idea that you shouldn't slaughter one animal in front of another because it causes stress, or even allow an animal to see the knife before it's slaughtered, is a million miles away from what people usually think, and what is too often practised.

Conversations about sex were much more startling.

'What? Are you a virgin? No way!'

Like just about all religions, Islam prohibits sex outside marriage. It's true that lots of people within those religions don't observe the rule; indeed, with our society becoming less and less religious, almost no one does. And when you're talking about young male footballers, it's a safe guess that almost none of them had ever thought that kind of abstinence was possible. Even the fact that I intended to get married young, like a lot of Muslims do, didn't make it easier for them to understand. If anything, that just made it even weirder, because I was an 18-year-old talking about marriage. I didn't feel like they were judging me for it – if anything, they were strangely impressed. It was more that they felt utter disbelief – as if I were from another planet.

When I got engaged in my second year of AFL football, at the age of 20, my teammates couldn't quite believe it. 'You're too young!' they said. 'You haven't even experienced what's out there – and you haven't moved in with her.' But the idea of 'experiencing what's out there' was just as odd to me. My attitude was that women weren't to be 'experiences' that you played around with and then left behind. I wanted to invest in someone.

Within the Muslim community, my approach was probably pretty standard. That whole 'locker-room talk' thing of guys bragging to each other about their conquests was completely foreign to me, because Muslims – at least the ones I knew – would never have that kind of conversation. But this wasn't the Muslim community, so there was no doubt who the strange one in this situation was.

Despite all that, nothing was quite as significant a point of difference as alcohol. When you don't drink, it becomes clear pretty quickly just how central alcohol is to life in Australia. It's everywhere. It's like Australians don't celebrate anything, mourn anything, socialise with others or unwind alone without alcohol. It's appropriate that a euphemism for being drunk is being 'well lubricated', because that's kind of how alcohol works in Australia: it lubricates so many of our social interactions.

That had serious implications for me at a new footy club. My peers were all fellow draftees, teenagers with few responsibilities and lots of time. They loved a night out, with all the drinking that entailed. Even in 2007, football wasn't quite as professional as it is now, so a fair bit of social 'lubricating' went on.

I felt extremely uncomfortable in that environment. Muslims approach this issue with different attitudes and varying degrees of strictness, but I knew that being around alcohol was deeply unsettling for me – like I was somehow wronging myself. I even found it difficult to attend club functions where alcohol was being served, but at that stage of my career I felt I had no choice.

All this meant that when I did have a choice, I'd stay away. I didn't go out partying with my fellow young teammates, and I never really identified with them much because I'd spent my whole life hanging out with older people. If anything, my lifestyle was far more aligned with that of my older teammates, but the culture of footy clubs doesn't really facilitate friendships between the different generations because senior players are often very busy with their families, and they tend not to open their social circles to kids who've barely played a game. There's a hierarchy in most football clubs based on experience and status as a player, and I found this foreign as it didn't exist in the other areas of my life. But it was common for senior players to show the young players the natural order of things by imposing themselves physically on them during practice games – it was a way of demanding respect. That certainly happened to me.

So at Essendon, while I'd have dinner with those players I mentioned earlier every fortnight or so, and I would definitely have called them friends, I didn't ever have really close friends whose friendship I knew would last well beyond football. I found myself in a sort of no man's land between the younger and older players, and I have no doubt that my aversion to alcohol, coupled with the fact that it is so ever-present in social situations, was one significant reason for that.

At Richmond it was a similar story for the first four years. I'd attend club functions and feel uncomfortable. I'd go to Mad Monday for the first hour or so, then leave the boys to it. But as I got older, more established and more confident, things started to change. I was more direct with the club about my discomfort, and I think the club trusted me more, so they understood I wasn't trying to avoid my obligations as a player. When I discussed it with the general manager, his response was very understanding and positive. 'You tell us what you need and we'll accommodate it for you,' he said. That's been Richmond's attitude every time we've discussed anything like this.

And my attitude has been to ensure that whatever steps the club takes to accommodate me also work for the club. So I'd avoid most functions with alcohol, but I recognised that there were some where my presence really was imperative: specifically, the season launch and the best-and-fairest presentation. And for the rest I'd come up with alternative arrangements.

There were the sponsorship functions, where people who had contributed to the club financially by sponsoring a particular player come along for a meet-and-greet. As you can imagine, that's a hard one for me to miss, because, like all the other players, there is a particular person or family who sponsors me personally. And they might reasonably take my absence as a bit of a slap in the face. So instead I'd arrange lunch or dinner at the football club with them, our own private event. I think that's been a better arrangement for them, too, because we could actually spend more time getting to know each other. And of course if they wanted to meet the other players, they could still go to the main club function.

The club's understanding filtered through to the players, too. I haven't been to a Mad Monday since 2014. The players know why, and they have no expectation that I'll be there. I can honestly say they completely respect my reasons. You can tell when people are pretending to. Maybe it's part of that special culture of 'connection' and love that we've fostered at Richmond, where we really accept people for who they are, but I can tell they respect my needs fully and from their hearts.

It really is remarkable how big a difference that makes, how much more comfortable I feel, and how much I feel I belong. And the friendships I've formed at Richmond with people like Trent Cotchin and Ivan Maric are the deepest I've known in football. One sign of that is that we don't feel the need to change who we are or compromise ourselves for each other. I think these friendships will last a lifetime.

The obvious starting point for my teammates on the issue of alcohol, especially in those early days at Essendon, was the question of why I don't drink. They knew it was for religious reasons, but they wanted to know what purpose that served. As it happens, much of the answer is fairly predictable. Even people who love a drink understand the damage alcohol can do in just about any setting, from the most public to the most private. They understand, even if only broadly, the potential health effects and the social problems it can unleash. 'They ask you about intoxicants and gambling,' begins the Qur'anic verse at 2:219. 'Say: "In them is great harm, and a benefit for the people; but their harm is greater than their benefit."' That verse almost seems like a transcription of those hot-and-cold bath conversations we had at Windy Hill.

Remarkably, I often found my teammates agreeing with me. Where we differed was that most of them figured they could drink responsibly, so they saw no reason to forgo the enjoyment alcohol brings them. That's why I'd usually be asked something like, 'Why can't you just have one or two drinks?' I have no idea what sort of drinker I would be, but the answer seemed pretty straightforward to me. 'Can you guarantee me I'd only have one or two?' I would ask. As the prophet Muhammad put it, 'Every intoxicant is unlawful and whatever intoxicates in large amounts, then a small quantity of it is forbidden.'

One of the most famous Islamic scholars, a man by the name of al-Ghazali who lived around the eleventh century, argued that Islam aimed to preserve five essential things for human flourishing: religion, life, intellect, lineage and property. That helps explain why Islam takes the question of alcohol so seriously: it compromises the preservation of several of these, but especially the intellect. The Arabic word for intoxicants (*khamr*) is derived from the verb *khamara*, which means to cover something with something else, or to obscure. Alcohol is *khamr* because it covers the mind, it obscures the intellect.

Something special happens when you have serious conversations like this with people. It creates a unique kind of bond, like you're connecting on a level you couldn't otherwise reach. Maybe it's because it requires us to make an effort to understand each other. Or maybe it's because everyone's a bit vulnerable in these situations, whether you're asking questions and hoping they don't cause offence, or you're the one being expected to have all the answers. Especially if something is happening in world events that has the potential to cause a lot of tension.

That's certainly how it was in 2014, when ISIS suddenly started dominating the news. It was a time of great fear and anxiety, and most people felt they had more questions than answers – at least, that's how it felt among my teammates at Richmond. The problem was that they clearly felt reluctant to ask me questions about it, probably for fear of offending me or making me feel attacked.

Mark Williams – or 'Choco', as we called him – was one of our assistant coaches at the time, and he was the kind of person who liked to deal with these sorts of things up front, so he arranged for me to give a speech to the players and staff. Suddenly, there I was, standing in the Graeme Richmond Room at Punt Road, equipped with PowerPoint slides.

I began with the basics, thinking I could then build up to the touchier subjects. As I ran through the Five Pillars of

Islam, the group seemed most moved by *zakat*, the requirement that Muslims give 2.5 per cent of whatever wealth they've held for a year to the needy. The word *zakat* means 'that which purifies', so the idea is that through this giving our wealth is purified – and that in its absence, our wealth is tainted. God may have blessed us with money, but others still have a right to it, because really it all belongs to God and we only hold it on trust. And by making it annual, Islam makes the requirement/practice become a habit.

When I came to the topic of jihad and terrorism, my message was a simple one. I spoke about the Qur'anic verse that 'whoever kills a soul other than for murder or spreading corruption in the Earth, it is as if he has killed all of humanity, and whoever saves one, it is as if he has saved all of humanity' (5:32). Then I ran through the rules of war laid down by the Prophet and the earliest Muslim community: do not kill women, children, the elderly, monks or workers who aren't fighting; do not mutilate dead bodies; do not destroy homes; do not wound animals except for food; do not even cut down trees.

Beyond that, I appealed to what they knew of me. They knew I was a practising Muslim, and that I was serious about it. And they knew I was the opposite of the people they were seeing dominate the news. All I wanted them to understand was that there were very good reasons for that difference. The club obviously thought the presentation was worthwhile, because they have asked me to do it for the first-year players and new staff each season since.

Probably the most important part of my presentation comes at the end. 'I'm sure there will be many more questions to be asked, and I'm sure lots of things will come up,' I say. 'Please, I want you to feel comfortable to come and ask me at any time. Just have the conversation. That's what friendship is about. I'll do my best to answer, and if I don't know something, I'll try to find it out and get back to you.'

Those conversations have become increasingly common at Richmond. Sometimes they arise spontaneously – when we have downtime after dinner on an interstate trip, for example. It begins with one person asking me a question, then other players start listening. Then they join in and ask their own questions. Then more do the same. Soon enough it ends up being like a roundtable discussion that lasts an hour.

All sorts of questions have come my way. Choco once asked me about the Islamic tradition of shaving a baby's hair off at seven days of age, weighing the hair and then giving an equal amount in silver to charity. He really must have been doing his research, because that's something some Muslims might not even know about. (For the record, my wife and I paid the money to charity but didn't shave our daughters' heads, because Rouba couldn't bear to do it!)

I also remember answering questions from Damien Hardwick on the differences between Sunni and Shia Muslims, which of course had become a big issue with ISIS. It wasn't an area I knew a lot about, because although I'm a Sunni Muslim, I'd never really felt any tension with Shias. In fact, one of my brothers married into a Shia family and it was never an issue. So I kept it simple and explained that it was mostly a political difference that began after the prophet Muhammad died – the groups were arguing over who should succeed him as the leader of the Muslim community. The Shia think it should have been someone from the Prophet's family – especially his cousin Ali – while the Sunnis think it should have been whoever was best suited to the job. But in the context of a footy club, we were going pretty deep.

A sign of how far things have come is that Richmond has recently started holding a club *iftar* – the meal at sunset to break fast during Ramadan – at the Islamic Museum of Australia. That's an unusual thing for a club to do, because typically it's left for a corporate organisation – such as the AFL – to handle. The best part was that it wasn't even my idea. Richmond had four Muslim employees for several years. One of them, a woman named Rana Hussain, came up with the *iftar* as a way of helping people at the club understand what Ramadan is and how it fits into a Muslim's life.

Having a formal *iftar* is a pretty immersive cultural experience for most people who work at a footy club. Suddenly they're hearing a recitation of the Qur'an and then the call to prayer, they're learning about the traditions around breaking the fast, and they're seeing the traditions in action and even participating in some of them – well, the bits that involve eating.

We start with dates and water, but then the Muslims pause to pray in congregation. Everyone else is free to dive into the food straightaway, but amazingly some usually choose either to watch the prayer or even join in, which they're welcome to do. Then I give a brief speech explaining how Ramadan works and what makes it special for Muslims, and take any questions, which can sometimes come in a rush and span everything from Ramadan to terrorism. Holding the event at the Islamic Museum encourages the guests to look through the exhibition and learn things they otherwise wouldn't about the history of Muslims in Australia, which goes back a long way – even to Macassan fishermen who'd make yearly visits to the north of the country from about the 1650s.

The club requires first-year players to attend the *iftar* as part of their education – which itself is pretty remarkable – but quite a few of the more senior players come along as well. Usually about a third of the playing list might be there. I can't discount the possibility that they're coming along mostly for the free feed – and the food really is spectacular – but you can never tell who might be interested in the cultural and religious aspects. Imagine having Dusty Martin tell you at training that he 'can't wait for tonight', and then seeing him in the museum, surrounded by Islamic calligraphy as he listens to me do the call to prayer and then takes in a presentation on the spiritual dimensions of fasting. Footy clubs can be incredible places.

But it takes special people to make them so, and I've been extremely fortunate to have some involved in my career at crucial times. One of the most important was waiting for me at Essendon when I first got drafted: John Quinn, the high-performance coach at the time. Quinny had been a running coach who had previously worked with two Algerian Muslim runners. As a result, he was already broadly familiar with how Muslim lives worked and what Muslim athletes might need. And through the club, he was also familiar with working with shy 18-year-old kids. Put that together and he knew instinctively what sort of support I might need as a kid from a minority background in an intimidating environment – even without me thinking to ask him.

'You don't pray anywhere else but in my office,' he said to me out of the blue one day. 'I don't want to hear that you've gone home to pray or anything like that. You pretty much have the key to my room. If I'm here and it's time to pray, you just tell me to piss off!'

That was one way to put it, but I preferred instead to walk into his office and say, 'Hey, Quinny.' That was all I needed to say. He would leave, I would pray and we'd get back to our business. Soon enough he'd gone and got me a prayer mat, which he displayed prominently in his office. 'You don't understand how many people walk into this office and ask me, "What's that?"' he later told me. 'I say, "That's Bachar's prayer mat."'

His thoughtfulness made a huge difference to me. Without John, I'd have been locking myself in the Windy Hill boot room to pray, hoping no one would come past and try to open the door. Imagine having to unlock the door in that situation and explain why you're in there with the door bolted! I didn't have to face that situation because Quinny was setting a culture in place.

Quinny didn't just want to help me out. He wanted to make sure everyone knew what he was doing – that it was what Essendon did. And it had an instant impact on match days, because the club provided a room attached to the change-rooms for me to use before or after a game, as I needed.

In my time at Essendon, Quinny often talked to me about Islam. He was interested, he was sympathetic and he always wanted to learn more about me and what mattered to me. He always had questions but I never felt he was interrogating me. When I gave him my answers, I found him unfailingly open and ready to accept them. I don't mean it to sound overblown, but it really felt like he was coming from a place of love.

We've long since parted ways professionally, but to this day Quinny still gets in touch every year on my birthday. I'm not entirely sure why we had such a strong relationship. Maybe he'd had really positive dealings with those other Muslim athletes and my arrival reawakened those impressions in him. Or perhaps it was just an expression of his character, because I know other players had that same sense that he was interested in their lives off the field. He'd have players around for dinner, or they might even stay with his family for a while if they were struggling. For me, though, his interest was so genuine that it was like having another Muslim at the club. From time to time I'd wonder aloud to him whether maybe, somewhere deep inside, he actually was a Muslim. 'I'm not far off!' he'd respond.

Quinny left Essendon in 2008, a couple of years into my career. Sheeds had gone by that stage, and from what I could gather Quinny didn't get along brilliantly with the new coach, Matthew Knights. To be honest, Quinny's absence made me feel like a part of me was missing – like I'd been suddenly cut adrift. 'What are you doing to me?' I remember asking him when I first heard that he was leaving. 'We've created something so special, and you've made me feel like this place is home to me. What am I going to do?' Of course, there was no way to change it, but I had to let him know how much he meant to me, and how much he'd helped me. I was only

20 years old, and was feeling genuinely worried about how things would pan out.

Above all else, I felt insecure. Maybe that was my fault. Maybe I'd let Quinny do the heavy lifting to the point where I wasn't proactive enough. But one thing was clear to me: all those conversations about praying, fasting and football – you know the ones by now – I realised I'd have to have again, only with someone new, and who likely could never be as under-standing, sensitive and familiar with the issues as Quinny was. And that's exactly what happened, with the end result that things at Essendon changed for me, even after all the ground-work of the previous years.

It didn't help that by this stage my footy wasn't going partic-ularly well. Quinny's departure coincided with my struggling for senior games, despite playing well in the VFL. All up, I was feeling exasperated and was lacking confidence. And I didn't feel like I could be myself or that I fully belonged. To put it simply, I was off to the boot room – for real.

I mostly prayed there for the next two years, unless I had long enough breaks during the day to get to the mosque and back in time. There was only just enough room to pray in the boot room, but it just seemed easier to do that than having to answer lots of questions from people.

I became more confident as I got older and more estab-lished in my career, especially at Richmond. These days I'm quite prepared to tell my coaches, for example, that I might need to miss a morning meeting to attend the Eid prayer, which is a little like a Christmas mass or Easter service. They're completely fine with it because they know I'm sincere and that I'm not being lazy. But I never would have done that as a younger player.

Probably the biggest landmark in that sense came in 2016. I was in the car with Rouba one day when she turned to me and asked, 'What are the chances of us going for *hajj* this year?'

As I've noted, the pilgrimage to Mecca is something all Muslims who are physically and financially able are required to do once in their lives. An indication of its importance is that those who cannot perform it for whatever reason will often send someone else on their behalf. *Hajj* is essentially a re-enactment of key moments in the lives of Abraham and Hagar, who Muslims believe was Abraham's wife. It matters to Muslims because Abraham's prophethood is such a big episode in the history of monotheism. The belief in a single God, without any partners, associates or rivals, is the most important and unshakeable foundation of Islam. And it's also what distinguishes the Abrahamic faiths – Judaism, Christianity and Islam – from other religions.

I'd been fortunate to have done *hajj* in 2013, but Rouba hadn't, and she felt that time was running out for her. Like Ramadan, *hajj* occurs at a specific time of year in the Islamic calendar. And that means it shifts through the seasons, getting earlier in the solar year each time. In 2016 it was due to fall in early to mid-September. In the years that followed it would happen during the home-and-away season, deeper in the Arabian summer, when the heat is extreme. We had one child at the time, who was two and a half, so it had been too hard for us to go before, and we could see that 2016 would realistically be Rouba's last chance to go for a long time. The only problem was that September is a pretty important month for footy.

All this was coming to a head about a month before the end of the home-and-away season. Richmond fans will remember that 2016 was an awful year for us, and by then it already seemed clear we wouldn't be making the finals, but it wasn't yet certain. That put me in a difficult position.

If I waited until we were mathematically unable to make the finals, it would be too late for me to organise *hajj* because it takes weeks to book it and arrange the special visas you need. But could I really start organising it now, more or less banking on us falling short? How would I explain that to the club? Wouldn't they be within their rights to insist that, at the very least, I make myself available for September? How would the coach take it when he was already so disappointed with how the year was going, and here I was planning my holiday? How do you even have that conversation?

But I had to. I spent what felt like forever trying to prepare a speech. I didn't want to say anything offensive or that gave the impression I didn't care about my football, but I was comforted by the fact that my audience would be Damien Hardwick. Even in those dark days I'd found him a great person to talk to because, like me, he's very family orientated, and he really values life away from football. Probably for that reason we had established a strong relationship of mutual trust and respect over six years.

'Dimma . . . this is going to be a serious conversation,' I began.

That wasn't how I'd planned my speech to start.

'I know this might sound like I'm getting ahead of myself in a way . . .'

I could sense him getting anxious, wondering what was coming.

'Part of our religion is to go at least once in our lifetime on the pilgrimage to Mecca,' I said, and then I launched into the best explanation I could give of what *hajj* was about. I've found that non-Muslims are often already familiar with the sight of it, especially the hundreds of thousands of people walking in circles around the *ka'bah*, the black cube-shaped building in Mecca that Muslims face towards when we pray. Dimma was familiar, which helped. But I found it just about impossible to convey the importance of *hajj* to someone who hadn't done it, because it really is a unique, life-defining spiritual journey.

More than two million people from all over the world suddenly descend on the holiest Islamic sites, all dressed in simple clothes that more or less obscure their worldly status. It's a moment where all the fake hierarchies we create in our lives are shown up for what they are, and the simple reality that we are all just creatures of God becomes concrete. It doesn't matter who's rich, or famous or powerful, because while you're there it's like the rest of the world just vanishes. Our petty hang-ups, rivalries and anxieties begin to seem immature because you're focused on the most important aspect of your existence: your relationship with your Creator.

And the idea is that you carry these things with you when you return home. You become humbler, more tranquil, more balanced, more tolerant, more patient, more understanding of people whose lives are different from yours. Or at least you should. Certainly that was my experience when I first went. What I hadn't experienced before was talking about it quite like this with my footy coach.

'Have you been?' Dimma asked me.

'Yes,' I replied. 'But my wife hasn't, and a few days ago she asked me if we might be able to go this year. I know she really wants to, Dimma, she really, really wants to go, and I feel like I really need to take her. It kind of has to be this year because we want to have more kids, and after that it will be really diffi-cult, so this could be our last chance for a long time. We really want to tick off this obligation.'

'Alright,' he said. 'So tell me – what do you need?'

'Well, don't take this the wrong way,' I began. Any sentence that starts that way is going to be a big sentence. 'Let's talk reality . . .' Same with that one. 'It's going to be hard for us to make finals. And if we don't, do you mind if I leave straight after the last game? It means I'd have to miss the season review and all that stuff. The problem is that I have to start organising everything now because it's not a normal trip. The visas take ages, you have to pay a deposit, and the travel agents need lots of time to arrange it because there's a big waiting list. But if we do make the finals,' I concluded, 'then I'm willing to wear the ten grand or whatever I've paid so I can take part.'

'Mate, if it's important to you, it's important to me,' Dimma said. 'Go ahead and book it. Do what you've got to do. Have a safe trip. Enjoy it. And make sure you send me some photos!'

He could easily have seen my request as evidence of someone not taking their football career seriously. He could have seen me as prioritising something that was part of my life, but less important in his eyes than football. That might even have been the natural way for him to have reacted while we were playing so badly and the club was under so much pressure, most of which Dimma took onto himself. People usually get strict and start asserting their authority in that sort of situation, and put everyone on notice. It's hard to grant people exemptions when you're losing. But he had total faith that my request wouldn't change how I approached the rest of the season.

Actually, if he'd said no, I would have understood and accepted the decision. I was confident that, whatever his answer, Dimma wouldn't question my commitment or my professionalism. We respected each other too much for that. I also knew that if there's one thing Dimma loved, it was honesty. He valued people who were sincere with him. I'm sure that's at least partly why he was so understanding in that moment. And I have to say, given the way that season panned out, it was a pretty good season review to miss.

That *hajj* was a special experience for Rouba and me. It was the first time we'd left our daughter at home while we travelled, and while we missed her of course, we were so immersed in the occasion that we weren't overcome with the emotion of that separation in the way we normally would have been. Rouba especially threw herself into the whole experience, buzzing with energy and excitement as we did all the rituals. Whenever we had to walk quite long distances in the heat, she was always at the front of the group. And because we spent almost the entire time together, it became an incredible shared experience. But it also turned out that Dimma's decision to let me go on *hajj* in 2016 was a momentous one for my football career.

Probably the climax of the pilgrimage is the day everyone spends on Mount Arafat. 'The *hajj* is Arafat; the *hajj* is Arafat; the *hajj* is Arafat,' said the Prophet, leaving no one in any doubt about the importance of that day. Imagine the scene: about 2.5 million pilgrims, gleaming in white, gathered on one mountain to spend the whole day in prayer. The images of people circling the *ka'bah* might be more famous, but if you ever get to see them, the aerial images of the gathering at Mount Arafat are just as striking.

In the Islamic tradition, this is believed to be the place Adam and Eve met on Earth after they left Paradise, and because Muslims don't have a doctrine of original sin, it's also the place we believe they were forgiven. For this reason it's also known as *Jabal al-Rahma*, or 'the Mount of Mercy', so it's a particularly good time and place for *du'a*, to seek forgiveness and then ask for blessings and favours. 'The best of *du'a* is on the day of Arafat,' in the Prophet's words.

If you're lucky enough to be there, you'll spend almost the whole day in supplication. It is an amazing thing to hear literally millions of people whispering in prayer, and very often crying quietly because of how moved they are by the experience. It's silent and audible at the same time, crowded and solitary. You're part of a massive crowd, but it also feels like you're alone, asking of God whatever you want.

You cover a lot of areas during that sort of prayer time – family, faith, friends, worldly things, spiritual things – but I reserved some time for my future in football. By the end of the 2016 season, I felt like I'd had enough. Football was meant to be the great love of my life but I wasn't enjoying it anymore. I felt like there was nothing to look forward to except going home at the end of each day. I spent my time at work thinking about how I could get out of there as soon as possible – I wished I was with my family, at the mosque, even fishing. Anywhere else, really. The idea of taking on another long season felt like a burden rather than a privilege. I was genuinely uncertain about whether I really wanted to continue. 'Allah, if football is meant for me after today, then allow it to be and show me the path towards it,' I prayed. 'Help me make a decision and give me what's best for me.'

When I returned to Richmond for preseason training later that year, it felt like a club transformed. It had suddenly become a fun, happy place to be, with a culture that made you love the place and everyone there. It was like the Richmond Football Club itself had been through a spiritual experience.

I launched myself into footy in 2017 and never looked back. I'm convinced that if I'd never gone to *hajj* – if I'd never spiritually recharged myself, and instead remained in the same environment in Melbourne, drowning in that feeling of not wanting to play – I would never have made it to 2017. And I never would have been praying *maghrib* in the changerooms during the third quarter of that amazing Preliminary Final.

My Preliminary Final dash into the rooms for *maghrib* may sound remarkable, but it's actually completely routine these days. The club understands it. The team understands it. It's just the way we do things now. When I step off a plane and arrive at a new stadium, the first thing that I find ready for

36

me is a towel and a prayer room for me to use. Or if it's Round 1 and we're still in daylight saving, and sunset occurs during the first quarter of a night game, I'll ask our property steward, Giuseppe Mamone, to have a towel ready for me at quarter time, so I can duck into the changerooms, made *wudu* and pray.

'No worries, it's all done,' Giuseppe says. Then he talks to my line coach or the assistant coach in charge of rotations, and they quickly assess what effect, if any, my absence might have. 'Do we need to start you on the bench in the second quarter?' they might ask.

'No, it's cool,' I'll say. 'I'll just be three or four minutes, then I'll come straight back out. But I won't be in the huddle at quarter time.'

'Oh, that doesn't matter – it's not important. By then I'll only be telling you what you've done really well, and I'll just tell you to keep doing whatever you're doing!'

At least, that's how it usually goes. There was a time Dimma started telling me off at quarter time when I wasn't there.

'He's in prayer,' said one of my teammates.

'What do you mean he's in prayer?'

I can't imagine it's a situation many coaches have had to face when they're trying to yell at a player.

But even that story tells you how far things have come. Dimma doesn't need to be told in advance every time I need to step away because we operate with such a high degree of trust. There was a time that wasn't quite the case – when if something came up that was slightly inconvenient, his response might have been, 'Can't you do that later?' But now he accepts that I know what I'm doing and will do the right thing.

In fact, Dimma has become so relaxed about it that sometimes he doesn't even realise Ramadan is approaching. He texted me one year, saying, 'I forgot about Ramadan – how are you going?' I was touched that he cared. The club doesn't see my practice of my faith as a trade-off, and that kind of support makes a massive difference.

This was probably never better illustrated than in the aftermath of the Christchurch terrorist attacks in March 2019, when 51 people were massacred at two mosques during communal Friday prayers. It came just before our season launch that year, which is one of the handful of must-attend events at the club, yet without any hesitation the club gave me the night off.

Then, the following Thursday night, Round 1 kicked off with our game against Carlton. I was scheduled to go to Christchurch the next day to visit the Muslim community there. Unfortunately, though, I injured my hamstring during the game. Whenever that happens, you're required to be at the club the next morning for the injury clinic, where you're assessed and begin your rehabilitation. It's an extremely important part of your recovery. But this time the club insisted I miss it and keep my commitment to go to Christchurch. They knew the magnitude of the moment, its importance to me and to a community in mourning, and they placed those needs above the club's. The point is that everyone at Richmond recognises how my practice of Islam isn't a burden the club has to bear. It might even be beneficial.

Given how everything has turned out, I can only be thankful that circumstance forced me to step up and talk directly to James and Daniel about being a Muslim during that under-16 national carnival all those years ago. Who knows how it might have been if things were slightly different? Even something as simple as the fact I was the Vic Metro captain was probably crucial, because had I not been, I reckon I wouldn't have had the courage for that moment. If I'd been a fringe player, there's no chance I would have said what I did. I'd have confined myself to a tiny corner of the hotel room. And I would have been worried. Very worried.

All this makes me realise just how important people in leadership positions can be, and how much of a difference role models can make, even when they don't intend to. The fact that I've been put in these positions throughout my foot-balling life means I have a responsibility to those who come after me. Even little things that most people might not notice can make big differences, like getting the AFL to put prayer rooms in its venues so Muslim supporters don't have to pray in the stairwell of a packed MCG, or run outside at half time to find a park and miss large chunks of the game – or, even worse, decide going to the footy is too much trouble. For me, if being the first practising Muslim to play in the AFL means anything, it's that.

In February 2020 I had the rare privilege of playing for Victoria in the State of Origin match to raise money for bushfire relief. That night, I needed to pray *maghrib* – it's always *maghrib* – at half time. As it happened, a lot of the Victorian team staff were from Richmond, and Giuseppe

Mamone was the property steward for the night. He knew what to do.

I did my usual thing in the usual way, but that time was unlike any other – because I wasn't alone. Praying at my side was another Muslim player, Adam Saad. It must have been the first ever congregational prayer involving players at an AFL game, and yet it was no big deal. How much has changed.

3

ON THE SHOULDERS OF GIANTS

IT WAS A SATURDAY NIGHT in April 2002. Dad was driving his taxi and listening to the footy on the radio. He was a big Western Bulldogs supporter at the time, and they were playing the Kangaroos. At three-quarter time the Dogs were up by 20 points and looking good, when a job came through to take someone from Altona East to Footscray.

As Dad picked up the passenger and started the trip, the footy started going sour. The Kangaroos piled on goal after goal, with the Bulldogs unable to stem the flow. At the final siren the Kangaroos had produced a six-goals-to-one last quarter and won by 13 points. Dad hit the dashboard in frustration and was nearly in tears, which startled his passenger a bit. But the passenger understood, because he was a Bulldogs man too.

They bonded over the footy and got talking about life. Unfortunately, at that time the shadow of the September 11 terrorist attacks still loomed over everything. It dominated the news and politics, and even conversations between friends and strangers. I suppose it was inevitable that Dad and his passenger would eventually get around to talking about what life was like for Australian Muslims.

As the trip neared its end, the passenger brought together the two big themes of their conversation. 'Don't worry, mate,' he said. 'In a few years' time we're going to have a Lebanese Muslim player in the AFL.'

'What do you mean?' Dad asked. 'Who?'

'Bachar, his name is. Bachar Houli.'

This guy had no idea who Dad was. And Dad certainly had no idea who he was. But here was a complete stranger telling him his own son would make it to the highest level.

Dad wanted confirmation. 'Who?'

'Bachar Houli,' the man repeated.

'A Muslim can't play in the AFL, can he?' Dad asked.

'Who told you that? Sport has nothing to do with religion, mate. I guarantee you, if this kid keeps going the way he's going, he'll be in the AFL in a few years. Believe me, I've been around footy a long time.'

Dad didn't know it at the time, but his passenger knew me firsthand because I played with his son at Spotswood. In fact, at that point he'd have seen me play much more than Dad had.

'What's your name, mate?' asked Dad.

'Ted Whitten Junior,' the stranger replied.

The thing about being described as the first practising Muslim to play in the AFL is that it sounds like you came from nowhere, as though you're one of a rare species or the fascinating exception to the rule. But the fact that there had already been a couple of AFL players from Muslim backgrounds, Sedat Sir and Adem Yze, tells you that these communities had been producing footballers for years. It might be true that Sedat and Adem weren't observant, but many other Muslim footballers were, so it was probably just a matter of time before one of them reached the top level. And there was a good chance that person would be Lebanese, given the size of the Lebanese community in Melbourne, and the fact that they were probably more religious on average than the Turkish and Albanian communities that produced Sedat and Adem. So, as nice as the idea of me being some historic figure who opened up a whole new field for Muslims might be, really I'm just the product of many others who came before me.

I grew up in a footy-mad community. Football was basically all the Lebanese community of Melbourne's western suburbs did when I was a kid, and they did it together. The Newport Football Club was almost entirely Lebanese, and every Saturday was like a community festival because everyone came out to watch the reserves and seniors play. I was always there because two of my older brothers, Mohamed and Khaled, were playing for Newport, and Saturday was easily my favourite day of the week.

But I was nervous while watching these games, because trouble was always brewing. Newport games almost always descended into fights, and just about anything could trigger one. The club had its share of troublemakers who hung out in gangs during the week, and they were always ready for conflict.

Every time someone got knocked over by a bump that had even a hint of being a bit rough, I'd wince. *Oh no, please no . . . Not now*, I'd think, hoping that this wouldn't be the spark that started the next fire.

My hopes were usually futile. Someone would fall to the ground with a bruised ego, then get up and try to restore things by throwing a punch. Then another player would join in, and then another, until soon enough there was a brawl. Before long, even crowd members would rush onto the field and join in. It was ugly and it was predictable.

A lot of games were called off because they disintegrated into a mass of people punching on. Many didn't reach half time. But even that wouldn't be enough, because once the game was abandoned, the fights would be taken down the road. This was the dark side of the community feeling that surrounded the Newport Footy Club. It's one thing seeing a teammate get knocked over, but when it's your brother or your cousin or your best mate, you're more likely to respond as though it's personal, and to expect others to defend you in the same way.

Once this started happening, it took on a life of its own. Other clubs knew that Newport players lost their heads easily, so they would provoke them because it would help them win the game. In the end, I'd say scuffles were more often being started by the opposition, but by then Newport's reputation was set. Eventually, the league banned the entire Newport Football Club. It took about 15 years for the club to be allowed to play again. It's still mostly Lebanese, but I'm glad to say it's now really well run and has a disciplined culture. Those problems are a thing of the past.

I can't tell you how much I hated what was happening at Newport. The longer the trouble went on, the worse it became. I felt like I was being robbed of footy, and of having a place to stretch my legs and kick the ball as far as I could. This was my only opportunity to be involved in what was already my passion, and it was being completely ruined.

More than that, I felt a kind of violence was happening within me. I'd never thrown a punch in my life and couldn't imagine doing so. Whenever I even saw people who looked like they were about to fight, I'd turn away as though by reflex because I found it too much to take in. It just wasn't something I wanted to witness, much less get involved in. I don't know exactly why this was, but for whatever reason I've always been a peacemaker, and something of a people pleaser. I can't stand conflict.

That's why, when Khaled finally took me to play footy, he took me to the Spotswood Football Club. He'd started playing there himself, looking for a more professional environment where he could concentrate on footy rather than fighting, and he knew that I needed the same thing. Whatever talent I had would probably have been lost at Newport in those days.

It's possible that's what happened to Khaled, because I know some good judges who think he was a gun player, fearless and with a ferocious attack on the football: harder than me in the contest, though not as good a decision-maker and less skilful. On talent, he might easily have made the VFL if he'd been guided when he was younger. But Khaled had no one. He played with his mates, and Mohamed was playing too, but they didn't really take their footy seriously or entertain the possibility that they might make a career out of it.

And Khaled certainly wasn't getting any support from Mum or Dad. They initially opposed my brothers playing, and even once they accepted there was nothing they could do to stop them, they didn't take an interest. Whatever Khaled achieved in football he did on his own. In a sense, he spent his whole life as a player kicking into the wind.

Khaled was determined that my football wouldn't suffer the same disadvantages. More than anyone else in my family, he was the most invested in my football, nurturing my talent right from the start and trying to surround me with people who could help me realise my potential. That might not sound like much, but it was a massive leap, given what Khaled had. After my first season of footy he could see I had the ability to play at a higher level, but he also knew that he'd probably reached the limit of what help he could give me.

Khaled and Mohamed were good friends with a man by the name of Mohamed Bakkar. Bakkar was Lebanese, and was also a practising Muslim, but his social and footy circles were much wider than those of the Newport crew. He grew up hanging out with people like Richard Osborne, Mark Arceri and Mick Martyn, who all went on to have successful AFL careers. He also knew recruiters and player managers like Brad Lloyd. And he was good friends with a guy named Saade Ghazi, a Lebanese bloke from Newport just like me, who ended up becoming a legend of the Williamstown Football Club in the VFA. Ghazi won the Liston Trophy in 1989 and is in the Williamstown Hall of Fame. Bakkar himself played for Williamstown too, under Barry Round.

Simply put, Bakkar knew his footy. He also knew what

players with a future in the game looked like, and his views were respected. He always told it like it is, so you could trust that his assessment was genuine. Khaled and Mohamed thought he would make an excellent mentor for me, and set about convincing him to take me on.

In my second year playing football, when I was 12, Bakkar agreed to come and watch me.

'What do you think?' Khaled asked.

'He's got talent, good balance, doesn't get pushed over,' Bakkar said. 'Good decision-maker, gets a lot of the footy, and delivers it at a standard way above the level he's playing. He's better than the other kids here by a country mile. But that's also because he's so much bigger than other kids. When he gets a bit older, they'll catch up to him, so I don't know how good he'll be then.'

Bakkar was right to raise the question. I was definitely an early grower, and by the time I started playing club football I was physically close to being a man. That did give me a natural advantage.

Bakkar kept coming to watch me. Within a year or two, he'd also managed to convince my dad that I might be a really good player. That confirmed what Dad had heard from my coach at Spotswood – and of course from that famous passenger who got into his taxi. Dad was initially against me playing football, just as he was with all my brothers. But once he understood that I might become a success, he viewed football in a completely different way to how he had throughout my brothers' childhood. It looked less like a waste of time and more like a legitimate activity.

Suddenly Dad was all in, taking me to training and games, everything he could. This was exactly the kind of support Khaled had never had. Dad and Bakkar were there when I kicked 20 goals 10 behinds one week, then 19 goals 7 the next. Now we were on a journey together. By the time I was playing for Vic Metro in junior national carnivals, Dad would put his whole business on hold to travel interstate with me.

Bakkar soon became convinced that I had talent that was worth developing, but the big question for him was whether or not I had the character to play at the top level. So he laid it out for me, and his criteria were clear. If I wasn't committed, honest, loyal, respectful and motivated, then it wasn't worth his time to mentor me. But if I was, then he'd give me every assistance he could. He was going to treat me like an adult, and I was going to have to behave like one.

I agreed. I was completely devoted to football, and because he'd known me since I was a little kid, Bakkar believed that I was genuine. I know that my religious commitment was also a significant factor for him, because he saw that it gave me a certain moral integrity and discipline that he could rely on and hold me to if I ever strayed from what was required.

Bakkar becoming my mentor was one of the most important things that happened in my young footballing life, because it set me on a path towards professionalism. He was the one who warned me not to waste my ability, who impressed upon me the importance of discipline, and who taught me what it meant to train. When I was 14 or 15, he arranged for Richard Osborne, who was only fairly recently retired, to come to my house and explain what sort of commitment and sacrifice was needed if I wanted to become a professional footballer. Bakkar even got hold of Osborne's old training program so I could do it.

Bakkar's philosophy was to take my strengths and make them elite, and then take my weaknesses and make them good enough. At that time my biggest weakness was my running. Until Bakkar arrived, I had no idea how to do anything about it, because about the only thing I could think of doing was just going for a run for half an hour. That actually isn't very useful for a footballer. You need to be doing interval training, repeat sprint efforts, things like that. You're always moving in footy, but the key is to be able to sprint whenever the game demands it – to put in 50 metres at top pace late in the final quarter so you can outnumber your opposition at a decisive contest. And you need to train specifically for that.

Soon, I was eating, sleeping and training like a professional player. Bakkar even had me doing recovery in the pool after games, which no other kid was doing. If I didn't have training on a given day he might get me to do a running program to build my endurance. I was even having my body measurements taken every couple of weeks to make sure I was on track.

The benefits of all this weren't just a matter of theory to me. I was fortunate to be able to see the path ahead because I had a distant cousin, Ziad Kadour – 'Ziggy' to everyone – who was also from Spotswood and went through the Western Jets system. Ziggy was three years older than me, and was one of my closest friends from the time I was 13 until about 19. We even looked alike, and people would often mistake us for brothers.

My parents liked and trusted Ziggy, so they had no problem with us hanging out for as long as we liked. I took advantage of this, often sleeping over at his house, and we did everything together, including training. We'd go to the local pools for rehab, kick the footy, ride our bikes or do runs together.

We grew up in similar families, too. Ziggy's parents, like mine, didn't approve of him playing football, though in his case that disapproval lasts to this day. He's won four premierships in local footy and got as far as playing a season for Port Melbourne in the VFL, but his parents haven't seen him play a single game. A few years ago, as a fully grown man in his thirties with a wife and kids, he got injured in a game and his mum told him off for playing.

I knew what I had to do: put my head down, get picked for the Vic Metro under-18 team, and have as good a carnival as I possibly could. If I did that, I had every reason to believe I'd be on an AFL list sometime soon.

Then suddenly it ground to a halt. I'd been picked for the Vic Metro side, but trouble struck when we played a practice game against Vic Country and I found myself struggling physically in a way I never had before. I'd go for a marking contest or kick the ball hard and feel a sharp pain through my back. At first I thought it was nothing serious – maybe a twinge or just a sore spot – but eventually it got so bad that I had to come clean to the team staff about what I was feeling. It was a disempowering experience, because for the first time in my life as a footballer, I was at the mercy of someone else's assessment. I overheard the trainers talking with each other about me needing an MRI scan – I had no idea what that was, but it sounded bad. My mind began conjuring up images of all kinds of awful machines. Frankly, I was scared.

Of course, the main thing to fear from a scan is the result, and in this case the scans revealed that I had a stress fracture in my lower back. The doctor delivered the news to me, along with the verdict that I wasn't going to play in the national carnival. It was only two days before the first game, so this was a lot for me to grasp.

I was devastated, but more than that I was shocked because it had never occurred to me that this might happen. Now it was a reality I had to deal with. The big positive was that it wasn't the end for me – I still had hope. Because I was 17, my chance to be drafted wasn't for another year, and I knew I was good enough to be picked to play in the carnival. All I had to do was get myself fit for the 2006 season.

The problem was I couldn't run. My body needed to heal, but still I needed to stay fit somehow. That's when the physio-therapist at the Western Jets introduced me to Pilates. I'd never heard of it, but suddenly I was doing it three times a week, with a focus on strengthening my core, which is a crucial part of healing a stress fracture in the back. I also did a lot of swimming: I'd do a kilometre at about 6:30 am, before I went to school, with the result that I'd often end up falling asleep in class around midday because I was so exhausted. And once I got home from school, if I didn't have to go in to the Jets for whatever counted as my footy training, I'd ride my bike to the physio, then do Pilates and come home. Cycling actually became a major part of my life. I was doing somewhere between 250 and 300 kilometres per week over about four sessions, using a bike Khaled bought for me. And in between all this I'd go to the gym to do whatever weights I could. It was exhausting, but I wanted so badly to make it to the top level that I was prepared to do whatever it took.

After four months that felt like four years, it began paying off. I was on the verge of running again, which would set me up perfectly so I could attack preseason. Then one night when I was riding home from a Pilates session, it all went wrong.

I'd been stationary at a traffic light when the lights changed. I went to take off, but my foot wasn't fastened into the clip on the pedal and slipped off, slamming my leg down into the chain. The next thing I knew was total agony. I looked down to see blood pouring out the back of my leg. The spikes on the chainring had pierced my Achilles tendon, ripping it open.

I called my brothers, my father, anyone I could think of, but no one was answering, so I had no choice but to ride my bike with one leg to the nearest hospital emergency department, where I was treated and put into a moon boot. The worst part was the psychological pain I felt once I realised the implications. It was November, and now I wouldn't be able to run for another three or four months. I was back somewhere near where I had started, but now the preseason was rapidly approaching.

In some ways this injury was even worse than the stress fracture, because my training was more curtailed. I couldn't cycle anymore, and even my swimming was limited because I couldn't kick. I didn't start my preseason until late February, by which time everyone else was way ahead of me. And when you're competing at an elite level, a bad preseason can ruin your year.

The timing could hardly have been worse. This was my draft year, and it wasn't just any year. As we headed into the season, this year's crop of young players was widely considered to be the best since the 'super draft' of 2001 that gave us Luke Hodge, Luke Ball and Chris Judd. It was a daunting situation, but at least I was back.

Then, after all the work, the frustration and the patience, the stress fractures came back. Now I was in a race against the clock. The under-18 national carnival was on the horizon, and I knew that if I didn't play in that, it was almost certain I wouldn't get drafted. In the space of a year, I'd gone from being a draft prospect ahead of my time to having a very real chance of not being drafted at all, and it was all beyond my control.

The latest stress fractures were less serious than the previous year's, probably because I was looking out for them rather than trying to push through them and making them worse, so I felt I could recover in time to save my season. But even if I did, the truth was there would be plenty of clubs who wouldn't risk drafting me because of my injury history. I knew lots of people now doubted I was physically up to the demands of the AFL. All I could do was make it to the carnival and offer my best, but I confess I wasn't terribly confident.

When the Vic Metro coach was telling us whether or not we'd made the squad and the moment arrived when he got to my name, I was expecting his next words would be 'sorry' or 'you'll be an emergency'. What I heard instead was that

I'd been named vice-captain under Leigh Adams, who would go on to play 104 games for the Kangaroos. And while I was happy with my performance at the carnival, I knew there were still plenty of doubters about my future. So it was a massive moment for me when I was invited to the 2006 draft camp. It meant that enough clubs had shown enough interest in me to justify me being there. I was in with a chance.

Bakkar kept hearing great things about me from the recruiters, but apart from my injury history, there was one weakness that kept coming up: my running. That meant they would be looking closely at my draft camp test results. There were some concerns over my stamina and my ability to get to contest after contest, but Bakkar told me I needed to work on the speed tests in particular.

Again, he developed a training program for me to get there, but it was a stroke of genius when he drew on his contacts again to get me a specialised running coach, Bohdan Babijczuk. He couldn't give me better genetics for running, but he could improve my technique – and that's exactly what happened, especially for the 20-metre sprint. Over a distance that short, the start is extremely important, and that's where I found my improvement.

In the 20-metre sprint at the draft camp, you aren't respond-ing to a starting gun. There are sensors that measure the moment you cross the starting line, triggering the clock to start. That means you want to have as much forward momentum as possible at the moment you pass the sensor. The secret is to realise that when you take off, you're really moving in two directions: forward and up. But if you do this at the same time, at least part of your power is taking you up, rather than forward. That means you'll spend the first few metres of the sprint building up speed, before you hit your top pace. That was exactly the mistake I was making. The most significant technique I learned was to separate these movements as much as possible, by first moving up without moving forward, so I could gain momentum without actually breaking the starting gate. That way, when I moved forward, I was doing so with a full running stride. Effectively, I was learning how to buy time by starting without setting the clock off.

Thanks mostly to this better starting technique, my times dropped dramatically, from 3.25 seconds before the camp to 2.96 seconds. That was enough for me to finish just outside the top ten. By the time I got to Essendon, I was clocking 2.82 seconds. The ridiculous thing about this is that I wasn't really running any faster – but the numbers said I was.

Even so, I had definitely improved as a runner. My draft camp results were beyond anything I had a right to expect as recently as a month beforehand. I finished in the top five for the three-kilometre run (in 10 minutes and 10 seconds) and for the beep test (14.7). At Essendon in my first year, I found myself finishing the 3.2-kilometre time trial in third place. Exactly as Bakkar had always demanded, I'd taken a weakness and turned it into an asset. Given where I came from, it's amazing to think that, so many years later, my whole game – indeed, my whole AFL career – is built on running.

My relationship with Bakkar didn't end on draft day. Our relationship came out of football, but it had quickly become much more than that. I'd talk to him whenever I wanted some grown-up advice – about the responsibilities I would have as a Muslim AFL player, about character, even about girls. After I joined Essendon, he remained my confidant and adviser. I talked things over with him when I wasn't getting games, when I was deciding whether or not to go to Richmond, basically any time I needed to talk to someone who understood football, Islam and me.

In time, Bakkar came to see me as one of his sons. He still does. To this day, we speak every week, and I still seek his advice because I know he sees the whole person when he looks at me, not just the AFL footballer. And he's still protective of me – he makes *du'a* for me every day, and rushes to my defence whenever he hears someone say something negative about me. If someone so much as says I should have gone harder in a contest, he'll arc up immediately. 'How many games did you play?' he'll snap. Even if it's my brother.

Bakkar was there the day I got drafted. To be fair, everyone was. I listened to the draft at home that morning with my family, watching everyone else get called. I felt myself getting nervous as it got past pick 30 and my name still hadn't been called. Then 35. Then 40. Finally, at pick 42, Essendon called out my name and the place erupted.

Dad was probably the most nervous of anyone, and so he was probably the most relieved and excited in that moment. He immediately took off to buy a huge amount of food because he knew what was coming. In a flash, we'd squeezed about 250 people into our courtyard at home. There were drums, lots of food and lots of dancing, even from me. This was a whole community celebrating. The party went until midnight.

At one point Bakkar sat down to speak with my father. Dad was still in tears of joy, just beaming. 'I'm going to ask you a question, but you have to tell me the truth,' said Bakkar.

'Yeah, I will.'

'What made you happier: your son becoming a doctor, or your son becoming an AFL footballer?'

'Honestly? My son playing AFL football.'

Some 13 years later, in the week leading up to my 200th AFL game, my parents recorded a video message that was played to me in front of the Richmond players and coaching staff. There was Dad, holding a sheet of paper that carried his thoughts, nervously reading out these carefully prepared remarks in his thick Lebanese accent. 'I would like to sank ze Rishmond Foodball Clabb . . . and Damyan Hardwick . . . for ze great obbortunity . . . I'm very broud of you, Bach.' And there was Mum, sitting right next to him. Looking stern, but clearly proud of what her little boy had managed to do.

But who knows? If there hadn't been a footy-mad community in Newport, and if my older brothers weren't part of it, I might never have fallen in love with the game. And if I'd been five years older and Khaled was still playing at Newport rather than Spotswood, I might have been just another kid whose talent never made it out of the Lebanese community. If Khaled wasn't so determined for me to be as good as possible, and if he and Mohamed hadn't recruited Bakkar into my world, I might never have realised my potential. If people like Mohamed Bakkar and Saade Ghazi hadn't first made it to the VFA and built their knowledge and contacts in the world of professional football as a resource for our community,

I might never have found my way through the maze that separates so many talented players from an AFL career. And if I'd never watched Ziggy do so much of it before me, and never soaked up so much of his experience, the path may never have seemed within my reach.

So everything I've achieved was only possible because of people you've probably never heard of until now, people who were trailblazers every bit as significant as me, just not as celebrated. These days I talk to young Muslim kids who love the game and have dreams my brothers never had. They have a discipline and focus their predecessors never did because they believe things are possible that once weren't. That's not something I did. That's something generations of people did.

4

A FAMILY OF OPPOSITES

WITH APOLOGIES TO RICHMOND fans, my love of football began with the Carlton Football Club. I always loved the game, but for me as a kid, Carlton *was* the game. And I was Anthony Koutoufides, crashing sideways into packs and taking marks from nowhere, darting between oncoming players, leaving opponents sprawling on the ground as they tried to tackle me. And especially picking up the ball and carrying it in one hand as though it were an apple.

Kouta played the game like a superhero, doing things I hadn't seen before and that no one else could do. When he entered a contest, he scattered it. When people tried to tackle him, he'd palm the ball in one hand and flick his opponent away with the other with such ease that it made everyone wonder why they'd even bother trying. He was stronger than everyone else but he wasn't a brute who stood in the goal square: he seemed to run faster and further than everyone else too.

I played footy in the street with a guy called Richard Hussein. Actually, his name was Rashid, but like a lot of Lebanese kids he used an Anglicised version of his name to get by. Whatever – I always called him 'Rash'.

Rash was 14 years older than me and was also a fanatical Carlton supporter. In our street football games, while I was always Kouta, Rash would be Greg 'Diesel' Williams or Craig Bradley. It never really occurred to me that this meant Carlton was playing against itself, but that didn't matter – I was living in my imagination, where things like that were possible. It was a full roleplay, with our respective driveways acting as goals, and we'd complete the scene with crowd noise and commentary. It was just like most kids do, only Rash was in his early twenties at the time.

He was extremely patient with me, because I never wanted the game to end. As soon as I got the hint that he was winding things up, I'd start pleading: 'Please, Rash, can we keep playing?' His body language would say that we really couldn't, but his mouth almost always said, 'Yeah, okay.'

As I got a bit older and Rash realised I was actually pretty good at the game – when I was around nine – we left our driveways behind and started kicking the footy in the local park. 'Kick on your opposite foot,' Rash would tell me, pushing me to get better and better. He'd see me launch the footy as far as I could, then he'd ramp it up. 'Wow, Bach! Alright, let's do 40 metres!'

His was the only other Lebanese family in our street, and

probably for that reason our families were extremely close. Even saying that doesn't really capture it. It's probably more accurate to say that our families were fused into a single unit. Our mums were like sisters, and I saw Rash's mum as my own. In fact, I probably saw her more than my own mum, because while Mum had six other kids, Umm Rashid (as we called her[1]) only had Rash and his sister . . . well, and me. She probably fed me just as much, too.

Umm Rashid might have been the best cook in the world – she was a professional Italian chef on Lygon Street – and whenever she got home from work she'd immediately start asking after me and my stomach. 'Where's Bachar?' she'd say in Arabic. 'I'll make him lasagne – I know he loves it.' In return, I'd go grocery shopping for her, or do whatever else a son would have been expected to do. I was playing in the under-15 national championships in 2003 when I heard that she'd passed away. It was like learning that my own mum had died.

As close as our families were, there was one important difference. My parents are from Mish Mish, a little town of fewer than 20,000 people in the Akkar district of Lebanon, where the Houlis are one of only about a dozen family groups that make up the population. The people there are mostly Sunni Muslims, and tend to be quite conservative. But Rash was from the big smoke: a city about 45 kilometres west of Mish Mish

1 Literally 'the mother of Rashid' in Arabic. This is a common honorific or polite way of referring to someone in Arabic-speaking cultures. So, for example, if someone wanted to address me politely, they might call me 'Abu Sarah', which means 'the father of Sarah'.

called Tripoli, second only to Beirut in size. People from the cities tended to be less religious, less conservative and certainly less strict in the way they ran their families. And that was true in our case. My parents were very strict, limiting what my siblings and I could do socially and how far we could travel. Rash, on the other hand, worked as a DJ.

Rash had some decks in a granny flat out the back of his house, and he'd always take me there so he could share his enthusiasm for music with me. 'Have a scratch,' he'd say, inviting me to do what he clearly thought was the coolest thing in the world. Or he'd shout, 'Can you hear that?' about some little detail, as though it was life-changing.

'Yeah, I can hear it,' I'd say, not really knowing if I was even listening to the right thing.

'What do you think? Do you like it?'

'Yeah, it's okay.' That was about all I could give him.

Rash loved to pump out 'Stayin' Alive' by the Bee Gees, presumably because he thought it was too good a song for me to resist, but it never really worked and was never going to. I'm not into music at all and never have been, but I enjoyed being with him so much that I was happy to go along with it. For a while, anyway, then I'd say, 'Let's watch the footy.'

Rash was serious about the entertainment industry, and he went on to have a long and successful career working for some of the biggest record labels in the world. It was no surprise, really, because he was always so passionate about the business of music. He was always reading classic self-help books like *Think and Grow Rich* by Napoleon Hill and *As a Man Thinketh* by James Allen, and he loved talking about the stuff he'd learned from them. It was like having my own personal amateur psychologist or life coach. I was barely a teenager and he was talking to me about the power of positive thought and the importance of goal-setting, then getting me to figure out what my plan was for achieving what I wanted. 'You've got to define what you want,' he'd say. 'You've got to be clear. The difference between you and someone else is focus and determination.'

Once I started playing footy seriously, Rash would debrief with me after each game. 'You got 25 possessions? That's fantastic,' he'd say. 'Alright, now let's set a goal. Let's go for 30 next week!' And if I didn't meet that goal: 'Don't worry about that, that's going to happen. Just keep going. You've got to deal with what you're given the best way you can.'

When I began to rise through the ranks of junior football and started attracting some local media attention, Rash got me a folder. 'Keep your press clippings in here,' he said. I'm sure Rash was dreaming big for his business, but he was dreaming big on my behalf, too. I don't think I understood it at the time, but I have no doubt he planted some ideas that have stayed with me forever.

From the youngest age, I saw Rash as a brother. Not because I needed any more – I had four of them, and two sisters – but because that's exactly how our relationship felt. I think my parents saw it the same way, because Mum would ask Rash to help me with my homework. About the only thing that caused any hesitation was when Rash asked my mum to let me sleep over. She wasn't keen initially, but Umm Rashid insisted, which made it inevitable, and soon enough it happened all the time.

Arabs have an expression, '*al-bayt baytak*', which basically means 'my house is your house', and that's exactly how it was. Even when I was just six years old, I'd been joined to Rash at the hip. And he, as a 20-year-old, thought nothing of hanging out with me all day, playing downball and watching movies – my favourites were comedies, and the 1995 Grand Final, when Carlton smashed Geelong.

Perhaps it would have been strange for some kids, but I grew up surrounded by older people, including my older brothers, who were 14, 12 and nine years older than me. I had friends my own age at school, of course, but generally I felt more interested in and even more comfortable with people of my brothers' generation. People often told me I was quite a mature kid, and that was probably why.

Rash taught me how to drive, long before I was legally old enough. I must have been about eight years old, and I'd sit in the passenger seat of his Gemini changing the gears of his manual transmission for him whenever he told me it was time. I must have loved that car because I would often come over and ask if I could help him wash it. When I think back, it must have been inconvenient for him at times to hang out with me when he had grown-up things to do. But he just incorporated me into whatever he was doing, and kicking the footy would be my reward afterwards. So we'd mow the lawns together, then kick the footy; clean the garage, then kick the footy.

But Rash wasn't the only major influence in my life. In fact, he wasn't even the only Carlton influence. Of all my siblings, two of my older brothers had far and away the biggest presence: Mohamed, who was 12 years older than me, and Khaled, who was nine years older. They were also especially close friends with Rash, and the three of them really were my world.

All were very different characters to me. Rash was a party guy with no real interest in religion. When I was about eight, I'd teach him how to recite certain chapters of the Qur'an because he didn't know that stuff. And my brothers weren't particularly religious either. Our household certainly wasn't irreligious – Dad would take us to the mosque, and he served on the mosque committee – but I was the most conspicuously religious of my siblings by far, especially after I moved from Newport Primary School to Werribee Islamic College. I prayed at school during the day, which built my religious commitment to the point that I found myself leaving the playground early to get to prayers on time, because I wanted to be there and let the feeling seep in. My older brothers went to Catholic schools, so they didn't have the same kind of daily experience.

Mohamed and Khaled weren't particularly diligent about doing the five daily prayers or observing the key rituals. Mum used to drop us off at the mosque at night during Ramadan, but as soon as we got there Mohamed and Khaled would take off with their mates in another car to hang out at 7-Eleven and have Slurpees, dragging me along. They'd time it perfectly and get back to the mosque just as the prayers finished and Mum arrived to pick us up again. They'd do this night after night and Mum was none the wiser.

Their behaviour was probably a consequence of growing up in a strict household where we were constantly being told we couldn't do things that other kids did. I had a friend in primary school whose parents were a bit laxer than mine and would let their children dye their hair. One day I joined in, putting a blond streak through the centre of my hair where a mohawk would be. When I got home, Mum hit the roof because even dyeing your hair was out of bounds. I was forbidden from visiting that house anymore.

I have no doubt our parents wanted the best for my siblings and me, and were trying to protect us, but the consequence was that whenever we could find a way to break a rule or step out of line, we'd take it. Or, rather, Khaled and Mohamed would take it and I'd tag along. Khaled even took me into nightclubs a couple of times when I was only about 16 because I could pass for 18 at that age.

To me, Khaled was the coolest guy in the world. Anywhere he went I wanted to be, and anything I wanted he'd give to me. He was very into fashion, and because we were the same size he'd let me wear his clothes. I was a 13-year-old walking around in snakeskin shoes worth hundreds of dollars. When I got those stress fractures I mentioned earlier and needed a bike because I couldn't run, he gave me the money to get the one I really wanted. He is still the most generous man I've ever come across, but at the time I didn't stop to think about how he could afford to be. I only saw someone who would do anything for me.

That meant I had real loyalty to Khaled. Whenever he and Mohamed got into a disagreement, I'd instinctively rush to his defence. I remember one fight in particular very well. Khaled had a girlfriend, which was pretty frowned upon in our culture, and he wanted to go to see her. So Mum asked Mohamed to hide Khaled's car keys so he couldn't leave – which, as you can imagine, Khaled didn't like. He decided to take it out on Mohamed.

No punches were thrown, but things got physical pretty quickly. I would have been about 16, and I threw myself into the fray. I grabbed Mohamed and dragged him off Khaled. 'Don't touch him! Let him go!' I shouted, even though I really believed Khaled was in the wrong. I didn't like that he was always the black sheep of the family, being picked on and singled out either by our siblings or our parents. Truth be told, that often happened because he loved mischief.

Khaled was the kind of person who saw rules as an invitation to break them. I remember how he got a job delivering pizzas, just like Mohamed did. The difference was that Mohamed had a driver's licence, while Khaled was too young. That wasn't an obstacle for Khaled: he just walked into VicRoads and impersonated his older brother. 'My name is Mohamed Houli and I lost my licence,' he said. 'Can I get another one?' Then he handed over Mohamed's passport, relying on the fact that the people at VicRoads wouldn't be paying close enough attention to spot that the person in the photo wasn't Khaled. And pretty soon he walked out with a licence in his brother's name. He even drove a taxi with it.

I loved that pizza delivery job he had because it gave me access to junk food and a way of spending time with my brothers. They would often get me to help out because I was good at spotting the addresses and directing them to the places they were going, and my payment at the end of the night was a pizza and some pasta. I would tuck in with gusto, without even thinking about whether the meat was halal. It's a fair reflection of the religiosity of our house at the time that this wasn't an issue. Even stuff that was cooked right alongside the bacon was fine. It wasn't even on my radar at the time that this might be a problem.

Throughout all this, footy was the glue in my life. It was everything to my brothers and me and our friends, and I still remember the feeling of those years. I feel like I can touch the plastic footy I had as a young boy, which was so different to a real football. If you gave it to me now I wouldn't be able to kick it, but back then I could kick it all kinds of ways and at all kinds of angles.

I used to dream of one day having a Sherrin – Kangaroo Brand, of course – because they were expensive and rare in my area. Whenever one of the local guys had one he'd cherish it like nothing else. He'd only bring it out occasionally, and even then he'd mostly polish it rather than kick it. And if you were going to kick it, it had better be on the highest-quality grass, miles away from the road or any asphalt that might damage the leather.

My brothers used Sherrins in the scratch matches they played with their friends at a nearby oval, and I'd stand behind the goals and watch, waiting for someone to take a shot. Whenever the ball came my way, I'd pounce on it, pick it up and then smell the leather for as long as I could before I had to give it back. It was like inhaling some kind of sacred incense.

Mohamed was as passionate a Carlton supporter as Rash, which gave me another reason to love the club. Mohamed had two main reasons for being a Carlton supporter. The first was the 1987 Grand Final, when the Blues beat Hawthorn.

The second was Mil Hanna, who played for the club in the 1980s and '90s. He was the first Lebanese player in the league – in fact, the only one until I arrived about 20 years after him.

Hanna was always a bit of a cult figure, both because of his unusual appearance – he had a completely bald head as a result of alopecia – but also because he was seriously good: a premiership player, an All-Australian and a Carlton Hall of Famer. The fact he had a long and successful career was a great story because he'd ruptured his anterior cruciate ligament on debut, before reappearing about a year later. Hanna was a big deal for Lebanese kids at the time: they'd never seen anyone like him on the footy field before.

Khaled, who always took a different path to everyone else whenever he could just for the sake of it, refused to barrack for Carlton. That meant there was only one option: Khaled would be a Collingwood supporter. That didn't rub off on me even though I was personally really close to Khaled, because he was nowhere near as passionate a supporter as Mohamed. Khaled was much more interested in playing than watching.

Mohamed did both. His and Rash's fanaticism for the Blues meant that, for an impressionable kid like me, the Carlton influence was much stronger. Watching Carlton win that 1995 Grand Final with them at our house at 17 Bunting Court, Altona North, remains one of my most vivid childhood memories.

Everything was great about that day, from me decking out the house in Carlton paraphernalia that morning to the riotous celebrations as Carlton destroyed Geelong from the first minute of the game. The Blues kicked the first four goals, and from then on it was an all-day party. No wonder I watched the tape so often at Rash's house over the years.

Every week, Rash, Mohamed and I would listen to the Carlton games on the radio at my place. We could rarely watch the Blues on TV because few games were shown back then, even on delay. This was the era when they'd show interstate games live and would give you updates on the other games that were happening after saying, 'If you don't want to know the scores, look away now . . .' It's unimaginable today.

Listening is different to watching because it requires you to put together the action in your head. There's so much going on in a football game that there's no way to describe it all, so you have to fill in the detail the commentary doesn't provide. That means it's a more active process than watching, and you have to concentrate more. There's more intensity. That made it a huge amount of fun for us, at least when Carlton was winning. But it all got too much for us when it went badly. Especially for Mohamed, who had a nasty habit of breaking the radio after a loss. Thank God the Blues were pretty good during that era. Even so, it got to the point that we ran out of radios at our place, so we had to relocate to Rash's house.

When I was 11 or 12, Rash took me to my first ever Carlton game. That was a big project, because it involved getting permission from my parents, and especially Mum, which was quite a task. Even my older brothers hadn't bothered doing that because they knew she would be too resistant. About once a month they'd take the risk of going to a game without telling Mum, taking precautions to ensure the news never made it back to her. They were so worried about it that they would sit in the top deck of the Ponsford Stand so they wouldn't be seen on TV. But my parents trusted Rash completely. Maybe that's what comes of being the one who helps out with your kid's homework. I don't know how he did it. All I knew was that I was off to the footy with Rash and my best mate from school, a kid named Waleed.

Mum might have re-evaluated if she'd understood Rash's full plan. This was Carlton versus Collingwood. At the MCG. In front of about 70,000 people. There are no quiet places in a crowd of that size, but Rash took us to the wildest place he could find: not just into the Carlton cheer squad, but into the middle of a group known as the 'Grog Squad'.

The name probably tells you enough, but let's just say the members of the Grog Squad didn't practise the kind of language, behaviour or . . . um . . . diet that my parents would have considered ideal. After every Carlton goal – and there were a lot that day – it was chaos. Limbs were flying every-where. At one point the Grog Squad suddenly threw me into the air. High. I landed safely back into their arms, surrounded by rowdy, unrestrained cheering. It was everything a kid loves, condensed into a single experience. My football team winning against their fiercest rival, a wild new atmosphere to absorb, and the thrill of being catapulted into the air like when a dad plays with his toddler: that feeling of danger while never really being out of control.

The noise, the colour and the excitement left a deep impression on me, but so did the characters. One of them I knew only as 'the Judge'. A slightly chubby guy who'd have been around 40, he spent the whole game with a beer in his hand and used to lead the singing after every Carlton goal. I don't remember the words exactly, but he always included the words 'hoo-ha' for some reason, which became a bit of an all-in refrain.

I'd eagerly wait for the next goal so I could anticipate it and sing the 'hoo-ha' bit along with the Judge. I found him hilarious and, because we were on the same team, really friendly. I was a shy kid, but I was perfectly happy for him to lift me up on his shoulders. I don't think I understood a lot of what was going on around me, but I knew the Judge and the rest of the Grog Squad absolutely loved me. And I knew I was having the time of my life. It was my first full-blown experience of being inducted into the tribalism of the game. I didn't shut up about it for the next month.

Seeing Carlton play was so rare for me that I was even prepared to forgo playing footy to do it. In my first season for Spotswood, I missed a game when Rash took me and Waleed to watch the filming of *The Sunday Footy Show*, and then to Optus Oval to see Carlton play. Our team were playing our closest rivals, Yarraville, and Waleed and I were the best players in the team. It seems like a terrible decision – okay, it was a terrible decision – but watching the Blues play was just so irresistible that as soon as Rash asked me if I wanted to go, there was only going to be one answer. But the worst of it was that we didn't let our coach or anyone else at Spotswood know. We just didn't turn up for the game. We spent the day eating as many pies as we could, and Spotswood lost by three goals.

Mohamed and Khaled were the first in my family to play at a club. They were born in Australia so knew the game as kids, but our family moved back to Lebanon when they were little. In the late 1980s they returned to Australia, and Khaled and Mohamed started playing junior footy at Newport a couple of years later. But they knew Mum and Dad would never approve. My parents were interested only in education. Sport, for them, was simply a distraction. That was a pretty common view in migrant families who had fled situations like civil war, and so lacked the social supports of home. Education often becomes the most important aspect of life, because it can give you a secure base and a reliable income.

In my family that attitude was probably entrenched by my oldest brother, Nezor, who had been a promising cross-country runner but abandoned it to focus on his studies. Eventually he achieved his dream of becoming a surgeon. He certainly never played football. The closest he got was playing hockey for his school team, but even that was only because the coach was his maths teacher. I don't think he ever actually got on the field.

Mohamed and Khaled didn't have that passion for education, and didn't share our parents' classic migrant mindset. Their lives were all about sport in a way that I think our parents found foolish – and even scary, given what they felt was at stake. So my brothers hatched a plan involving our auntie – Mum's younger sister – who lived nearby.

Her husband used to work the night shift, which meant she was often at home alone. One night someone broke into her house and robbed her – a terrifying experience that left psychological scars. Afterwards, she was scared of being home alone at night. Like the good Lebanese boys they almost were,

Mohamed and Khaled decided to visit her each evening and sleep at her place to make her feel safer.

Once they started playing footy, this provided the perfect cover story. They'd leave home around 5:00 pm, go to footy training and then head to our auntie's place afterwards. Mohamed and Khaled trained on different nights, which was handy because it meant that one of them was always there, so if Mum dropped by and asked about whichever of them was missing, the other could provide an excuse: 'Oh, Khaled went to the milk bar with some friends . . .' Of course, our auntie knew what they were up to, and she would occasionally threaten to tell Mum. Mohamed and Khaled would respond by using the only leverage they had: 'If you tell Mum, we're not going to sleep here anymore . . .' That sorted it.

It didn't always work perfectly. Mohamed couldn't find a way to get to training during Grand Final week in his under-18s year. That meant, to be fair to the other kids in the team who had trained, he spent most of the game on the bench, coming onto the ground only for 15 minutes in the last quarter, by which time his team was already in front by 100 points. It's the most miserable premiership anyone has won. He also won the club's best-and-fairest that year, but he left the trophy with a cousin of ours because he couldn't risk bringing it home.

Despite all their efforts to conceal what they were up to, my brothers' scheme came crashing down about three years later when someone kneed Khaled in the face during a game, breaking his jaw. That was something he couldn't hide. The pain and the swelling was so bad that he couldn't even take his footy jumper off, so he had no choice but to go home wearing it. It was all going to come out.

Dad had been working a night shift, so he was asleep when Khaled got home in the early afternoon, but Mum was very much awake. She didn't seem terribly interested in treating the injury or rushing Khaled to hospital. 'Wait until your dad wakes up!' was her immediate reaction.

Actually, Dad wasn't really the problem. He's definitely the quieter of our parents, and the truth is he mostly went along with Mum's objections. She was strongly against her sons playing football, and Dad wasn't about to intervene. So once my brothers were exposed, things went slightly better for them than they might have expected. Slowly, over time, Mum and Dad let them play. But it was more an admission of defeat than it was a change in policy. Mum decided that she'd failed with these two boys, so she'd focus instead on her younger ones. By the time I came along, the ban in our house on playing footy was as strong as ever.

That didn't mean I couldn't go along and watch. Nothing could stop me from being there every Saturday to watch Khaled and Mohamed play for Newport, although my favourite moment was when the siren announced the end of each quarter and I could run onto the ground myself and kick the footy. All I wanted to do was the one thing I couldn't do: play.

Those few minutes during breaks in play were the greatest. I'd charge on with all the desperation you'd expect from a kid wanting to do his favourite thing, eager to show off to any grown-ups who might be watching, but knowing the clock was ticking. If I had no one to kick the ball to, I'd kick it to myself, and if there was any room at all, I'd start bombing the ball at goal from 50 – or, at least, that was what I imagined I was doing. Sometimes I think I could kick the ball further as an eight-year-old than I can now.

As Khaled got closer to playing seniors, he decided to leave Newport to play his footy at a higher standard. Spotswood were in the highest division, so he went there. One night at training in 2000, he noticed that the under-12s didn't seem to have enough players.

'Where are all your boys?' he asked the coach.

'We need some. Do you know anyone?'

'I've got a brother, but I don't know how good he is . . .'

And so Khaled hatched a plan. He was good at that. 'Jump in the car,' he said to me one evening. I was 11, and by this time I was getting a bit weary of helping my brothers deliver pizzas. But this time Khaled was insistent, and eventually I gave in. I got into his car and he drove. And kept driving.

'Where are we going?' I asked.

'I'm taking you to the Spotswood Football Club.'

'What for?'

'You're going to start playing footy,' he told me.

It was the best moment of my young life. I loved the game with a passion, and my friend Waleed was in that Spotswood team and I was desperate to play with him. I knew how my parents felt and had always assumed I'd never be allowed to play, but Khaled wasn't having any of it.

However, there was a problem. Khaled could take me to training, but how was I going to get to games? I couldn't get a lift with him because the under-12s played much earlier than he did, and he'd have no way of explaining why he was leaving so early. And Khaled often went out partying on Friday nights and would be in no fit state to take me anywhere the next morning anyway. I needed someone with a car who was free, and who wouldn't arouse any suspicion if I was with them.

There was only one person who fitted that description: Rash. He was perfect. I was with him all the time anyway, he loved footy, he knew how much I loved footy, and he came from a far less strict family than mine so he considered my parents' policy unreasonably restrictive and figured they just didn't understand.

I'd sneak over to his house the night before a game. 'Rash, I'm playing tomorrow,' I'd tell him quietly. 'Can you take me – please, please, please?' The next morning I'd sneak back to his place with my footy bag and knock on his window. Often he was a bit groggy because he'd been out doing his DJ sets until 2 am. 'I'm ready,' I'd whisper, and Rash would drag himself to his car, take me to the ground, then go home and sleep. A couple of hours later he'd come and pick me up.

If Rash ever needed to explain where he was taking me, he would say I was going shopping with him, which would provide the cover story for the few hours we needed. After the game I'd get changed at Rash's house. I'd leave my footy bag there before going home, because I didn't want my parents to see me carrying it and start asking questions. I'd go back and get it from Rash that night.

The plan worked brilliantly. After a little while, even Umm Rashid was in on it too. And if Rash couldn't take me for some reason, my under-12s coach would get involved. I'd walk down the street and wait for him at a service station on the corner of Bunting Court and Millers Road.

It wasn't neat, but I was finally doing what I most wanted to do in the world. And it went smoothly enough that I was able to get away with it for the whole season. The scheme only began to unravel when I won three trophies at the best-and-fairest night: Spotswood's best-and-fairest, the league's best-and-fairest, and the league's top goal kicker. I probably should have followed Mohamed's lead and given my trophies to someone else, but it didn't occur to me to do that. I couldn't think of anything to do but bring them home.

'What are those trophies for, Bachar?'

The game was up. The secret was out. I was in the same situation my older brothers had been in all those years ago. 'Look at what I've achieved playing this game,' I argued. Khaled stood up for me, like he always did. 'You've got to let the kid play and enjoy what he's doing,' he pleaded.

The best we could hope for was a stalemate. My parents wouldn't approve, but they also knew it was pointless trying to stop me. For the next year I didn't speak to them about football and they pretended to forget I was playing. It took until the end of that second season for them to accept what was happening. In the end, I'd got what I wanted. And so, in a sense, had Khaled.

I suppose the only reason I ever started playing footy was that Khaled was such a maverick. If he was straighter, like my other siblings, he never would have smuggled me down to Spotswood to play. I might never have played a game of football at all. Maybe, as I got older, and my older siblings married and started their own families, my parents might have relaxed a little. They did certainly become less strict over time: my older siblings were never allowed to go interstate, but by the time I was 18 my parents let me go to Queensland for a holiday with a mate. And when it was my younger brother's turn, he was allowed to go to Bali! But who knows how old I would have been before they would have reached the point of letting me play football? If I'd started playing football fairly late, I don't think I would have made it anywhere near the AFL. It's probably the biggest irony of my life that my whole career is the result of my brother being the kind of person who behaves in a way I would never dream of doing.

Khaled got into a lot of mischief when he was young, but of all the rules he broke, this one had the soundest reasoning. He knew how much I loved footy: he'd leave the house in the morning with me kicking a ball to myself, and then see me still playing with it when he returned later that night. He knew how much I loved going along to watch him play, and how eagerly I waited for the siren so I could run out onto the ground and kick the ball around. More than anyone, Khaled knew what I was missing out on, and that my parents' position was over the top. He could also see that I had talent and would be a better player than so many other kids who had the opportunity. I think that, in Khaled's mind, taking me to play footy wasn't so much getting up to mischief as righting an injustice.

That sort of thing motivated my brothers, whatever their misbehaviour along the way. The fact they were wilder than me – especially Khaled – didn't change the fact that deep down they really cared about our family. Maybe nothing shows that more than the day my dad's career as a taxi driver came to an end. He had picked up two passengers at the airport, a man and a woman who had been prevented from boarding their flight, almost certainly because they were on drugs. The job was to take them to the Chadstone shopping centre, which Dad did, but they fell asleep on the way. When they arrived, Dad tried to wake the woman, but the man woke up in a rage and bashed him.

It was a horrible time for taxi drivers generally, with many being assaulted and some even stabbed. For Khaled, the thought that anything like that could happen to his father was unacceptable. He hit the roof and made it clear to everyone that Dad had to get out of the taxi industry straightaway, and then he set about making that happen. Mohamed was running a fish-and-chip shop at the time, so my brothers figured out that this would be the best escape route for Dad. Mohamed sold Dad half the business for next to nothing and they became partners – and Dad had a new, much safer line of work. When something really mattered to my brothers, they stepped up.

Football was definitely one of those things. In fact, it seemed to be the one area of life in which Khaled was determined to keep me on the straight and narrow. At the end of my first season, I went to Lebanon for a couple of months, spending lots of time with my older cousin. While I was there, I picked up a habit of smoking shisha, or what the Lebanese call argileh.

Argileh is to Lebanese culture what coffee is to Melbourne. It's available everywhere, is consumed by everyone and carries no real stigma. My cousin had a corner store that got about two customers a day, and we spent the rest of the time drinking Coke, eating chocolate and finishing it off with some argileh. By the time I returned to Australia I'd been having four or five argileh sessions a day. I was 12 years old and I was addicted.

Back in Melbourne, I needed to figure out a way to satisfy my cravings. So I pulled my own little operation together, heading to the shop on my own, choosing my favourite flavour – 'Double apple, thanks' – and smuggling it home. What I didn't realise is that everyone could smell it. One day I was hiding in the corner of our garage with my younger brother, Louay, and we were getting stuck in when Khaled walked by.

'Bro, what are you doing?' he asked. I could tell he was angry.

'What?'

'What's that smell?'

'It's nothing.'

'It's not nothing – you're smoking argileh. That shit is bad for you. If keep going down this line, you're not going to be a footballer. Do you want to play football or not?'

I stopped right there and then. I had a sense, even at that age, that I wanted to be really good at football, and I didn't want to destroy my chances of success. Argileh never came back into my life, especially as I got older and more serious about religion and came to believe that smoking is prohibited in Islam (a view which, clearly, many Muslims don't share).

So while Khaled's approach to life was about as opposite to mine as you could get, he was a real authority figure for me in all sorts of complicated ways. If he thought something was wrong, I decided, then it really must be, because my brother was the guy who seemed to have so few boundaries.

I knew Khaled got into fights occasionally, but I was never privy to the whys and wherefores of his escapades, and in time he chose to take a path that has led to him becoming a successful businessman and family man.

Despite there being so much I didn't understand, there was one thing I definitely did: this wasn't at all my scene. I loved and admired Khaled so much, but at the same time I knew we were completely different people. Back then he was instinctively a rule breaker who loved doing whatever he could get away with. I wasn't a troublemaker. I didn't even like seeing someone else get into trouble. So watching Khaled make poor decisions, and seeing what he was putting my parents through, left a deep impression on me. I knew this wasn't right, and I saw the consequences. I wanted my life to be different.

My natural personality is much more like that of my dad, who's a very quiet, patient, religiously inclined person. My oldest brother, Nezor, was also one of these responsible, rule-observing types. But the truth is that because of his career and the age gap between us, I barely saw Nezor, and was socially and emotionally much closer to Khaled. Somehow I've ended up a completely different person from those who were my biggest influences.

But that very fact might be a big part of who I am. I'm different. I'm comfortable being different. But I'm also comfortable around people who are totally different to me. When I look at people who behave in ways I could never condone, I still see the good in them because that has been my whole life.

I could never be a member of the Grog Squad. My attitude to alcohol couldn't be more different to theirs, and I don't accept the harmlessness of drinking. But they were warm, generous people who gave a kid the time of his life and made one of my happiest football memories.

Rash and I could hardly be more different in our approach to religion, but he's one of the most important people in my life; to say I love him like a brother feels like I'm understating the depth of our relationship. Similarly, I don't love my cousin in Lebanon any less because he lives in an environment where giving a kid tobacco is no big deal.

I might be someone who follows rules, but I owe my career to my brother Khaled's preparedness to break them. Khaled might have done some things I can't defend, and that he wouldn't defend today, but that's exactly why he was one of my most significant teachers in life, even if only by giving me an example I knew I didn't want to follow. I can't pretend he is anything other than one of my biggest influences. And beneath it all, he has a huge generosity and a heart of gold. These days Khaled is a husband and father who runs his own business and sends his kids to an Islamic school. Mohamed, too. We're all evolving.

People talk a lot about diversity, about different worldviews and values systems. Usually they mean we're diverse because we have different cultural or religious backgrounds. But it's often surprising where the differences and the common ground exist. I grew up surrounded by Lebanese Muslims, and Islam is central to the way I look at the world and how I live my life. But the fact is that it was football, rather than Islam, that was at the centre of my closest and most influential relationships from childhood. And today, strangely enough, it's Islam, rather than football, that's at the centre of my relationships with my closest non-Muslim friends, who I see daily at Richmond.

5

COME AS YOU ARE

ROUBA AND I WERE what you might call family friends. My sisters and hers were really close, and she would visit our place occasionally, but she and I didn't have a lot to do with each other. No one within our families would have had the slightest inkling we'd end up getting married. We went to the same high school, and spoke to each other only once. It was at the library. I was in Year 12, she was in Year 10, and she was sitting with some friends at a computer, so I pulled up a chair a few stations down and asked how her sisters and the family were doing.

That conversation would have meant nothing to her at all. But it was very deliberate on my part. Rouba had been on my radar from the time I was about 14, when my cousin Ibrahim became engaged to her older sister Ramzia. It was he who started getting in my ear. 'She's the one for you! I'm telling you, get onto it!' I'm not sure exactly how, but Ibrahim's insistence must have reached my mates at school because they started up as well. 'One day she'll be your wife,' one of them said, not so much to tease me as to state a fact. In the Muslim community, you talk about these things quite young, and I'd always had the intention to marry early. I denied it at the time, of course, but they were completely right. I had definitely noticed her.

It was her eyes that got me: they were a sparkling green that seemed to pop whenever I saw them and pierce straight through me. For as long as I'd been interested in girls, and for as long as people had asked me what my 'type' was, green eyes were always the thing I'd mention. The fact she was wearing a hijab as part of her school uniform probably enhanced the effect, because with her hair covered, her eyes really stood out. Every time she walked past, I'd think, 'Whoa! *Masha Allah. Tabarak Allah!*' These expressions – which mean 'This is what God willed' and 'God is blessed' – are commonly used by Muslims whenever they come across something astonishing or beautiful. It's a way of recognising God as the source of that beauty.[2] That way, we channel a feeling that could be quite base into something that reminds us of God's presence. It didn't mean I was any less impressed.

By the end of high school, I'd become good mates with Rouba's cousin Wally. He kept vouching for her too. 'She's

---

2   They are also used in a lot of other contexts – for example, when giving someone a compliment. I might say, '*Masha Allah*, my friend is very intelligent.' The idea is to direct the credit for this to God, so that my friend doesn't become arrogant and I don't fall into envy. It helps both of us recognise that God wanted it this way, rather than it being something we control.

my favourite cousin,' he'd say. 'She's exactly like her mum.' That really meant something, because although I didn't know Rouba's mother very well, everyone seemed to agree she was a gem.

All these things were aligning. Rouba came from a good family who I knew and liked, and who seemed to have values very similar to mine. I knew from my own experience that people within families can vary a lot, but I'd been told by people I trusted that she represented the best of her family's characteristics.

Then one day during my first year at Essendon, Wally mentioned to me in passing that Rouba had started wearing the hijab. To wear it at school was one thing, but it's a big decision for a Muslim woman in the West to wear it in her daily life, because it often comes with all kinds of prejudice in the community. Obviously, people wear it for many different reasons, but based on my impressions of Rouba, it felt like a sign she was at least as religiously committed as I was, and that we probably had similar approaches to Islamic life. I decided it was time to make my move.

Both of us came from traditional Lebanese Muslim families, though, and we were both also fairly traditional people, so if I was going to approach her, I had to do it right. I couldn't just start courting her. Neither of us would have found that Islamically appropriate, and her family definitely would have intervened once they found out. I knew her dad a bit because we used to go hunting together as part of our family visits. He was a lovely, gentle man, but he was also very strict with his kids. A bit like my parents.

So I did the most obvious thing I could: I got Wally to talk to Rouba for me, to see if she had any interest in getting to know me better, with a view to marriage.

This is how things work in lots of Muslim communities. Because premarital sex isn't accepted, there's no real dating scene to speak of, and relationships commence with the idea that marriage is in play. That doesn't mean there's any expectation or obligation. It just means everyone's intentions are clear from the very beginning. Some cultures and families will be more or less relaxed about how much interaction is appropriate between unmarried people, but there was no doubt in our context that the whole thing would have to happen with the permission of our parents, and with no chance of something untoward happening.

I can't say for sure how much interest in me Rouba had at that time, but it was enough for her to begin getting to know me. What I can say is that being an AFL footballer made no difference to her at all. She didn't follow the game and didn't seem to think that me playing for Essendon was anything special. In fact, it was probably a disadvantage because I had to convince her I wasn't after the high life of a footballer. Rouba wasn't the kind of person to be impressed by someone pursuing what others see as a glamorous life, along with whatever version of fame it offers.

The reason we were so suited is that we were both quite mature for our age. In a situation like ours, your lack of seriousness can get exposed pretty quickly because the conversation soon turns to the big questions of life, including when you'd be looking to start a family. Marriage is a big deal for Muslims:

'When a person gets married he has completed half of his religion,' said the Prophet. Much of our conversation was about confirming we had taken that to heart. So it actually didn't take very long for us to agree we were both serious about this.

The next step for me was to convince my parents. And just as with playing football, Dad was the easy part. As far as he was concerned, if I felt it was important and he had no moral objection, he would support me. Mum was a different story. Partly that's because she had strong ideas about who I should marry, which effectively meant someone she had recommended. But she also resisted for the same reason she originally opposed football: it would interfere with my education. For her, marriage should wait until I'd finished university and established myself in life and financially. It took lots of back and forth before I managed to convince her that actually I already had a good job that could provide a house for us, and that since university was just something I was doing part-time, it made no sense to make graduating a prerequisite for me getting married.

Rouba and I began discussing the possibility of getting engaged, and how that might work – which was a complicated process. First, my family would have to approach hers and ask their permission for me to ask for her hand. Then we'd set a time for me to come back formally and propose, and if she agreed, we'd then hold a more official engagement ceremony. We agreed that was where it was heading, but Rouba thought we should proceed more slowly than I did. By the conversation's end, we had agreed that I would set things in motion in a week or two.

I showed up the next day.

Not by myself, I should confess. In fact, to be honest, I barely showed up at all. I arrived at her place with Dad, but as soon as we got there, Dad took over. 'Go. I'll tell you when I'm done,' he said.

I didn't even stay in the driveway. As Dad went in to speak to Rouba's father, I drove off, killing time for an hour, getting more and more nervous as I agonised over what was being said.

Rouba was caught massively by surprise. She had no idea we were coming, but she knew exactly what it meant. Immediately, she got very shy about the situation and ran to hide in her room – which, to be fair, was kind of what I was doing too. But I had high hopes that the conversation between our fathers was going well. Our families liked and trusted each other, and in Lebanese culture the idea that you are marrying into a family is a common one.

The next month was like torture. Silence. Nothing. It wasn't a rejection – in some ways it was worse, because I had no idea what the hold-up could possibly be. Had I misread the situation? Had Rouba decided I wasn't for her? Did her dad have an objection we didn't know about? Were they just too embarrassed to tell us the bad news? The longer it went, the more nervous I got about it, but I felt powerless to do anything.

As time went on, it became a topic of conversation within my extended family. Among whom was my uncle Sleiman, Dad's brother, who was the kind of outgoing, up-front person who would always say what was on his mind. One day he brought it up in his no-nonsense way. 'Have they given you an answer yet?'

'No,' I said.

'What do you mean no? They haven't called? Enough's enough. I'm going to take your dad to their house right now and sort this out.'

'Um, okay,' I said. 'I'll get ready.'

'No, you stay here. We'll take care of this.'

He was gone before I knew what was happening. Sleiman could do this because, like Dad, he knew Rouba's parents well. He could be forthright without it being taken as rude. So when he got there, he just asked bluntly what the reason for the delay was.

It turned out that Rouba's dad hadn't even spoken to her about it.

Sleiman didn't like that. 'Go inside and ask her!' he said. 'What are you waiting for? Do you have a problem with it? If you don't have anything against it, what's the problem?'

Rouba's dad was more or less forced to ask her there and then. She said yes almost straightaway, and a time was set for me to propose formally the next week.

Finally, I was on the home stretch. She'd agreed. Our families were happy. Even my mum was content. I knew for sure the hard work had been done when Rouba, our mums and I all went shopping together for an engagement ring. This was happening.

About a month later came the formal engagement ceremony, which naturally (like everything else) involved drinks and Lebanese sweets, but it centred on the families gathering and reading the first chapter of the Qur'an, called *al-Fatihah*, together.[3] It's more a cultural practice than a strictly Islamic one, but it's very common in the Arab world and is something traditional Lebanese families do.

But like everything else in this saga, it dragged on forever for no good reason. We all knew why we were there – after all, it was the result of a big process – but everyone seemed to think about 45 minutes of small talk was in order first. It was like everyone was skirting around just getting on with it. I know 45 minutes isn't much in the grand scheme of things, but by this point each minute felt like a year.

Rouba and I were now officially engaged, which meant people knew of our relationship and we could spend more time together legitimately – just not alone. I visited her house a lot at that time, and stayed as late as I could, but we were never alone together behind a closed door. Every now and again I'd ask her father if she could visit a close friend's house with me. I was petrified each time I asked because I knew how strict he was, but if I wanted to spend more time with Rouba then I knew I'd have to pluck up the courage. And it was just as well I did, because her dad always said yes.

---

3 *Al-Fatihah* literally means 'the Opener', but often appears in Qur'anic translations as 'the Opening', and is in some ways similar to the preface of a book. It is short – only seven verses – but sets up the Qur'an's key themes. It is expressed as a kind of prayer asking God for guidance, leading some scholars to describe the rest of the Qur'an as the answer to it. The prophet Muhammad called it 'the greatest chapter in the Qur'an' and the 'mother of the Qur'an', and it is the most recited chapter in the Qur'an because it is a compulsory part of *salat*.

This continued for about nine months, until we finally got to the stage of getting married. Often in Muslim cultures, marriage takes place in two ceremonies. Think of it as having the ceremony and the reception separated by months instead of hours – but food is involved in each stage.

The first, called the *katb al-kitab*, is smaller but arguably more important, because it's the moment you're considered Islamically married. It's the time you exchange vows and sign contracts in front of witnesses and guests, mostly just family. But even then people usually still consider the couple to be engaged, and the marriage to be incomplete until the second event, called a *walimah*, which is really just a party. Ours was a fairly small affair of about 300 people – modest by Lebanese standards – with the men and women holding separate functions. That usually means the women have more fun. In the absence of the opposite sex, dress and behaviour codes are relaxed, so the women typically really go for it and dance up a storm.

Not that I knew this firsthand, of course. And not that I cared. What mattered most to me was that I was a married man. I was 21, and at the end of my third year in the AFL. I seemed young to everyone else, but to me it felt like it had been a long time coming.

When I explained all this to Trent Cotchin one day, he was blown away. He couldn't get his head around the number of rules surrounding engagement and marriage, the multiple stages you go through and especially the role that parents play. He couldn't believe that until Rouba and I were finally married we weren't even spending time alone. It must have sounded to him like an arranged marriage, even though it certainly wasn't, because Rouba and I were the ones who pushed for it. Even so, it was a million miles away from the way marriages in the West usually occur, with couples often living together and even having children before they consider getting married, if they choose to get married at all.

Someone with Trent's background could therefore be forgiven for being shocked, and even finding it all a bit weird, as my teammates at Essendon had at the time. But his response was open and curious. He wasn't put off or judgemental – he seemed really interested, even excited to be learning about something so different from what he knew. I think he was even quietly flattered that I'd let him in on this kind of thing.

I loved Richmond as soon as I got there, but it wasn't yet what it became from 2017. The club culture was a bit shallower back then, and the players didn't have the profound connections that would come years later, so it wasn't the done thing for players to talk about particularly meaningful things. But Trent did. And because he knew that Islam meant so much to me, he became very interested in talking to me about it. He asked about it all the time, and we ended up comparing notes on how Muslim relationships work. It was inevitable that the subject would come up, considering how much we both cared about family.

By the time I arrived in late 2010, Trent was already in a serious relationship with Brooke, and was looking to get married young and start a family, while I was already married and wanted to have children soon. That already marked us out as different in a footy club, even before you considered that we were both quiet, unassuming people who didn't drink and didn't like big nights out. According to most people, we were both far too young to have those kinds of attitudes. The other players used to call Trent 'Grandpa' because of that, but they probably spared me something similar because they accepted I had religious reasons for my choices. But even though we were from wildly different backgrounds, we were both definitely old souls, people who took life seriously from a very early age. We often talked about how football was important, but that there were more important things in life. That wasn't an attitude that was typically expressed around football clubs at that time. Our discovery that we shared this worldview was significant for both of us, and created an especially strong bond between us.

There have been times in Trent's career when he felt he had to be something he didn't want to be just to be normal, but with me he was never that way. It meant that he could turn to me with his frustrations because I was one of only a few people who would genuinely get it, and he often did, especially after he became captain. A role like that comes with certain expectations among his teammates that his position on drinking and partying just didn't allow him to fulfil. Often, the boys would ask him to come out with them more, and when things weren't going well they'd criticise him for being distant.

It irritated Trent that this could even be an issue – that he would be marked down for not involving himself in those things. In fact, judging by the way he vented to me over coffee one day, it was probably the one thing that really got to him.

'I'd like to think I'm not a bad role model in the way I live my life,' he said to me.

All I could do was support him by affirming who he is. 'Do what makes you happy, bro,' I told him. 'If people can't respect that about you, then they aren't worth worrying about anyway.'

It was a big theme in our friendship because it showed we were there for each other in the tough times, at moments of vulnerability. I suppose it was a preview of how Richmond's culture changed in the lead-up to the 2017 season. It was at that time that Trent decided to tackle the issue head-on. 'This is just who I am,' he told the whole playing group. 'I'm not the partygoer. I'm not a big drinker. But I love having a joke, taking the piss – I love physical pranks.'

Trent and I based our relationship on life outside football, and that meant we felt safe with each other, comfortable in each other's presence, and that we trusted one another. We have nothing to hide from each other, because whatever differences we might have in our beliefs or the way we live our lives become interesting rather than strange.

Probably the clearest sign of this for me is that I don't think twice about inviting Trent to join me on a family trip. That might sound simple, but it's not something I do lightly, because being a Muslim has lots of facets that can make it difficult: making sure the food is halal, for example, or having to pray each day within specified times. It takes an understanding travel companion for you to feel at ease doing those kinds of things, and it takes a genuine bond for them to feel at ease too.

On one of our recent trips, my daughter Sarah and I went camping with Trent and his girls. Trent left the tents to get something while I started the barbecue, and on the way back his eldest daughter, Harper, rushed ahead and reached us first. At the time she arrived, I was praying, which she hadn't seen before, so she immediately shouted out: 'Daddy, Bachar's head's on the ground! Is he okay?'

Because I was in the middle of the prayer, I couldn't respond, so Trent explained what was happening. Being a kid, Harper just took it all in her stride. She'd been exposed to something she never would have seen if they'd gone camping with most other people, and the whole experience seems to have left an impression. To this day, she still calls lamb '*lahm*', which is the Arabic word for meat, because she heard Sarah calling it that. When Harper got home she decided she'd draw a picture of Sarah's family, and she depicted my beard and Rouba's hijab, apparently without giving it a second thought.

In the week of the 2019 Grand Final, Trent sent every member of the team a video with a quick message. The one he sent me captured the essence of our friendship:

> Bachar, my brother . . . I just wanted to say how much
> I respect you . . . I cherish our friendship. I cherish the
> values you continue to live by but also teach me about.
> You're a very humble man. I hold you in the highest regard
> and I just wanted to thank you for our friendship, your love,
> your support. And I love being a part of this journey: the
> journey of football but more so the journey of life together,
> and I can't wait to watch our kids grow up and live life in
> a very similar way to what we have to date. I'm looking
> forward to the Grand Final Parade and sharing that with
> you and all the little moments across the next few days,

but more importantly the ones going forward in our lives.

Keep smiling, brother! Love you, and I can't wait to run out with you on Saturday.

My friendship with Ivan Maric arose just as quickly and for similar reasons. 'You'll love this guy,' promised Richmond's list manager, Blair Hartley, when he told us he was bringing Ivan to the club from the Adelaide Crows. 'He's exactly like you!'

And he was right. In fact, Blair asked me to give Ivan a call to welcome him to the club: he thought we were so similar that I'd be the best person to introduce him to Richmond. I'd only been at Richmond a year, but my transition had gone so well, and I felt I belonged enough, that I was only too happy to make the call. It took one five-minute phone conversation for us to hit it off, but in our case the starting point was ... well, being wogs: having funny names, growing up eating funny foods. He was Croatian and I was Lebanese, but in these respects we came from a similar background.

From a distance, you'd never know just how deeply that sense of cultural difference had always affected Ivan. He felt it very sharply from a young age, being the one who didn't speak English at home with his parents or relatives. His mum would insist that he correct people if they mispronounced his name – 'It's not *eye*-van, it's iv-*aan*' – which he felt embarrassed doing, but he did nonetheless.

His school lunchbox included nothing that came in a packet. Other kids had jam on white bread, but Ivan would have a gourmet roll with salamis, cheeses and lettuce. Sometimes he felt so self-conscious that he wouldn't eat his lunch at school, but would scoff it on the way home instead. By then it was safe to do so, and he was starving.

It probably didn't help that he was a big soccer fan. When all the other kids were talking about going to the footy on the weekend, he was off to watch Melbourne Croatia play in Sunshine or St Albans. Footy was probably his third favourite sport after soccer and basketball, and when he did watch the AFL he tended to notice the non-Anglo players, like Mil Hanna or Danny Del-Re, who played for Footscray in the 1990s.

Ivan's parents didn't want him to play footy, and like me he started playing without their knowledge. But in his case it was due more to cultural identity than to an emphasis on education. When he asked his father if he could take up footy, his dad's response was: 'What do you want to play that Aussie shit for?' Playing soccer and basketball was no problem – in fact, his sister and younger brother were playing basketball too – but footy represented something else altogether. His dad wasn't keen on cricket either, for the same reason.

In a role reversal of my case, Ivan's mum was less strident. He would sneak over to train and play footy with Keilor when he was 16, but once they had to play away games, he came clean and asked his mum for a lift. He only played eight games in that year before the phones started to ring from representative teams like the Calder Cannons. The following year, when people from the Brisbane Lions came to visit him, his dad's opinion about footy changed pretty quickly. All that sounded very familiar to me.

In that first phone conversation we had, Ivan and I talked mostly about changing clubs. I spoke about my experience coming to Richmond from Essendon, but for Ivan it was an even more significant change, because he was coming home to Melbourne after seven years in Adelaide.

That was important for him, because however different he felt in Melbourne, it was magnified in Adelaide. He didn't know the Croatian community there so he had no solid connection to that culture, and when he was starting out in his AFL career he really just wanted to fit in. That meant he spent years burying that part of himself. It was only late in his time at the Crows that he had the confidence to unearth it, and he started making connections with the Croatian community and attending Croatian festivals.

So he returned to Melbourne with a real yearning to embrace his roots and reconnect with Croatian culture. But Ivan can be surprisingly tentative at times, and can second-guess himself. It was like he needed someone to convince him that his instincts were correct.

I was definitely that person. Everything about my life involves my family. For us, family's not something that happens on festivals and holidays. It's an everyday thing, and it's big. To this day – or at least until COVID-19 hit – my whole family catches up weekly for dinner at my parents' place – there are about 40 or 50 of us, once everyone brings their spouses and kids. Some people might call that Christmas. We call it Monday.

Damien Hardwick got to witness it once. In fact, it was only the second time he'd met me. The first was when he and Blair Hartley invited me to the club to talk to me about why they wanted to recruit me and how they saw me fitting in to the Richmond side. But despite their interest, they'd failed to reach a trade with Essendon, which meant they had to get me via the Pre-season Draft. I think they felt I was worried about this, so they wanted to catch up again to let me know they were still keen. Usually a meeting like that would happen over a coffee, and I'm pretty sure that's what Dimma was expecting.

'Come and meet me at my parents' place,' I told them when they rang to see if we could catch up.

Dimma had no idea what he was walking into. Blair knew me a little better at that stage and told him there might be some family around, but even that didn't capture it.

Forget the front door – I showed them into our garage out the back, which in typical Lebanese fashion had been decked out as a living area, complete with a traditional fireplace. As they arrived, they were greeted by a small village. There weren't as many kids in the family back then as there are now, but even so, my parents, Rouba and my brothers were all there, making the usual cacophony. Blair and Dimma were welcomed with hugs by people talking loudly and pas-sionately about footy with a depth of knowledge that caught them by surprise.

Coffee? Sure, if you like. Try this Turkish coffee we just made. But that was the least of it. As soon as Dimma and Blair sat down, out came the meat. It must have looked like a tonne or two of lamb. They could smell it cooking from the moment they'd arrived, and they could hear the commotion inside of people organising themselves to serve food, but even so they would never have expected this much food.

We weren't meeting – we were entertaining! At least, that's how it would have looked to Dimma and Blair. To us, it was just what you do when someone comes to visit. Food and hospitality are deeply ingrained in Lebanese culture. You would never host someone without feeding them, and you would never feed them without ensuring there will be plenty left over.

As far as I could tell, Dimma loved it. He definitely loved the food – and he still does, often nudging me to bring in some of Mum's food if I haven't done it in a while. One reason he and I are close is that we're both family people. But I don't think he understood what that really meant for me until he saw it up close, and even then he mightn't have realised he'd just caught the end of a routine gathering. He walked away that day knowing that if I came to Richmond, about 100 new members were coming with me.

When Ivan came to the club in late 2011, I invited him to hang out with my family all the time, and he revelled in it. He loved the big characters and the chaos that is so common in Mediterranean cultures. It made him feel normal. 'Your cousin reminds me so much of mine,' he'd say. Or: 'My uncle's exactly the same!'

Looking back, it's incredible just how quickly and completely Ivan became like a family member. My brothers started inviting him to lunch independently of me because they saw him as one of their own. He came along on our end-of-year family holiday trips without anyone so much as pausing to consider whether it would be strange. After seeing me so fully embrace my family, and through being welcomed himself to the extent he was immersed in it too, I think Ivan found the confidence to take the same approach to his own family. He knew he had friends at his football club who would support him in doing that, and who wouldn't find it strange.

Ivan – like Trent – was really interested in how Islamic weddings worked, and he also liked to compare our non-Anglo cultures. Ivan has always considered himself a religious person. He comes from a Catholic family, and grew up going to mass every week. His wife, who he met in Adelaide, also comes from a religious Catholic family. He always felt very positive about religion because it was at the centre of the things he loved in cultural and family life, especially at all the big moments: weddings, births, funerals. For him, it was something that brought people together. I remember inviting Ivan to a cousin's wedding once, and he was there in the same room watching us all pray together in congregation. He loved it because it reminded him so much of the role he saw religion play in his own family.

Maybe it was coffee that ultimately brought Ivan, Trent and me together. The starting point was that Ivan and I would meet for coffee or breakfast before training, or perhaps lunch if we found time during the day, along with our property steward – and another guy with a funny name – Giuseppe Mamone, who Ivan knew previously from his time at the Calder Cannons. It didn't take long for Trent to join us, because he and Ivan quickly found they shared common ground.

For them it began at our preseason training camp in Arizona during Ivan's first season at Richmond, when they roomed together and found they shared similar values based largely on family. Even at that early stage, they were talking about serious stuff like marriage and their futures. Their relationship was cemented by the fact they played together in the midfield and therefore trained a lot together, and they also lived near each other and would sometimes give each other lifts to games.

Other people would join us too. Brandon Ellis was often there because he was good mates with Trent and me, but there was no doubt that Trent, Ivan and I would tend to drive the topic of conversation. Over the years we spent countless hours over countless coffees talking about anything and everything that was happening in our lives, and about how we viewed the world. There might be a bit of small talk, but usually we dived straight into some pretty profound stuff.

One of the biggest topics of conversation at this time was the fact that Rouba and I had been trying unsuccessfully for a long time to have our first child. We'd been trying since about five months into our marriage, and we felt completely ready, but for three and a half years nothing happened. There didn't seem to be a particular reason, either. We had every test we could, and all the results said there was no medical issue. It just wasn't happening.

As time went by, the pressure from our families (mainly mine) grew – it was well intentioned and came from a place of care and concern, but it was pressure nonetheless. We found ourselves fielding lots of questions about how things were going or what the doctors had been saying, and that took a toll, especially on Rouba. There were times when it all got too much for her, and she was in tears. But happily that tough time came to an end, and I'll never forget the day Rouba told me things had changed.

Rouba called me when I was at a mate's house. 'Hurry up! Come to my mum's house,' she said.

'What's wrong?'

'Just come!'

I got there and she was in tears. 'What's wrong?' I asked.

'I'm pregnant!'

'No way!'

Everyone in the room, especially Rouba's mum, was incredibly emotional. I definitely got teary too.

Ivan, Trent and Brandon lived that journey with me through countless conversations. These weren't typical conversations between teammates at a footy club, but we spoke about it all effortlessly because that was the level of our friendship. And through these conversations, we ended up talking about our approaches to the big questions life throws at you.

'We believe, in our faith, that if it's meant to be, it's meant to be,' I remember saying one day. 'I'm definitely not willing to give up, but we can't force someone to arrive on this Earth. It's all down to the will and plan of God. Maybe this is being prevented for a good reason. We can only take the positive out of every situation, not say "why me?". One of the meanings of the word "Islam" is "surrendering to God", so that's what we do.'

It was the kind of reasoning that applied once Rouba was pregnant, too, when we considered whether we should tell people. Ultimately, we decided we would, because people had to know so that they could look after Rouba if she needed anything. If something happened to the baby along the way, there was no need for us to be shy about it because that would be from God just as much as the pregnancy was. We've been through three pregnancies now, and have taken that approach with each of them.

In Islam, we call this concept of relying on God and trusting in His plan *tawakkul*. I've been seriously invested in this idea for a lot of my adult life, and it's hard to overstate how powerful it has been in giving me comfort or tranquillity in situations that could have been stressful or even crippling. It certainly came to the fore in the early stages of COVID-19, when the 2020 season was shut down after Round 1. Like all players, I had my pay cut in half, and like a lot of them, I watched my ambassador roles disappear one by one. And as the whole country entered lockdown, there was no telling if or when the competition might restart. It was possible I had played my last game, and that my income wouldn't recover for the rest of my life.

I admit I was in a good position to absorb all this because my life is now relatively established with a family and a mortgage paid off, but even so, having *tawakkul* as a foundation made a huge difference. It meant I resolved to accept whatever was coming as a test. How would I respond? It was one thing to talk about *tawakkul*, but this was a chance to live it. That was my job.

For me, that meant things like not panic-buying, because that would probably be me trying to be in control and doing the wrong thing by other people because I can't accept that I'm not. It would be me failing to recognise that I could always ask my in-laws for, say, toilet paper, and that I could always just go without a few things if necessary. And it meant that if the pandemic ended my career, I would go with a smile on my face, ready to work in Khaled's landscaping business or my younger brother Louay's fish-and-chip shop. I wouldn't particularly want to, of course, but I couldn't be too proud to do it. *Tawakkul* has always worked as a guiding principle for me, in my life and in my football career.

My closest friends at Richmond weren't Muslims, but they certainly appreciated the concept of *tawakkul*, and we'd talk about it surprisingly often. That sort of discussion would lead us to talk about related ideas, which, in later years, would become a big part of our approach to football as a club. Specifically, we'd talk about how important it is to remain present in the moment in life, rather than failing to appreciate what we are experiencing because we're too busy worrying about the future or the past. Then we might discuss the importance of being humble and grateful for what we have, rather than always being obsessed with what we don't have or envious of what others have. Ivan particularly liked a statement of the Prophet I mentioned once: 'If the son of Adam [i.e. human beings] had a valley full of gold, he would want to have two valleys.'

What I took away from our conversations was that these were people who not only had similar values to me, but who also had great character. They embody so many of the characteristics I value so much: they're extremely respectful, they're calm and balanced, and they're fair and understanding. In short, they show all the traits Muslims are meant to have. I hope they wouldn't mind me saying that they're probably better Muslims than a lot of Muslims.

Religion came up a lot in our chats, mostly because Ivan kept trying to get me to talk about it. He seemed to feel it was a good conversation starter – as if he wanted Trent to hear what I had to say. Ivan seemed especially motivated by media misrepresentations of Muslims, because I think he had a general distrust of the way media often worked. Part of that was because when he started playing professional football and compared what he knew with the reporting he saw in the media, he saw that the reality was so often different from the reporting. He'd also grown up reading about 'Croatian soccer hooligans' in the paper, and that stereotype didn't reflect the people he knew. When it came to Islam in the media, he only ever seemed to hear about terrorism, but because he knew me personally he could see that wasn't even close to the full picture. That drove his curiosity.

This is what makes Ivan the kind of person who will stand up and correct people if he hears something amiss. So, for example, if he hears someone using the stereotype of Indigenous people as drunks, he'll stop and have a conversation with them about the Indigenous people he knows who aren't like that at all, or he'll talk about the impact of the Stolen Generations and how that sort of trauma creates social problems. Ivan's a very warm, gentle person, but he's prepared to make people uncomfortable if there's a good reason for it. He's often done similar things when it comes to Islam. He might be at a pub with friends when someone says something like 'they're all terrorists anyway'. Ivan knows that if he doesn't say anything, he'll end up being upset about it. So he does.

In March 2019, on the day of the Christchurch terrorist attacks, I ran into Ivan at the club. By this time he had become a coach.

'Have you heard what's happened in New Zealand?' he asked.

'Yeah, someone just told me something about that,' I replied. At that point I had only heard about it briefly while I was on the massage table, and I hadn't fully grasped the news.

We were about to start training, and Ivan's mind immediately turned to whether I would be up to it. 'Don't do anything if you don't feel like it today,' he told me. If I needed to be released from training, he said, he was happy to arrange it.

'It's all good, I'll be okay,' I said. But now it was dawning on me that this event was taking on a size I hadn't appreciated.

I went into a bathroom and closed the door to be alone, then I looked at my phone to catch up on the news. My WhatsApp was running hot with videos of the attack. It looked almost unreal, like a video game, but that changed when I saw that a three-year-old boy had been killed, running towards the attacker. Then it really hit me: this stuff was real.

The boy's name was Mucad, and his father had taken him to the mosque that day, exactly as my daughter Sarah pleads with me to do. Maybe that's because the imam usually gives her lollies, but whatever the case, she loves joining us, being part of our community gathering. Mucad's story was too close to home for me.

I came out of the bathroom and went straight to Ivan's office, and the words poured out. 'That's my daughter,' I said in a rush. 'She could have been in the same position . . .' Then I broke down in tears. 'To see this happen like that, especially at a place of God . . . an innocent young kid who just wants to be with her dad. A young kid doesn't deserve to die. I can't do this. I've got to go home. I've got to be with my family.'

Ivan made the arrangements with the club. I think he understood what I needed so quickly because he felt it himself – and that's probably the best illustration of the relationship I have with him, and with Trent. It's deeply moving to see them feel pain on my behalf when something like Christchurch happens, or when they see Muslims being vilified in the media, or when stories emerge of someone in the crowd calling me a terrorist. It's like they've become personally invested in the perception and treatment of Muslims, so they take on some of the weight we carry around all the time.

For Trent, I think it's primarily his connection to me as a friend that means this sort of thing affects him. The same is true for Ivan, but he also has the experience of having grown up in a cultural minority, and thus of understanding how prejudice works. He remembers teachers referring to him as Yugoslavian rather than Croatian, without a thought for how much that might hurt, and he saw how angry it made his father. It means Ivan can't stand seeing people form opinions about people they know nothing about, without bothering to educate themselves first.

That education process isn't always comfortable, of course, especially when you encounter points of difference rather than similarity. Probably the clearest example of that came within my first couple of years at Richmond, when I invited some people from the club over to my house for a barbecue. When Trent and Brooke arrived, something completely normal but quietly awkward happened: Brooke leaned in and greeted me with a kiss, and Trent did the same with Rouba.

For Muslims, physical contact between the sexes is quite carefully regulated. The most orthodox opinion is that there should be no physical contact between men and women who are not family. We won't even touch the opposite sex when we line up for prayer. This rule is actually meant to facilitate, not hinder, contact between men and women – by trying to remove any potentially sexually charged interactions, men and women can engage with each other purely as people. Men and women still greet each other warmly, we just don't touch.

This is why you occasionally hear of Muslims not shaking hands with people of the opposite sex. A lot of people think this is either because Muslims regard non-Muslims as unclean, or because Muslim men regard women as inferior, and so refuse to touch them. All that is completely untrue, and is not based in any way on Islamic teachings.

Muslims often shake hands or hug people of the same sex – whether they're Muslim or not – and Muslim women are just as likely not to shake hands with men as the reverse. It's all to do with Islamic etiquette about proper interaction between the sexes, and has nothing to do with anyone being superior to anyone else. So, if even shaking hands with the opposite sex is something many Muslims avoid, you can imagine how they might approach greeting people by hugging or kissing them.

Of course, lots of Muslims don't follow this rule, which is why men and women shaking hands is very common across the Muslim world. Some people take a more lenient view that physical contact is not prohibited where there is no desire being aroused, which they might apply generally to something like shaking hands. Others just ignore the orthodox rule altogether, while still others probably think it would be worse to cause embarrassment or offence to people than to be staunch about the rule. I have to admit, social distancing during the COVID-19 pandemic definitely made all this easier!

Personally, I accept the more orthodox position, but I'm also aware that these things need to be kept in perspective. I'm not about to start offending people by being strict over something like this. If someone meets me for the first time and greets me with a kiss, there's no need for me to make a scene about it. I'll just leave it be. But if I sense it's likely to be an ongoing thing and I get an opportunity later to explain my view, I'll do so as sensitively as I can.

Given my ongoing relationship with Trent, I knew I couldn't leave the matter unaddressed. The best course of action, I sensed, was to wait for the right time and have a word with Trent, to let him know that Rouba and I didn't do physical contact between the sexes for religious reasons.

There's a risk in such a situation, of course: handle it wrongly and people might think you're arrogant, that you think they aren't good enough for you, or that you regard them as somehow immoral for observing different rules. So it was important for me to explain to Trent that it was nothing personal – it was just a blanket rule we tried to live by. Nor was it a judgement of anyone: I understood that people in different cultures had different customs. The fact that other people did things differently didn't make them better or worse than me.

An opportunity arose the next day, and I didn't hesitate. I knew Trent and Brooke were only greeting us that way as a matter of habit, and I was confident he would understand our position, especially as we already had a friendship based on mutual love and respect.

It turned out Trent and Brooke had already been wondering whether Rouba and I felt comfortable greeting people that way. Maybe they sensed an unease from us, or maybe they just wondered independently whether there were cultural sensitivities around such things. I got the feeling that if I hadn't brought it up, Trent would have asked me anyway because he wanted to respect our feelings. So I wasn't at all surprised when he said they were completely understanding of our views.

I've never had a hint that Brooke was any less respectful. Probably the best illustration of that came a couple of years later, when she and Trent got married. Brooke momentarily forgot and greeted me with a kiss. 'Oh my God, I'm so sorry!' she said immediately, clearly anxious that she had upset me. Of course, she hadn't.

'Relax! Take it easy,' I said, trying to reassure her. 'It's your wedding day! I'm sure you have a million more important things to worry about.'

Who knows? Maybe these sorts of things become a subtle barrier that prevents Rouba and me from catching up more often with people if I'm not quite as close to them as I am with Ivan and Trent. Maybe they don't. I'm not pretending these things are easy or comfortable. They certainly aren't for me.

There have been times I've avoided social situations because I'd rather not have to deal with the awkwardness involved if I think there will be lots of greeting kisses.

Perhaps that's not the best response to the issue, and I should be less discouraged. I get that, for non-Muslims, and maybe even for some Muslims, this might seem like a strange hang-up. But if my faith is important to me, that means I need to make sacrifices that might not make sense to other people. I can't deny that there are times it's just hard being a Muslim because there are things you can't do that mark you out as different, and that you're liable to being misunderstood by others. I hate offending people, and I'm desperate to avoid it. But I also know that I have to be true to myself, and that means being true to the demands of my faith, even when it's not convenient for me.

In the short term, that might limit my friendships or restrict my socialising a little. The same is true for Rouba, who inevitably misses out on certain social events with people at the club when I'd rather not go. It's not like she's missing out on things she's desperate to experience, but she worries that the other players' partners might regard her as a snob if she doesn't do enough with them. I have similar concerns sometimes too. But you can only go so far in a relationship with certain people when those relationships rely on things you can't do or take place in environments that don't suit.

In the end, it matters more to us to be respected than to be especially popular. And in the long run, it means we can look ourselves in the mirror with a clear conscience – and know that the friendships we do have are deeper and more enduring.

That's the thing about diversity. When it really works, it's because people are coming to the table as they are, and being respected for who they are. There's a magical meeting point where people can appreciate the differences we have from others, and even encounter differences they could never accept for themselves, but still fully see the human being in the middle of it all.

The key to this isn't sameness; it's openness, understanding and respect. In my experience, that only becomes possible when you have a clear sense of who you are. That way, differences – even ones you don't approve of or want to practise yourself – stop being threatening and start being part of what makes life and human relationships so interesting and enjoyable.

Trent and Ivan know who they are, and that's exactly why I think they can be so open and supportive. For the three of us, the fact that we can love each other without having to compromise ourselves for each other is wonderful. It's rare. But when it happens, it's one of the greatest things in the world. And I'm blessed to have relationships like that.

6

RAMADAN

THREE WEEKS BEFORE MY draft camp in late 2006, my under-18s club, the Western Jets, decided to put me through some tests. The idea was that they would help me figure out how well positioned I was, and where I might have to improve while I still had time. The main suspects were the 20-metre sprint and the beep test. My results weren't great. My beep test score of 12.4 was particularly poor.

In fact, it was so bad that the Western Jets' regional manager, Shane Sexton, was stunned. 'What's happening?' he asked, in exactly the way you might expect someone to when they're genuinely lost for an explanation.

I had to tell him straight. 'I'm fasting.'

To the unfamiliar ear, that sort of thing just sounds crazy. For starters, fasting isn't something people commonly do anymore. It used to be a part of many communities' lives, probably because just about every religion has a version of it. But these days? You're probably most likely to hear about fasting as part of some new weight-loss fad diet. One place you don't tend to hear it is from a prospective draftee three weeks out from the AFL draft camp.

'What are you doing to yourself?' he asked me. 'It's going to be an embarrassment if you turn in this sort of run. Do that in a few weeks and no teams will even look at you.'

On that point he was right, and I knew it. But his message went further than that: he thought I should stop fasting ahead of the draft camp.

When I look back on it now, I understand where he was coming from. We were talking about my career, and the draft camp would conceivably be a make-or-break moment. It's not exactly your only shot at the AFL, but it's not far off it — and it certainly looks like that when it's just a few weeks away.

Imagine how the situation must have seemed to Shane: he had an AFL-level talent on his hands, and he didn't want to see me apparently sabotage what I'd spent so long working towards. And for reasons he almost certainly didn't fully understand. Shane's job was basically to help as many kids as possible get drafted to AFL clubs. And the kids he was dealing with wanted nothing more than that in their lives. That was probably why he was such a hard taskmaster, and had a reputation among the players as ruthless and relentless.

I was fortunate in that I'd always had a really strong relationship with Shane, maybe because I was one of the better players at the club and had earned his respect. But now I was testing it. Our relationship hadn't seen anything like this moment. It was the eleventh hour, and now I was throwing this at him?

'Put this fasting to the side,' he advised me.

I didn't take it well.

'Who the f★★★ does he think he is?' I snapped to my mentor, Mohamed Bakkar, later that day. It's fair to say it wasn't the most pious language, but I was genuinely annoyed by the situation. 'I'm not changing the person I am. I'm not changing my faith for anything. I don't care.' I've always had a stubborn streak, and when it came to religion, I was especially unprepared to compromise.

Fasting is a big deal in Islam. It's not some obscure aspect of Islamic practice which is observed by relatively few people. It's so foundational that it's the fourth 'pillar' of Islam, one of the chief obligations a Muslim has. You'll even find Muslims who aren't especially observant doing it because it's so baked into the lives of Muslim communities. That's an amazing thing when you consider the discipline required throughout Ramadan: every day, between the first thread of light (usually an hour or two before sunrise) and sunset, we're required to go without food, drink and sex.

No, not even water.

So, it's a month of mastering control over your most basic desires, of consciously submitting yourself and sacrificing your wants for the sake of something greater. A month of pushing this world to the background, of increasing your worship, of reading the Qur'an more and of making God your focus. A month of constantly running into your limitations as a human being, of highlighting just how dependent you really are on the blessings God has given you – and of understanding how quickly you become vulnerable when they're taken away. A month to learn what it means to go hungry, and to taste the smallest sample of what life is like for so many people less fortunate than you. And a month that demands the highest levels of conduct: extra patience, extra charity, extra kindness, extra reflection and extra humility.

'Whoever does not give up evil and ignorant speech . . . Allah has no need of his giving up his food and drink,' said the Prophet. And: 'There are people who fast and get nothing from their fast except hunger and thirst.'

Exemplary character under distress is the point, so that once you're no longer battling hunger and thirst, you are able to maintain that character. And it's the fact of doing this every day for a month that makes it so transformative. It's the spiritual equivalent of a great preseason, and no less compulsory. Just as the preseason makes the season possible, Ramadan makes a Muslim's spiritual life possible. That's why breaking your fast without a valid excuse is such a grave thing for a Muslim to do. I was never going to do that.

But Bakkar was really worried. He'd seen me do the beep test, and how I struggled. He'd seen Shane Sexton's reaction. He'd seen my unnecessarily defensive response. 'They really should have done the beep test at night, after you'd finished fasting,' he said, consoling me. But he agreed with Shane on one point: my beep test results had to change, and we couldn't simply rely on the fact that I was fasting as an excuse. Bakkar let me blow off some steam, but then he made the point clear.

'You're a midfielder,' he said. 'If you don't get your beep test up to 14, you're dreaming.'

He wasn't making this up. He'd spoken to recruiters and managers, and they'd all made it really clear that 14 was the score I'd need. We had to fix this. I could huff and puff all I liked, but none of it would change my chances of getting drafted if I kept putting up junk running times. If I was going to be serious about both my faith and my footy, I had a mountain of work to do.

'Bach, I know you can do it,' said Bakkar. 'I know you can do 15. My heart tells me you can, my mind tells me you can, and I've seen you can do it because you're committed.'

So we got to work.

One of the key features of life in Ramadan are the long evening prayers at the end of each day, known as *taraweeh*. They set the tone for the whole month as a time of community, spirituality and devotion. Traditionally, you aim to recite the whole Qur'an in these prayers over the course of the month, which means reading roughly a thirtieth of the text each night. Not every mosque does this, but either way the Qur'anic recitation is a highlight of the month. It's not uncommon for mosques to fly in people from all over the world who've memorised the entire Qur'an and are known for their beautiful recitations to lead the prayers. It also means the recitation each night can be quite lengthy, taking anywhere from 40 minutes to a couple of hours, depending on the speed of the reciter.

I began meeting Bakkar at the *taraweeh* prayers at the Newport mosque, and we'd head off to start training afterwards.

He'd spoken to his mates Richard Osborne and Saade Ghazi about the situation, and they'd helped come up with a program that would improve my fitness quickly. Saade swore by the benefits of running on sand, and Bakkar embraced this whole-heartedly – much to my exhaustion.

Bakkar took me to a beach that was lit by lampposts roughly 50 metres apart. Those provided the landmarks we'd use. Imagine a series of three posts in a row. Bakkar made me sprint from one post to the one in the middle, then jog to the one at the opposite end, then sprint back to the middle post and then jog back to my original starting position. I'd have to do this 20 times, without letting my time for each set drop. It was no good me racing through the first set and then dropping dramatically in speed, because that's exactly what would lead to a poor beep test result. So I needed to produce roughly four kilometres, two of them sprinted, without dropping speed. On sand.

Then he'd make me do it all over again, but this time with 20-metre intervals rather than 50, again with the emphasis on not dropping speed. Then I'd jump in the water for a swim to aid my recovery.

It was a brutal program for an emergency situation. Deep down, Bakkar was scared that he was going to overwork me and I'd pick up an injury. He didn't tell me this at the time, of course, saving those anxious conversations for his wife. But he persisted because he felt he had little choice. I had to improve significantly in a very short period of time to have any real chance of being drafted, so it was a calculated risk.

We got started pretty late on those nights. Once you enter daylight saving in October in Melbourne, the sun sets around 7:30 pm, concluding a 14-hour day of fasting. The temptation when you break your fast after such a long time is to eat everything in sight as quickly as you can – a bit like one of those American hot-dog eating contests. It's also the wrong thing to do, on every level.

For one thing, it's not the example of the Prophet, who would eat and drink slowly and avoid overeating. And when you go a whole day without eating and then gorge yourself on (usually rich) food, you feel properly awful. Then you lie down and fall into a food coma. I can also tell you, from experience, that eating like that is an especially stupid thing to do when you're about to sprint along sand dunes more times than you ever imagined.

'You can't even run! Why did you eat so much?' Bakkar would ask on those days I got it horribly wrong. I'd try to pretend he was wrong, but there was no hiding it and eventually I'd have to come clean. It's fair to say I learned pretty quickly: minimal eating at *iftar* time, eat well after training.

It took a lot of discipline, over the course of a few weeks. When you fast longish hours, it's not really the length of the days that's the problem so much as the shortness of the night. Sunset at 7:30 pm meant *taraweeh* began about 9:15 pm. If that took around an hour, I'd start running on sand dunes around 10:30 pm, finishing by about 11:30 pm. Add in some recovery time, and I'd probably be done by midnight. Then I'd go home to eat. But the next day's fasting would begin before dawn, at around 5:30. That means I'm up at 4:30 or 5:00 am to eat and hydrate before fasting again. I suppose I was fortunate I was training only three or four times a week. Imagine keeping up a schedule like that daily!

The draft camp itself fell in Ramadan too. Obviously, that created a dilemma, and even some disagreement within my family. My parents and siblings were telling me not to fast. Potentially, my future livelihood relied on my performance on this particular day: everything I'd built up to this point came down to this moment. For it to evaporate because it happened to fall in Ramadan seemed a particularly heavy consequence. But for me, missing a day of fasting in Ramadan was a heavier one.

Breaking your fast isn't breaking some garden-variety rule, it's violating something central and fundamental. Despite what my family was saying to me, I felt the burden of this duty. I couldn't resolve it simply by arguing that the draft camp was really important to my career or even my life. This was about something bigger and more important even than that. One's life and career are fleeting, Muslims believe, but one's deeds before God are eternal.

There was really only one way through it: I had to be convinced that there were legitimate religious reasons for me not to fast. And ultimately, that's what I ended up asking my family to prove to me. Eventually, we agreed that we'd consult some Islamic scholars we knew for their opinion on whether or not I had a valid reason not to fast for the draft camp.

Islam provides several exemptions from fasting in Ramadan. The common thread between them is that they are circumstances where fasting will be harmful or constitute a significant hardship. Probably the most obvious case is illness, especially where fasting would worsen your condition or slow down your recovery. Some scholars even hold that in such a situation, breaking your fast isn't merely permissible, but encouraged because of the harm it does to oneself – so fasting actually becomes the wrong thing to do. A similar exemption applies to pregnant or breastfeeding women, because fasting in those situations can harm not just the mother but the child as well. Pregnant women might fast if they feel comfortable doing so and if their doctor doesn't think it's dangerous, but very often they won't.

In situations like these, you're simply required to fast the number of days you missed at a later date, when you're in a position to do so. It's slightly different if someone is too fragile to cope with the rigours of fasting and is likely to be weakened significantly by it. This is usually the case for old people, but someone might have a chronic medical condition that means they will never be able to fast safely. Obviously, they can't make up the days they miss, and in this case Islam requires them to feed a poor person for every day of fasting they cannot do. That would mean giving money or food that is sufficient to feed around 30 people each year. The payment is called *fidyah*.

One of the most common exemptions applies to travel. The Qur'an specifically mentions it along with illness: 'Whoever is sick or on a journey should fast the same number of other days instead. Allah wants ease and not hardship for you so that you might complete the number of days required' (2:185). There is some debate about what sort of journey makes you a traveller for this purpose, but most scholars have concluded it means journeying around 80 kilometres from your hometown.

In my case, this was the decisive exemption: the draft camp was in Canberra, so I would be a traveller and could legitimately break my fast. Had the camp been in Melbourne, the discussion would have been more complicated. The opinion we were given stated that the circumstances were exceptional enough that I could break my fast anyway, because my future livelihood was dependent on my physical performance on this particular day. That's not a clear-cut exemption in the way the ones I've mentioned above are, which is partly what would have made the situation so difficult. It was a moot point on this occasion, but it would become an important line of reasoning later in my career.

Because the Islamic calendar has a 12-month lunar year, it lasts around 354 days – 11 days short of the solar year. That means Ramadan gets about 11 days earlier each year, moving gradually back through the seasons. In 2006, my draft year, it ran from late September to late October. By 2008, it would land entirely in the finals series, running for pretty much all of September. By 2011, Ramadan would be entirely within the home-and-away season. The way things fell, if I had a decent football career, then Ramadan was going to be a factor during the season for most of it.

This was something I'd never had to think about as a junior, when Ramadan was exclusively a post-season event. Because of when I was born, Ramadan was arriving in the AFL season at about the same time I started playing senior football. That meant I needed to figure out a Ramadan plan that made me as comfortable as possible, religiously and professionally.

The way my career panned out ended up giving me a few years to formulate one. Essendon only played finals once during my time there, and that was in 2009, when we finished eighth, and I wasn't being selected in the senior side at that time anyway. And since Ramadan was mostly in September until 2011, fasting didn't really arise as an issue for me while I was at Essendon. Except once.

It was a VFL elimination final in 2010 – what turned out to be my last game as a Bomber. VFL games were always played during daytime, so the game happened during fasting hours. By that stage I hadn't really settled on how I felt about the fasting issue. I'd heard different opinions from different Islamic scholars, but that had been the opposite of helpful because I felt overloaded with contrasting views, which only made me more confused.

Basically, those different views boiled down to the question of just how significant work is. Either I could break my fast because my livelihood was at stake, or I couldn't because it was only work, which should rank well behind the more import-ant things in life. I understood both views, but in my heart I was never really content with the more lenient one. I instinc-tively understood how paramount fasting in Ramadan is, and I knew that my situation didn't fit within the well-established exemptions. It was clear that, religiously speaking, the safer option was to fast.

And then there was the fact that, as far as my time at Essendon was concerned, I felt I had nothing to lose. I'd decided I wanted to leave the club and figured that I was likely not going to be there next year. That meant I thought the risk to my livelihood was minimal. Putting it all together, I decided to fast through the game, with the proviso that if it all became too much for me, it was the equivalent of being sick and I'd break my fast.

Actually, I started the game well. I remember dominating the first quarter and a half, kicking two or three goals and gathering about 15 possessions. Then all of a sudden I hit a wall. The drop-off was alarming. I couldn't cover the ground quickly enough to get to contests – and when I did get to them, I had nothing to give. Whenever I got knocked over, I felt dizzy and could barely get up.

I all but completely disappeared from the game, much to the confusion of my coaches, who couldn't understand where I'd gone. Not that it made any difference, because we were down by almost eight goals at half time anyway – a fact that ended up being decisive for me. Since the game was all but gone, I felt there was no point breaking my fast. I figured I could slow down however much was necessary for me to get through to the end. I was wrong. By the game's end I'd lost five kilograms and my vision was blurred. It's probably the worst I've ever felt.

A few days later I met with Blair Hartley and Damien Hardwick. I'd had to wait until the season ended to be allowed to meet with them, but by then I'd made up my mind that I wanted to join the Tigers. 'What happened in that game?' they asked. 'We noticed you just kind of shut down after half time.'

'Yeah, I was fasting,' I said. 'But rest assured, I won't do that again.'

That wasn't a lie. Playing an AFL game is on a different plane to playing any VFL game. The intensity, the speed, the physicality and the amount of running mean they can hardly be compared. If I'd become that unwell fasting in the VFL, there was no telling what the damage would be if I tried it at AFL level. My guess was that I'd last about ten minutes. If I was playing a day game, I realised, I simply couldn't fast, not even if the game started only half an hour before sunset and I could break my fast around quarter time. It was just too dangerous.

The only real alternatives would be to make myself unavailable for day games during Ramadan, which clubs would almost certainly not accept, or get another job entirely. And on that last point, the scholars I'd consulted felt that effectively making professional football off-limits to Muslims would be an unreasonable restriction. My presence as a representative of Islam in the broader community, and as a role model of sorts within the Muslim community, meant that my career brought important benefits that extended beyond my own financial interests. Taking it all together, those scholars advised me to proceed.

I've made my peace with that position. Sort of. Whatever days I miss, I make up for by fasting them after Ramadan. But I carry enough guilt about it that I also make the *fidyah* payment. It makes no sense for me to do this because it only applies to people who aren't capable of making up the days they've missed. I've asked scholars about it and they all say the same thing: it has nothing to do with my situation. I know this, but I do it anyway because it helps me clear my conscience.

'What do you do during Ramadan?' is probably the most common question I get asked. Everywhere. In countless

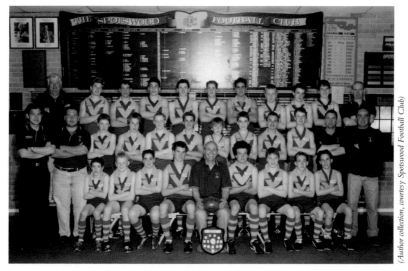

(Author collection, courtesy Spotswood Football Club)

Being told by my brother, Khaled, that I was going to start playing footy at Spotswood was the best moment of my young life. He nurtured my talent right from the start, and surrounded me with people who could help me realise my potential.

(Author collection, courtesy School Sport Australia)

The All-Australian Team from the 2003 School Sport Australia Championships, held on the Gold Coast. Nick Smith (back row, far left), Nathan Jones (back row, far right), Joel Selwood (front row, second from left) and Leigh Adams (front row, centre) would all go on to have great careers at the highest level.

The 2003 Vic Metro squad. Future Sydney Swans captain Josh Kennedy is pictured in the middle of the second row behind me.

The Vic Metro Schoolboy squad for the 2004 NAB AFL Under-16 Championships. My roommates that year in Adelaide were James Arundale (number 9 and sat next to the coach) and Daniel Beckwith (next but one to me, number 15).

Rash Hussein cultivated my love for footy as well as my skills. He was instrumental in getting me to Under-16 level – and beyond.

The Vic Metro squad that won the 2006 NAB AFL Under-18 Championships, a team including future greats Tom Hawkins (number 9; Geelong) and Robbie Gray (number 26; Port Adelaide).

The 2006 Western Jets TAC Cup squad, coached by Mark Neeld.

Getting ready for the 2006 NAB
Draft.

In action for Vic Metro at the 2006
NAB AFL Under-18 Championships.

On my wedding day with a number of the Essendon boys. From left:
Hayden Skipworth, Henry Slattery, Tayte Pears, Heath Hocking, John
Quinn, Angus Monfries and my manager Nigel Carmody.

During the Round 16 VFL match between the Sandringham Zebras and Bendigo Bombers on 28 July 2007.

(Greg Ford / AFL Photos)

(Greg Ford / AFL Photos)

(Andrew White / AFL Photos)

Top left: Celebrating my second ever goal and first win for Essendon, two matches into my career with the Bombers. *Top right:* Pursued by Robert Harvey in the Round 5 game against St Kilda in what would become a stretch of seven straight losses. The losses don't get any easier. *Bottom:* pictured with Mark McVeigh and Kyle Hardingham in my first loss as a Tiger against Essendon. Seven weeks later, we beat them.

Often in Muslim cultures, marriage takes place in two ceremonies. These photos are from the second event, mine and Rouba's *walimah*. With Mum *(above)* and my parents, Malek and Yamama *(left)*.
Top: From left: Marwa, Louay, Khaled, Mum, Rouba, Bachar, Dad, Nezor, Mohamed, Safa.

(All author collection)

There had already been a couple of AFL players from Muslim backgrounds before me, Adem Yze *(top left)* and Sedat Sir *(top right)* – trailblazers every bit as significant as me. ***Bottom left:*** With Adam Saad before the coin toss at a Round 22 Tigers–Bombers game in 2018, and *(right)* at the 2020 State of Origin for Bushfire Relief match in February 2020. We are simply the product of many others who came before us.

(AFL Photos)

(AFL Photos)

(Michael Willson / AFL Photos)

At the beginning of my professional career when teammates such as *(top left)* Adam McPhee, Henry Slattery, and Mark and Jason Johnson *(top right)*, asked me about Islam, I appreciated their curiosity and willingness to learn. The friendships I've formed with people like Trent Cotchin *(above)* have a solid foundation in openness, understanding and respect.

(Andrew White / AFL Photos)

(Scott Barbour / AFL Photos)

I share with Trent and Ivan Maric an approach to football and life that it is ultimately about service. This provides a focus during training sessions *(left)*, and makes the rewards of hard work all the sweeter – celebrating a goal against the West Coast Eagles in 2012 *(above)* and *(below)* at Cotch's 150th match for the Tigers in Round 20 2015. We beat the Gold Coast Suns by 83 points.

(Michael Willson / AFL Photos)

I've been extremely fortunate to have so many special people involved in my career at crucial times. *Clockwise from top left:* John Quinn, Essendon's high performance coach; my specialised running coach, Bohdan Babijczuk, found by Mohamed Bakkar; Richmond's backline coach Justin Leppitsch and assistant coach Mark Williams, with whom I've had many conversations about faith and community.

Above: Kevin Sheedy was a pioneer for inclusion at Essendon. My time with Sheeds laid an invaluable foundation for me.

Left: Pictured with senior Tigers coach Damien Hardwick during post-match celebrations at the 2017 Grand Final. Our mutual trust and respect are the bedrock to my successful career at Richmond.

It's hard to overstate the importance Islam places on humility. I appreciate every award nomination, knowing that my achievements help to elevate the club and the game.

(Michael Willson / AFL Photos)

(Darrian Traynor / AFL Photos)

(Kelly Defina / AFL Photos)

(Dylan Burns / AFL Photos)

Clockwise from top left: Among my fellow 2008 Rising Star nominees. Little did I know back then that Jack and Trent would become future Premiership teammates; accepting the David Mandie Community Award at the 2019 Jack Dyer Medal (another honour I was lucky enough to be a two-time winner of), just days after our second Premiership; at the 2019 All-Australian selection; receiving that year's Yiooken Award for best on ground at the Dreamtime game against Essendon.

(Scott Barbour/AFL Photos)

(Getty Images/Darrian Traynor)

The Jed Lamb incident really tested me – the emotional intensity of the episode ran me down physically – but after the hearing I was glad to tell the media I accepted the tribunal's decision. And to know that Jed was okay.

(Alex Coppel / Newspix)

For me, religion has reinforced footy and footy reinforced religion, because
the disciplines and the lifestyle involved in each are similar.

interviews. At every school visit. It's an extremely difficult one to answer, especially when I'm being asked by Muslim kids, because there's always a danger they'll take my response out of context and use it to their advantage. My 14-year-old brother-in-law was playing in a grand final during Ramadan one year, and at about 9:00 am I heard the gas stove ticking over in that way it does before it catches flame. I walked into the kitchen to find him making noodles.

'But it's okay for you!' he protested.

He'd clearly decided that whatever dispensations applied to me as a professional footballer in the AFL applied to someone playing junior club footy. The idea that fasting through an AFL game would seriously harm my health, but doing it when playing juniors wouldn't, seemed lost on him. The same goes for the idea that playing in the AFL is a job you're obliged to fulfil rather than a hobby. But here he was, violating a religious obligation and using me as an excuse! I feel a heavy sense of responsibility for that sort of thing.

But actually it arises as an issue less than people think because so many games are played at night or interstate. A night game in winter usually starts about two hours after sunset, which gives me plenty of time to fast that day, break my fast, then eat in time to be fully ready to play. And if I'm travelling, I'm not obliged to fast, so I can just prepare as normal. That means it's only in daytime or twilight games in Melbourne that fasting becomes an issue.

One of the good things about playing for Richmond these days is that we tend to have a lot of games in high-profile slots, which are usually at night. In 2019, for example, we played in Perth in the first week of Ramadan, faced Hawthorn at the MCG in a twilight game the following week, then had the Dreamtime at the 'G game against Essendon the following Saturday night, before finally playing a Friday-night game against North Melbourne. Only one of those games – the Hawthorn game – interfered with fasting. The year before had a similar mix of night and Perth games, so only our Round 10 match against St Kilda was in question. In 2017, our game against Sydney at the MCG was the only day game during Ramadan. In 2016 I'd broken my wrist and was injured for the month anyway, while the whole league was shut down for all of Ramadan in 2020 due to the COVID-19 pandemic. So, for the most part, all I've needed to figure out is how to manage training, and then what I'll do with fasting for one game per year.

I begin preparing about three or four weeks before Ramadan by fasting two days a week. As it happens, the prophet Muhammad used to fast Mondays and Thursdays, so while it isn't mandatory, Muslims are encouraged to do the same. I take it as an opportunity to get my body used to fasting, so that doing it every day doesn't come as a shock. That means I'm training as normal while fasting occasionally, which then becomes more or less how it continues throughout Ramadan when I'm fasting every day.

In a normal week there are two main training sessions, the first of which is just getting us moving again after the game. We run four to five kilometres, which is pretty light for us. The second is more to do with structure, but also involves some contested work and tackling drills, which usually happen at the end of the session. Occasionally I start feeling a little light-headed by the time those drills arrive, and the club's happy for me to sit them out if I need to. Usually I'll do them, though, and then maybe just do a bit less in my weights session afterwards, which is pretty light during the season anyway. Really, it's a matter of making adjustments for how I'm feeling on the day.

The club gives me a lot of control over this because they trust me to know how I'm feeling. In fact, the whole thing is based on trust. Nothing works without that. I'm sure if you asked Dimma in a quiet moment he'd tell you that even though we'd spoken about it before Richmond drafted me, he was worried in the lead-up to my first Ramadan at the club. He was even concerned that he might not be able to select me. He'd had no experience with this sort of situation, so his nervousness when he asked me about it at training one day was perfectly understandable.

'I've been doing this my whole life,' I reassured him. 'I have a really good understanding of how it works.'

As a result, there's no program the club develops and then holds me to. If I were a younger player or didn't have a record of performance in Ramadan, it might be different.

The biggest adjustment I've experienced was actually in 2016, when I was injured through Ramadan with a broken wrist, because I was at the point in my rehab where I was training hard and running a lot. I trained early in the morning, around 6:30, before it was even light. I remember wearing a headlamp as I ran around Punt Road Oval. Actually it was easy for me because, like many fasting Muslims, I would get up about two hours before sunrise to eat – a meal called *suhoor*. (This isn't just a good idea – it's a religious act in itself, encouraged by the prophet Muhammad: '*Suhoor* is a blessed meal, so do not omit it, even if one of you only takes a sip of water.') So by training early in the morning, I was exercising not long after I'd eaten, and I was fully energised. It felt like I wasn't fasting at all, really. I'd be done by 7:30 am or so, and would be ready for the 8:00 am main team meeting. By 9:00 am I was done for the day, so fasting had no further impact. About the only difficulty I experienced was that I'd occasionally get thirsty and a bit headachy by about 3:00 pm, but that can happen sometimes when you're fasting anyway.

Game day is a little more complex. There are no health concerns with me fasting until the game starts, so I'm not in the same position as someone who is ill. Really, my situation is analogous to that of a traveller who is exempt from fasting – and there's some important detail in the way the traveller's exemption works, concerning the point at which someone becomes a traveller. Are you travelling the moment you wake up intending to travel? Or do you have to be travelling before you can break your fast? If so, how far into your journey do you have to be? Is it the moment you close your front door?

Most scholars would consider you a traveller only once you've physically left behind the built-up area of your home city, town or village. It's possible, for example, that you might intend to travel but, for some reason, that doesn't happen. Maybe the need for your travel changes, or maybe your flight is cancelled or your car breaks down before you leave, or maybe your child comes home from school sick and you have to stay to look after them. If something like that were to happen and you'd already broken your fast, then you'd have missed a day of fasting despite not having travelled anywhere. For that reason, people who are intending to travel begin the day fasting and break their fast only when the journey out of their hometown has begun. It's then up to them whether or not they want to continue fasting.

The same logic applies to my situation. I might, for example, roll my ankle getting off the couch to go to the game, or pull a hamstring in the warm-up, or maybe the coaches will decide I'm out of the team for whatever reason. I can't know these things, and I can't assume they won't happen: in fact, it did happen once when I was warming up for a game against North Melbourne and I felt some hamstring soreness and pulled out of the game. All that means I fast as normal for the day until I get through the warm-up and am about to start playing.

Once I get to that point, I'll eat something that gives me a burst of energy I can use straightaway: perhaps a carbohydrate gel and some Gatorade and water. I probably should have some high-energy food, but the truth is my feeling of guilt prevents me. I know that doesn't make any sense because you're either fasting or you're not, so once you've broken your fast it doesn't matter how much you eat. Similarly, if we're playing an early game at 1:10 pm and we finish at around 4:00 pm, I don't eat any food until after sunset.

Some scholars say that there is an unusual case where if someone is suffering from unbearable hunger or thirst when they're fasting, they can eat or drink a tiny amount, after which they must continue fasting for the rest of the day and then make the whole day up later. But that isn't my situation, so I can't claim that sort of reason. My behaviour here isn't rational; it's more from the heart. It's just psychological baggage I carry with me. On some level, I feel like I'm only entitled to take the minimum amount I need in order to get through the game.

That feeling probably captures how grave the whole matter is for me, and I hope it reflects how sincere I am in wanting to fast and how reluctant I am to break it. My worst-case scenario came in 2018, when I broke my fast just before the St Kilda game and then got injured in the first five minutes and sat out the rest of the game. If I'd known that was going to happen, I wouldn't have broken my fast at all. But there I was, sitting on the bench for the whole game, not eating or drinking, but not fasting either. It was incredibly frustrating.

Obviously, this is a departure from my normal match-day routine, but it's a smaller one than most would assume. I eat very little in the lead-up to a match anyway: game day typically involves just a couple of pieces of Vegemite and avocado toast for breakfast, or, if it's a night game, two packets of two-minute noodles (with the water drained and then the flavour added at the end, which is clearly the best way to have them). At the ground before the game, our club trainers give us each a banana and a muffin; I usually only eat the top. You don't actually get your energy for the game in the last six hours before the bounce; you get it 48 hours beforehand. That's when I normally start loading up with carbohydrates (which I don't eat much during the week) and hydrating thoroughly.

The same is true for Ramadan, so what I eat two nights before the game matters most. But game day itself also requires some specific planning. I'll get up far earlier than normal for *suhoor*, to give myself plenty of time to hydrate because it's my last chance to do so until just before the game begins. Then I'll eat a substantial meal to give myself whatever energy reserves I can so I don't enter the game undernourished. After that, it's about sleep. I know I'll need to conserve my energy and be as fresh as possible, so I sleep for as long as I can into the morning.

It turns out that my Ramadan routine might actually be a masterstroke. It can't be an accident that for most of my time at Richmond I've played my best footy during Ramadan. Dimma's often told me privately that he can't wait for Ramadan to start, and in 2019 he slipped it into a post-game press conference after the Dreamtime game. I'd just been given the Yiooken Award for best on ground, so someone asked him about me. 'It's amazing,' he said, 'it's Ramadan at the moment and he just seems to play better and better every year. I'm going to put in an [application] if I can, to get it extended for him.' I suppose I should just move to Ramadan mode every week. If only I didn't enjoy my coffee and food so much.

I do feel physically different going into games during Ramadan, because I've eaten even less than normal. The biggest difference is that I feel extremely light, which is significant for someone like me, whose game is based on running. That's even true for night games when I've fasted all day and then eaten two hours before: I know from my time running on those sand dunes as a kid that the worst thing I could do would be to eat a lot. So I break my fast in the way the prophet Muhammad did, and Muslims traditionally do: with dates (three of them, in my case). Then I'll eat a banana and honey sandwich, like I always used to eat before games as a junior.

It's a pretty weird *iftar*, but I find it gives me just the right kick for footy because it's basically just carbohydrates and natural sugars; the banana is chosen specifically because it helps prevent cramping. Then I'll drink a substantial amount of Gatorade and water. And that's it. It's amazing how little you need to feel fine after you've been fasting, and how much better you feel if you don't rush food into your mouth.

I don't eat properly until after the game, at which point I have the traditional dinner of elite athletes: a big lamb kebab (extra meat, no salad), a hot dog (extra cheese) and large chips. I don't even order at the kebab van anymore when I see the guy who runs it. He knows.

Oh, and I finish off the rest of that muffin.

I was born at exactly the right time. Ramadan was never an issue for me as a junior, and by the time it arrived in the home-and-away season during my AFL career, I was an established player at a club that was really keen to recruit me, so I had enough authority and confidence to speak to the club about the situation and how we'd best handle it. It might seem strange to say it, but I'm really fortunate that Ramadan has landed during the season in my career. The adjustments are simple enough, and my track record shows that, if anything, it helps my playing.

It might be a completely different story for the next generation of Muslim kids who dream of playing in the AFL, because they'll start playing when Ramadan lands in the middle of preseason. In 2029, for example, it will be from mid-January to mid-February, when the training is brutal, the weather is hot and the days are long. Who knows what the training schedule will look like then, but if it's anything like mine, there will be three main running sessions a week where we're covering somewhere between 12 and 14 kilometres. For context, that's about what we cover in a game, and with a similar breakdown of high- and low-speed running. The weights sessions are also heavier than during the season.

The closest thing I've experienced is fasting through rehab sessions, but the comparison really doesn't go that far. Rehab training often involves one-on-one sessions with the rehab coach, but clubs usually want preseason running sessions to be done by the whole group. And even if they were happy for a player to train individually with a coach, the model I've used in rehab of starting just after *suhoor* becomes much more complicated in summer, when that meal has to be about 90 minutes earlier. So what was a 6:30 am start during the season turns into a 5:00 am start – and which coach is going to come in for that?

I could head home after rehab early in the morning, too, but in preseason that's not really an option because you have to stay back for some gut-busting tackling or contest drills, or maybe some intense handball drills or whatever. And overall, there's the fact that a rehab training session involves only about half the running that a preseason one does.

All that means hydration becomes a big issue. That 3:00 pm thirst and occasional headache would probably be worse, and there would still be close to six hours of fasting to go. And then there's the quick turnaround to the next day's training after a short night. When you put all that together, fasting through each of those big sessions could be nearly as difficult as fasting through a game.

I can't say I know for sure how you'd solve all that. But I think it could be done if clubs put their minds to it and are flexible enough with their training schedules to ensure players get the work in at those times that are safest for them. It would have to involve some kind of personalised training program, which is really the direction sports science is heading anyway. You could possibly draw lessons from other sports around the world – plenty of Muslims have played elite-level rugby league and soccer – but the demands of Australian Rules football, especially the amount of running combined with the collisions, make it unique.

You'd have to find a solution to it somehow, because I can't imagine Muslims coping particularly well with being forced to break their fast three days a week throughout Ramadan. Whatever it ends up looking like, the basic principles that can make it work will be those that have applied through my career: a club that is very understanding, a high level of trust between club and player, and a creative approach. There's no doubt it would be a bigger challenge than anything I've had to face in my career. I'm thankful I never had to face it. But it's a challenge whose day is coming.

7

INSECURITY

YOU COULD NEVER TELL from the way he played, but Dustin Martin was a bundle of nerves all week in the lead-up to the 2019 Grand Final. 'What do I do if De Boer tags me?' he'd worry. 'What if I can't back up my performance in 2017? What if we let another chance slip?'

I found myself reassuring him on the day: 'Bro, I can feel it, today is your day. I know for a fact you are going to blitz. You're going to demolish the game. You're going to own it. And you deserve it because you're the best player in the league.'

I wasn't making it up. I could just tell he was going to do something special as easily as I could tell he had doubts. Apparently, a Brownlow medal, three All-Australian selections, two club best-and-fairests, countless media and peer-judged awards, and a Norm Smith Medal weren't enough for him to believe in himself. So he went and won another Norm Smith.

I suppose these doubts are a matter of your personality. And I know that my personality can be quite insecure too. In football as in life, I'm a confidence player. If the coaches show vision of me making a mistake as part of the post-match review, it takes me days to get over it. I don't respond well to criticism that isn't expressed in a constructive way, or that doesn't reassure me of my strengths. I'm the kind of person who gets defensive until I've had time to go away, process the feedback and realise what's true in it. That's why I avoid reading newspapers and try to look past any negative media coverage about me: I know it will get into my head. Really, I thrive on positive feedback, and Damien Hardwick knows this and coaches me accordingly.

I'm the opposite of Jack Riewoldt, who seems to be motivated by criticism – Dimma often yells at him, even in front of the group. 'Not good enough, Jack! That's shithouse!' The coach lets Jack have it because he knows that brings out his best. I can't remember the last time he said anything like that to me, even when I've deserved it.

That's why moments of positive reinforcement, even apparently insignificant ones, can have a huge impact on me. Take our jumper presentation in 2019, right before we were about to play an intra-club practice match. As he handed each player his jumper, Damien Hardwick said something about them. I've been number 14 ever since I got to Richmond, so I knew exactly when my moment was coming, and I was hanging on every word.

'Over the whole time I've been at this club,' he began, 'I consider this young man to be the most consistent player I've ever picked up. He's a big-game player. I can't remember one big game he's ever played in where this man hasn't performed.'

I've done a lot of things in football, but I'll remember that little moment for the rest of my life. I was best on ground in that practice match. Then I went on to have the best season of my career. I don't think it was a coincidence.

It might seem strange, because my best games have often been big encounters in front of massive crowds, but I think I'm quite sensitive to external pressure. Some players need the excitement of the crowd to be at their best, but I'm not the kind who looks forward to playing in front of 90,000 people. For me, crowds usually make the game seem harder than it is. I really enjoyed those first few games of the 2020 season which were played without crowds thanks to the COVID-19 pandemic. I loved the lack of build-up before the game, which meant I often didn't think about it all week. I loved that I came to each match feeling extremely calm. I even loved that it felt more like a heavy training session with an opposition than a full-scale match. Crowds are great when you're flying, but I suppose I tend to experience them more as pressure than inspiration, especially when there's plenty of opposition support there.

My most insecure moments always seem to come when I'm in long-term rehab. That's when that I start to lose perspective, when my insecurities surround me. I'm the kind of person who usually lets the past go, but when it comes to the anxiety of being injured and wondering if I'll get back in, I remember the details vividly: 2016, injured scaphoid, 12 weeks, returned playing a half in the VFL against Box Hill, then returned to the senior side the next week against Greater Western Sydney in Canberra; 2018, groin injury, missed seven games, came straight back into the team. I remember these so well because it's in these periods that I feel doubts, and it's probably become worse as I've got older and closer to the end of my career.

There are times I even talk myself into feeling insecure when there's no need. The coach might just have shown the team some vision of the weekend's game and highlighted the things that were missing because I wasn't there, or clips from when I was playing to show the younger players what's required and what's missing. *Yes!* I'll think. *They're realising the importance of my role!* Then I'll start worrying: *Now these young boys are going to be pumped up, running like mad, and they're going to play well and I'm not going to get back in . . .* It's in these moments that I feel jealousies at odds with what I want my character to be. That's an actual failure. Overcoming this is something I am still working on.

It didn't take long for the insecurities of life in the AFL to find me. I'd started my second season, in 2008, particularly well, playing ten of the first 11 games and sitting in the top few of our best-and-fairest to that point. The game I missed came after Round 7, when I began to notice sharp pain in both groins. After a week off I came back, but I couldn't kick the ball as far, and I had an awful sensation every time I tried to sprint, like all my muscles from my groins to my lower abdominals were going to tear apart. I'd lost my pace and my power, and every week it just got worse – to the point that I could barely walk after games, or even sometimes after training. It felt like my body was being eaten from within.

I spoke about it to John Quinn, the high-performance coach at Essendon and he knew exactly what it was: I had a condition known as osteitis pubis. I can't be sure exactly what caused it, but generally speaking it's an overuse injury that happens as a result of repeated strain on the muscles around the pubic bones. Maybe it was partially a result of all that intensive running on sand I did before my draft camp in 2006. Or perhaps it was a consequence of my battle with stress fractures, and the extra strain other parts of my body were taking on to compensate for weakness in my lower back. It could also have been a result of all the extra training an AFL career demanded, or all of these things may have played a role. Whatever the case, a few days later I was booked in for surgery and my season was over.

It was a scary injury to get. Osteitis pubis was a big issue for young players in the 2000s. Lots of us were being diagnosed with it, and my guess would be that about half never made a full recovery. I knew of many examples of young players who lost their careers because they never regained their speed, power or form as a footballer.

I'm glad to say that is mostly a thing of the past now. Sports science has come a long way since then, and in fact the term 'osteitis pubis' is hardly ever used anymore. Players these days are usually diagnosed with pelvic problems before they experience much pain, let alone after they've been trying to play through it, and the treatment is totally different. Back then it was two or three months of rest before you did any rehabilitation, which was why it ended my season. Now they have you doing muscle-strengthening work straightaway. I got basically the same injury in 2018 and was back playing within a couple of months. But back in 2008 I was one of those young players thrown into the lottery of this debilitating condition.

For two seasons it looked like the injury was going to get the better of me. I spent the first season just trying to get back to running again. But the second was even more worrying, because I'd returned to playing but I was a shadow of my former self. Throughout the 2009 season I put heat patches on my groins just so they'd feel loose and warm enough for me to play. Even then, I could still feel the muscles as I ran and kicked. It was mostly discomfort, but occasionally I felt sharp pain. I had officially recovered, but I didn't have any confidence in my body, and I certainly lacked the power I'd had before. I played the whole game at one pace because there was no way to accelerate my body.

Towards the end of the 2009 season, I'd finally fought my way back into Essendon's senior team. In our Round 19 game against Brisbane, though, Luke Power accidentally kicked me in the leg, which was left looking badly bruised. I battled with it through the next week at training, but I couldn't get through the last session before our game against St Kilda. I returned to the changerooms so the doctors could do a few tests, then started taking off the strapping to ice my leg. I pulled at the tape, and then – *crack!* Everyone turned around when they heard the noise, which gives you a sense of the agony I felt. I'd broken my fibula. My season was over, and I began to feel like I was cursed.

But 2010 brought at least some relief. As I worked my way through preseason training, I felt I had fully recovered. At last

I could start playing football like myself again. But having finally triumphed over my body, I was then confronted with the deflating experience of rejection from within my club. I did everything right but I just couldn't find my way back into the senior side. For two years I was constantly in and out – mostly out. If I played and the team didn't go well, it felt like I'd be the first to be dropped – like a scapegoat. I'd play out of my skin in the VFL then watch as other players who'd done much less, by any reading of the stats, were promoted ahead of me. I came second in the VFL team's best-and-fairest that season, even though I only played 13 games. It still wasn't enough.

This sort of thing happens a lot in football. Sometimes the coaches, for reasons they probably don't even understand, only see a particular player negatively, downplaying their strengths and obsessing over their weaknesses. Sometimes it's just a feel thing: the coach might not have a clear reason for not liking a player, but has a gut sense that means he won't back him. If you want to know why Damien Hardwick is such a great coach, watch the press conference he gave after we beat Hawthorn in 2019, when he talked about his attitude to Brandon Ellis.

Brandon had been dropped from the team in late 2018, missing the entire finals series, and had started 2019 on the outer as well, missing Round 1 before reclaiming his spot the following week. That particular day against Hawthorn came in Round 9, and might have been his best ever game: with 20 kicks, 15 handballs, 13 marks and five clearances, it was a monster. Hardwick could have just acknowledged how well Brandon had played, but he went further. 'I was probably looking at areas of his game, they're not poor, but they're probably below in some areas,' he told the media. 'But what I sort of forgot as a coach, and it's really poor on my behalf, is that he's great in a lot of areas. I've got to remind myself to look at those areas.' Every coach has done something like that, but very few would admit it in public so readily.

The worst thing about being in that situation as a player is when you don't really have a clear idea why it's happening and you can't see a path back. That's certainly what I found in those years at Essendon. The coaches might tell me to go work on a particular aspect of my game – say, my defensive running or the defensive side of my game generally – and I'd go and excel in that area, only to find it made no difference to their attitude towards picking me. I thought I was good enough, but you never know if that's just wishful thinking.

It wasn't as though the senior team was winning, either. We were churning through players at selection, trying to find the right mix, but it felt like everyone was getting picked except me. As time went on, I had conversations with my teammates about it, and they seemed just as confused about it as I was. Some of the senior players even asked the coach, Matthew Knights, why I wasn't getting played, given that the team was losing and I was dominating at VFL level, but they never got an answer they felt was satisfactory. About the most reassuring thing my teammates could say to me was that with the way things were going, Knights wouldn't be at the club the next year. But even that didn't especially help, because I never had anything against Knighter. If there had been a personal issue between the coaches and me, that would at least have been something solid I could understand, but I never had the sense it was that.

I definitely began to feel isolated at the club. Partly because people don't tend to get along so well at a club when the team is losing, but also because – through a combination of my own avoidance of socialising around alcohol and the general turn away from understanding cultural diversity at Essendon after Kevin Sheedy left – I never had strong relationships with the coaches or those in charge at the club. Our relations weren't strained so much as hardly there. We weren't communicating particularly well, and I found myself feeling increasingly distant from the people in charge. One week I had to seek the coaches out myself to find out if I was playing. Ordinarily in a football club, if you're on the verge of selection the coaches will talk you through their thinking, or at least tell you their decision. 'No, we're going to go without you this week,' was the reply when I finally asked. *Any chance of anyone telling me?* I thought to myself.

I was frustrated. One day I even broke down in tears while talking to Rouba's cousin Wally (who you might remember facilitated my relationship with Rouba) because I was at such a loss. That tells you how close to breaking point I was, because I almost never show that kind of emotion to other people. Among my friends, I'm famous for being unemotional and in control. But now everything I'd been building since I was a kid was up in the air, and I had no real understanding of why. I began to assume I was out of chances. I'd played 26 games, which I think would be pretty close to the average length of an AFL career, once you consider that lots of players who are drafted don't even get to their debut. And after only 12 senior games in two years, and with no sense of direction, I thought my career was over.

My last senior game for Essendon was against Carlton in Round 19 of 2010. We were slaughtered that night. They kicked ten goals in the last quarter to beat us by 76 points. It was after that game that I finally decided I was done. There was simply no reason for me to stay at Essendon anymore. I wasn't getting chances professionally, and the culture had changed so much that I felt no real connection to the club personally. I had no relationship with the coach, no relationship with the assistant coaches, and some good relationships with a handful of teammates but none that was so deep it would hold me at the club. And most of my best friends there – Jason Johnson, Mark Johnson, Adam McPhee – had already left the club or retired by then anyway.

'Enough's enough,' I said to my manager, Nigel Carmody. 'I need to make a move.'

'Yeah, I agree. I'll see what clubs are interested.'

I could quite easily have given up on my career and accepted it was over. Even as Nigel looked elsewhere for a suitor, I couldn't assume he'd succeed. I believed I was good enough, but I hadn't had the chance to show it, so how could I expect anyone else to have seen it? When I put it that bluntly, it seemed scary. And while I did have my moments, generally I kept myself calm by maintaining a kind of spiritual resignation. What was destined to happen would happen, I told myself, and whatever that was would be for the best.

I said a lot of prayers in this period – not of the kind we do five times daily, but the type called *du'a*, in which you're free to say and ask for whatever you like. 'Allah, keep me steadfast,' I'd say most often. 'You know what's best for me, so provide it.' I had to be open to the possibility that being an AFL player wasn't good for me, and that I might be saved from something terrible if it was taken away from me. 'Perhaps you hate a thing and it is good for you; and perhaps you love a thing and it is bad for you,' says the Qur'an (2:216). That idea defined my mentality through that period. The truth is that we so often don't know what's good for us, or even what will make us happy. The mistake we make is to confuse what we want with what is good.

I knew I was going through a rough patch with football. I didn't know how it would end, but I knew that my job was to give it my best and then accept the result. You do your rehab seriously, you prepare for games as professionally as possible, you work on your psychology so your mind is clear under pressure. But there's no guarantee these things will mean you win more games or have a successful career. Success might take a long time, or it might not come at all. But that doesn't change the work you do. I recognised this was a moment that would take a lot of patience.

The Islamic term for patience is *sabr*, and it's one of the most important ideas we have. There are too many Islamic texts on this point to mention. 'Give glad tiding to the people of *sabr*: those who say, when afflicted with calamity, "to Allah we belong, and to Him is our return",' says the Qur'an (2:155–156). 'No one had ever been given anything better than *sabr*,' said the Prophet. 'There is no faith for the one who has no *sabr*,' said the Prophet's cousin, Ali. In some ways, 'patience' isn't a good translation, because we tend to think of patience as just waiting for things to happen without getting agitated. Maybe it's better translated as 'patient perseverance'. *Sabr* is really about calmly persisting with doing the right thing even when it's tough. The sign that you're really practising *sabr* is when you face setback after setback but they don't cause you to deviate.

And after all that, you also accept there are no guarantees, because the result is entirely in God's hands. This is that idea of *tawakkul* I mentioned earlier. Like *sabr*, it's not a passive concept. Muslims believe God is in control of everything, but He has created cause and effect too. He has created a world in which work and effort often bring results. He's given us responsibilities to ourselves and to each other, and requires us to work.

To say everything comes from God is not to say we should stand around and wait for provisions to fall from the sky. A famous story has the Prophet noticing a Bedouin dismounting from his camel and leaving it untied. 'Why don't you tie down your camel?' asked the Prophet.

'I put my trust in Allah,' came the reply.

'Tie your camel first, then put your trust in Allah,' said the Prophet.

That phrase – 'tie your camel' – is now shorthand among Muslims for the concept of *tawakkul*. It is not an excuse for inaction. It is instead an encouragement to take action without fearing whatever hardships or difficulties might arise. Think of it as a much bigger, divine version of when footballers talk about 'trusting the process', rather than worrying about the result. By training as hard as I could and doing my best in the VFL while my manager looked for other opportunities for me, I was tying my camel.

It worked. One day, Nigel told me that someone was interested. I felt like I'd made it through to the other side, that a new beginning was possible. I sincerely believe that if it wasn't for my faith, and if it wasn't for the *sabr* and *tawakkul* my faith teaches me, and which I take seriously – if I hadn't truly surrendered myself to the idea that God's plans are better than mine – then I wouldn't have made it through that final year at Essendon. I don't think it's a stretch to say that Islam saved my career.

I had a lot of reasons to be grateful. To God, obviously, but also to a man who believed in me. A man who, about five years earlier, had been an assistant coach at Hawthorn when my name was apparently on the board there listing young players they wanted to draft, and who had apparently remained interested in me as a player even when I was struck down with stress fractures at Essendon. A man who had since taken a head coaching job at a different club.

A man by the name of Damien Hardwick.

When the season ended, I met Dimma and Blair Hartley, Richmond's list manager. They gave me a full presentation on the role they saw for me: specifically, they wanted me to play on the wing. As it turned out, I never did – Shaun Grigg, who they recruited at the same time, ended up playing there instead – but I was impressed by their belief in me.

And so I went from being a fringe player at Essendon on $100,000 plus match payments to a starting Richmond player with a fixed salary of $230,000. I left the club that didn't want to use me for whatever reason, and joined one that seemed keen to have me and was basically guaranteeing me games. In the end, it was an easy decision, but it wasn't an easy situation.

There's a period when you're changing clubs, before things are official and maybe even before they're fully agreed, when it feels like you're carrying a dirty little secret with you everywhere. That's how I felt. I didn't go to the Essendon best-and-fairest that season in order to avoid the awkward conversations that would inevitably happen; I didn't want to end up lying or saying something stupid. It was difficult for me, because distancing myself like that, and for those kinds of reasons, doesn't reflect the person I am. I worried that I was leaving my teammates with a poor impression of me, especially those who had been really good to me in my time at the club.

That was a big deal, because I always worry about what other people think of me. I don't need to be the most popular person in the room, but I can't stand the idea that people feel they have reason to speak badly of me. I don't want a single person to have any ill feeling about me. I feel this to the extent that if I meet someone who I know has been speaking badly of me behind my back, even if it's an open secret, I won't raise it with them. In fact, I'll do the opposite: I'll greet them warmly and ask about their family, because I don't want to make them feel awkward and potentially hold it against me. So even though I later explained the situation to some of my teammates, looking back I think avoiding the best-and-fairest was the wrong thing to do. It still doesn't sit right with me morally, and I wouldn't do it now.

A few days later, I ran into Jobe Watson at the airport; we were both heading to Adelaide for Henry Slattery's wedding. There was an obvious elephant in the room. Jobe knew the signs. 'I understand, mate,' he said to me. 'It's hard what you went through.' He suggested I look to the future. As it happened, Matthew Knights had been sacked as coach on the same day I played my last game in the VFL, so Essendon would soon have a new regime. That might mean new opportunities for me.

'You do know that most likely Hirdy's going to get the job?' Jobe said. 'You played with him – he rates you really highly.'

'Yeah, but I'm very hurt at the moment,' I replied. 'I don't want that feeling of resentment to come back to me next year if I stay and don't end up playing.'

When I got back from the wedding, James Hird began calling me. So I did what my manager advised me to do and ignored his calls. Just saying that sounds ridiculous. But Nigel knew that, with Hirdy's reputation as one of the best players ever to have played, and with my inexperience, I could end up making the wrong decision for myself. 'He's very smart,' Nigel would say. 'He has a marketing background – he knows how to sell an idea to you.'

I could see where he was coming from, but in the end I just couldn't cope with it. However bad it sounds for a nobody like me to be shunning someone like James Hird, it felt even worse. *Who the hell do you think you are?* I remember asking myself. *He's a champion of the game, and you're just some guy who's played 26 games. How dare you? This is not me.* I also felt it wasn't right Islamically.

I decided to ask Mohamed Bakkar for his advice, because while he understood the business side of the equation, as a practising Muslim himself he'd also understand the moral discomfort I felt.

'Hirdy's done nothing wrong,' he told me. 'So out of respect, go have a meeting with him. Open your heart to the guy, and listen to what he has to say. But don't commit.'

I called Hirdy back. 'Yeah, let's catch up.'

We met at a cafe in Docklands, and I confessed to him that I felt hurt by Essendon.

'Yeah, I know,' he replied. 'But I want to keep the whole list. I want to prove to everyone that the players we have are good enough to make the finals and be competitive. And you're part of that. You're part of our best 22. You're important to my system. You're going to be playing week in, week out. I really want you to stay. I don't want you to leave, and I value you as a player.'

It was exactly what I was desperate to hear. But I also heard a nagging voice in my head: *How do I know I'm in your best 22? Show me the evidence. Show me a contract that proves it.* The reality was that there was no way he could do that. Any offer from Essendon would have been on similar money to what I was earning before, just with a promise to play me more often.

The key thing about Richmond's offer wasn't the money per se. In fact, if I played every game at Essendon, I'd only have been earning slightly less. It was that by making that investment in me, by putting me on a contract without match payments, Richmond really had to give me games. No club puts a player on a contract like that unless it intends to play them in the seniors, because otherwise it'll have to give games to someone else who is on match payments and blow its salary cap. So the Richmond offer came with *security*.

I texted Hirdy back that night and told him I'd made up my mind to go to Richmond. He never replied.

Now I just needed Essendon and Richmond to reach a deal. It didn't go well. Essendon played hardball, bluntly rejecting the trades Richmond offered. I don't know why they did that, because it meant they ended up getting nothing for me. If two clubs can't reach an agreement to trade a player who is coming out of contract, that player heads into the pre-season draft, where he can be picked up by any club. That was actually a risk for me, because West Coast had the first pick in that draft, with Richmond second. I'd already negotiated a deal with Richmond, so according to the rules West Coast could only select me if they were prepared to match my terms.

I suppose Essendon wanted to force me into the pre-season draft so I'd get nervous about the possibility of West Coast choosing me instead, and decide to stay at Windy Hill. But by the time the draft came around, I'd been training with Richmond for a month. I already felt like a Tiger. The chances West Coast would come from nowhere were pretty slim, so I took the plunge. I still worried, but it was never really in doubt. West Coast took a WA player as expected and Richmond selected me with pick two.

But if my thirst for security played its part in leading me to Richmond, that didn't mean it was quenched upon my arrival. Insecurity never really goes away. It's there through the form slumps and the injuries, of course, but it's especially present during contract negotiations. The final year of a contract can be a hard time for a footballer, because you spend a lot of the year waiting to hear if you'll get a new offer while the club tries to figure out who it wants to keep, who it will let go and how it will fit all its players under the salary cap. That last point makes life particularly difficult, because often one player's contract depends on what happens with another. Say Richmond are trying to re-sign Dusty Martin. Lots of other contracts probably can't happen until that has been finalised, because only then will Richmond know how much money they have left to spend. Contract renewals therefore only happen after a lot of hurdles have been cleared: the club has to want you to stay, it has to know what sort of salary it can offer you, and you've got to decide whether the offer's acceptable – and, if you have any reservations, who else might be interested in you.

That was exactly the situation I was in during 2016 when my contract with Richmond was coming to an end and my contract negotiations (like the team) weren't going particularly well. The most Richmond would offer me was two years, and the financial increase initially was also fairly modest. That would take me to the brink of 30, which is exactly when getting new contracts becomes significantly harder and your earning potential drops. If I signed for two years, there was a real possibility I could be on the scrap heap after that. But if

I signed for three or four, then at least I'd have some security. If I moved to single-year contracts on low money after that, then at least I could say I'd got the most out of my career. Given how much I crave security, you can imagine how much the situation unsettled me.

In situations like this where I needed to talk through something or let off steam, I often found myself venting to Ali Fahour. I first met Ali when I was 16. We were both playing for Lebanon in a competition called the AFL Harmony Cup, which also involved an Israeli team, an Indigenous team and an Italian team. The tournament was held at Princes Park, which would have been familiar to Ali because he was playing for Carlton's affiliated VFL team at the time. A couple of years later he moved on to Essendon, which turned out to be fortuitous because by then I was there too. In addition to playing in the VFL, Ali was Essendon's head of community, and one of the first things he did when I arrived at the club was show me where he used to pray: basically a cupboard hidden away in the media room, which was unused for a lot of the week. On Fridays we'd drive to the mosque together for the congregational prayers.

We started to become close in those dark days at Essendon when I found myself on the outer and began considering leaving. When I felt the world was crashing down around me, Ali was one of my most important sources of guidance, consolation and patience. At the time in my career that I was lowest on confidence, he always called me on match day to tell me how good I was – a habit he would keep up for years, even after I got to Richmond. Ali understood my insecurities completely.

Ali was the AFL's Multicultural Manager at the time, and I'd been working with him for years. In 2012 we established the Bachar Houli Academy together, a football and leadership program for promising young Muslim players. It was an enormous and extremely meaningful project for me, and it brought us even closer, to the point that I counted him among my very closest friends. But as close as we were, he clearly still had the ability to surprise me, because as I complained to him about my contract situation with Richmond, he said the most startling thing: 'I want to try to get you to GWS.'

From his perspective as an AFL employee, it made perfect sense. Where better to have the AFL's most senior Lebanese Muslim player than in Western Sydney, the unofficial capital of Lebanese Muslim Australia? I had good connections among the Muslim community there, and one thing I knew for sure was that they're loyal. I had no doubt they would come along in droves to see a Muslim play, especially if he was Lebanese. It might even be worth 5000 more members to the club, with a fair chunk of them coming most weeks. The AFL clearly wanted the Giants to make inroads into Sydney, and engage multicultural communities there more successfully, so it was a no-brainer.

Probably for exactly that reason, AFL CEO Gillon McLachlan was really supportive of the idea. To this day I cannot understand why GWS hasn't recruited a Muslim player. When I was coming out of contract with Essendon in 2010, Kevin Sheedy, who had been announced as the Giants' first coach, said he was interested in getting me there, which made sense given his awareness of the potential of multiculturalism in football. But nothing ever came of it, possibly because the Giants knew that, with the way the draft worked that year, every other club would have a chance to take me before they got a shot. And maybe after that they figured they had already recruited Israel Folau to appeal to the people of Western Sydney. But that experiment ended in 2012, and there's been nothing since.

'No, no, no, I don't want to leave Richmond,' I told Ali.

But Ali's good at what he does because he's relentless. He wasn't about to let it lie like that. He had a good relationship with Wayne Campbell, which he formed when Wayne was working at the AFL as the umpires' boss. Wayne, who of course is a former Richmond captain and a club legend, had since moved on to be a senior member of the GWS football department. Ali texted him: 'Bachar?'

'Can we talk?' Wayne replied.

They did. Ali knew the Giants had some salary cap issues, so his proposal was to include a new ambassador role in my contract, which the AFL would pay and which would therefore sit outside the cap. The ambassador role, along with the chance to secure my future with a multi-year, financially lucrative deal at a club climbing up the ladder, was something to at least consider for a moment, given everything that was happening.

Apparently, it was an interesting enough idea for the Giants for it to escalate all the way to the head coach, Leon Cameron. Ali arranged a secret meeting with Leon and Wayne midway through the 2016 season. No one else knew. Not Richmond. Not even my manager.

'Should we be doing this?' I asked Ali. 'Dimma's been so good to me . . . I feel bad.' Actually, I felt worse than bad. It felt like I was having an affair.

'It's the right thing to do,' he assured me. 'It's a business, and you've got to look after yourself.'

I was very nervous, and didn't want to go. But a deal to take me beyond 30? Even the possibility of that was simply too much for me to walk away from without even a meeting. Rouba has family in Sydney, so it was probably the only place outside Melbourne I'd ever consider playing. I was flying to Sydney anyway for the AFL *iftar* dinner, so I met them at a cafe while I was there.

The meeting was productive, and we ended up discussing that if this was going to happen, it was going to need to be well in advance of what Richmond could do. But Leon and Wayne seemed to be at odds on how they rated me as a player.

Leon was a fan: 'You're the sort of player we're looking for, Bach, you're a gun. We love what you do at halfback. We've always wanted a left-footer in that position. You'd fit into this team really well and probably be in our top ten players.'

But Wayne was less complimentary: 'I'll be honest with you, we have a really strong list, so please don't think you'll be a walk-up start into our best 22. We have a couple of halfback flankers that we think are ahead of you.'

There's no way of knowing for sure, but it's possible I'd be a Giant today had Wayne not said that. I was confused. Why would they even entertain an offer of that size if they didn't rate me really highly? And if you do, why start on that note? I took it like a dagger in the heart. Still, I didn't dismiss the idea straightaway. I gave myself time to think it over and reach a decision I was comfortable with.

Muslims have a special prayer for those moments in life when they feel they need guidance while making a decision: *salat al-istikhara*. It's like any other prayer, really, but it includes a specific supplication that effectively asks God to give us what is best for us, and for us to be pleased with it, whatever the outcome. Here's a translation:

> Oh Allah, I'm asking You for goodness through Your knowledge, and I'm asking You for strength through Your divine ability, and I'm asking You from Your infinite grace. Because You're completely able, while I am not. You know everything, and I do not, and You know everything that's unseen. Oh Allah, if You know that this decision [which the Muslim then mentions] is good for me in my religion, my worldly life and my afterlife, then decree it, facilitate it for me with ease, and bless me through it. But if You know that this has bad consequences for my religion, my worldly life and my afterlife, then get it away from me and get me away from it, and decree what's better for me, whatever it may be, and make me content with it.

After this, you simply proceed and trust that the outcome will be the right one. That's exactly what I did.

About a month after the meeting, Wayne called to say that they hadn't forgotten about me, but that things were developing slowly. I don't know what the delay was, but I wonder if they were working towards a deal with Brett Deledio – who did end up leaving Richmond for GWS that year – and couldn't take things further with me until that was sorted.

Whatever the reason, the security equation had changed. Richmond's improved offer was solid, and GWS's wasn't yet. Richmond also offered me the near certainty that I'd be playing games, while GWS's position on that was unclear. And because I never wanted to leave Richmond, I needed a good reason to do so. The fact that I felt bad even having a meeting probably told me all I needed to know. Taken together, I took all this as a clear enough answer to my prayer for guidance. I decided to stay at Richmond.

And thank God I did! No financial benefit or job security could possibly have replaced the two premiership sides I've been so fortunate to be part of. And of course I cannot help but be aware of the irony that both those premierships were only possible because we beat GWS in the finals: the 2017 Preliminary Final and the Grand Final in 2019. I hold nothing against the Giants or Wayne Campbell, of course, but I will admit that every time I played GWS after this episode, I desperately wanted to do well.

Ali saw the irony too. He texted Wayne after we won the 2017 Grand Final: 'Is he still not in your best 22?'

'He had a ripper game!' replied Wayne.

Ali messaged him again after we beat the Giants in 2019. That one might have been a bit rough.

8

FAILURE

FOOTBALL IS MOSTLY ABOUT FAILING. Most years you don't win the premiership, and most players never achieve it at all. Every week, only half the teams can win. Because of the AFL's many equalisation measures, a player will almost certainly spend a good part of his career, if it lasts a decent length, playing for a team that's losing. And when it's finally your turn to play in a team that wins enough games to make the finals, you're most likely to end your season with a loss in a big game, which will hurt. That's why it feels so great to win a premiership. It's really, really hard to do.

Most footballers never make it to the AFL. And most of the ones who do will barely play. Something like 90 per cent of players never make it to 100 games. Less than a third will make it to 50. Every year around 10–12 per cent of a team is sacked, traded or retires to make way for new draftees – and that was in the good old days before the COVID-19 pandemic threatened to gut the league. Imagine that in any other industry.

You'll get injured. You'll wonder whether you're going to get your spot in the team back. Coaches might reassure you – 'you're really important to our structure', 'there's a big hole when you're not playing' – but you'll still be wondering: what if they don't really mean it and they're just telling me that to make me feel better? What if someone arrives and fills that hole in the meantime and the team looks better without me? What if I'm out for a while and I have to come back through the VFL and then I struggle? The longer you're out, the more you'll worry. You'll start to doubt yourself. You'll start to question whether you belong. You catch yourself hoping that the players stepping into your role go well but not too well, and feel relief when they don't. Then you'll recognise how terrible that is and feel awful about it.

I've played 200 games, won premierships, made the All-Australian team and represented Victoria. And I've thought all of these things.

You'll lose form. You'll be dropped. You'll be recalled, then dropped again. And even when you're playing every week, you won't feel secure about your place. Very few ever do, really, and they're the superstars of the competition. Even those players will one day face a time when they're getting too old and too slow and people start wondering whether they should be dropped or forced into retirement. Jarryd Roughead won four flags and a Coleman Medal, and is a Hawthorn legend and former captain. He played most of his last season in the VFL.

If they can have this conversation about Gary Ablett Jr, they can have it about anyone.

Then, if you're blessed enough to get through all that, you'll retire. You'll lose your cultural relevance, and maybe even your sense of identity. You'll lose the camaraderie, the structure, the routine, the relentless purpose that a football club provides. You'll lose one of the things you love most, and you'll lose it forever. You grow up as a kid dreaming of playing in the AFL, but no one dreams of retiring from it. That one just comes and finds you. I haven't been through that yet, but I've seen enough examples of players falling into that abyss to know how serious it can be.

I'm not saying footballers have especially hard lives, or that we aren't extremely fortunate to have the jobs we do. I understand that in the grand scheme of things people endure far more serious hardships: they lose loved ones, they live through droughts, famines and wars. One of the remarkable things about the COVID-19 pandemic was how quickly things like football were put into perspective.

What's different about the life of a footballer is not that it's more serious or important. It's that failure and hardship are such a frequent part of your everyday professional life, because success is so rare. The bottom line is that if you're going to play elite sport, you're going to have to handle these things. You're going to need a way to manage your own insecurities. Either that or they'll break you.

Unsurprisingly, my answer has always been anchored in faith, centred on the idea that I have a greater purpose in life than football. I know that's not unique to me because I used to have that conversation reasonably often with Anthony Miles when he was at Richmond. Milesy is a devout Christian and often approached things similarly to me. He has been through a lot in his life, and developed his faith as a teenager a little while after he lost a cousin to cancer, so he understands its power. Even as a footballer he's been through a lot of ups and downs, being traded from one club to the next, struggling for game time despite often playing really well. But I noticed how he always had a smile on his face, he was always in good spirits, his wellbeing was solid no matter what was going on. 'We're always strong,' he said to me once, explaining how it was that his faith got him through things.

I can only get close to achieving that feeling when I have the broadest perspective possible. I play because I enjoy footy and I'm okay at it, but everything comes and goes: jobs, money, even family. The only thing that doesn't is God – and, if I'm fortunate, my faith. And that is my true purpose. To lose that would be truly devastating for me, because I know that, once lost, faith can be very difficult to retrieve. And when things don't go my way, when all else seems lost, my faith gives me something to turn to.

I don't mean to imply that faith is some kind of safety net or consolation prize. It's central for me. As Muslims, our relationship with God isn't something to be put into a separate compartment of life; it's the focus of everything we do. Even mundane things like housework or sleep can be transformed into acts of worship if they're done with consciousness of God. So, there's vacuuming – but then there's vacuuming with an awareness that God loves cleanliness in humans, or that performing these sorts of chores can be an act of service to other people, and that God loves those who serve others and work hard to maintain good relationships with their spouses, children, parents or community.

Similarly, you can sleep mindlessly, or you can recognise that sleep is a sign of your own weakness and dependence – unlike God, who doesn't sleep because He is independent of everything. He has no needs; we have countless needs. He is eternal; we will die one day. He is perfect; we are not.

And that's not a problem – it's something to be embraced, because it reminds us who we really are. It frees us from the mental anguish of perfectionism and self-obsession. The prophet Muhammad captured it nicely when he said: 'If you did not sin, Allah would replace you with people who would sin and they would seek forgiveness from Allah and He would forgive them.' Of course, we are meant to do our best to avoid these sins, but we are not angels. We are meant to be imperfect. We are a mass of flaws and limitations. And it's fantastic.

For me, having this sense of purpose means bringing it to everything. I love to win. I really love to win. But if I want my football to be something with a higher purpose, then it matters more how I go about it. How do I handle the pain and the exhaustion of preseason? How do I handle the rejection and failure along the way? Do I do so with the character and humility Islam requires of me? Do I take these setbacks as a valuable opportunity to improve myself as a player, and even as a person, by learning to control my ego? In short, do I play in a way that reflects Islamic ideals or do I not? If I do, then

I've succeeded without winning a single game. If not, then I've failed, no matter how many premierships I win.

That's the theory, anyway. But faith isn't even or complete. It's not perfect. Mine certainly isn't. I'm a work in progress, and will be forever. Faith shrinks and grows and wavers, and with it so does my clarity of purpose. But like anything, I suppose, the more I focus on it, the better I get, and the stronger I become mentally – but also the freer I become, because I know there are so many more important things to life than football.

Realising this made me enjoy football more, and do it better, because it means now I play with a more carefree attitude. What's the worst-case scenario coming out of a football game? That we lose and I get dropped the following week? That we lose a Grand Final? That's not the end of the world. It's not even important in the grand scheme of things, just as winning can't fill a hole inside you if that's all you have to fill it. If I can internalise that knowledge fully, then I have nothing to fear in football. Why fear failure, if failure itself isn't a soul-shaking problem?

The prophet Muhammad put it like this: 'Wondrous are the believer's affairs. For him there is good in all his affairs, and this is so only for the believer. When something pleasing happens to him, he is grateful, and that is good for him; and when something displeasing happens to him, he shows patience (*sabr*), and that is good for him.'

That doesn't always come naturally, though. You need to keep reminding yourself, practising patience, consciously choosing to respond to hardships in that way. Like every player, I have that feeling after a bad loss or when I'm playing badly of wanting to hide, of wanting not to go out to cafes or the shopping centre because it feels like even having conversations with people is a hard thing to do. So I pause and think about it quite deliberately. What's the worst that could happen? How am I going to bounce back? Then I force myself to go out and approach people immediately, to make sure people can see me, because the reality is that football is just a game.

I'm probably like a lot of senior players in that I realised this particularly strongly once I got married and had kids. That was when I was hit by the enormity of it all: of suddenly being responsible for people, of the love you feel for these lives that are in your care. It made me realise the full weight of the blessings I'd received, and how reliant I was on them.

It's not uncommon that people become better players once they become parents, even though they might spend less time devoted to football, or get less sleep. Maybe they're just getting older, more seasoned and more mature. Maybe they're home more often, which helps them lead more responsible lives. But I'm sure one factor is that they have a new perspective. They see football for what it is – something they love and that matters a lot to them, but that ultimately isn't that important – and they can then play with greater freedom and less pressure.

That's why, even though it might seem odd, so many of my conversations with teammates are about making football mean less. Probably the best example is Brandon Ellis. He's a fair bit younger than me and so didn't have the life experience older players have, but we're also just such good friends that I can tell by looking at him when he's being eaten up inside because he's had a bad game. I'd take him out for coffee and we'd chat, but the message would always be pretty much the same. 'Footy doesn't define us as people,' I'd say. 'We're human, so we're going to have bad games, but that doesn't make us bad people. Keep smiling, brother.'

I really believe that. But it can be an easy thing to forget when you're in the middle of your career, and there have definitely been times when the downside of football has got the better of my love for the game. The end of 2016 is the clearest example in my mind. In Round 6 that year I broke the scaphoid bone in my wrist. It's a tiny bone, but because it doesn't have a steady blood supply it takes about twice as long as other bones to heal. I ended up missing three months of football. That was the worst of all worlds, because I was able to do everything except play. I could train almost fully, so I stayed really fit, but it meant I was doing all of the difficult work of training with none of the fun of playing.

Not that there was much fun to be had that year, as we spent most of it getting beaten. We were playing football that was difficult to watch and even less enjoyable to play. By the time I came back, our season was all but gone, and it felt at the club like everyone couldn't wait for it to end.

Football works when we see the games as meaningful; otherwise, it's just a bunch of people kicking around a bag of wind. It feels like there's no bigger picture. In 2016, after three seasons in which we made the finals and felt like we were making progress, all that progress had stopped. It felt like we were done. We had failed to climb the mountain. Basically, we'd just walked up a hill. I didn't cope with it particularly well and, as I've said, was seriously contemplating what would have been a premature retirement.

A lot changed in 2017, including with my mindset. In the lead-up to a big game or whenever I could sense myself losing perspective or overthinking my football, I started writing reminder notes to myself on my phone. Mostly, I was just reiterating my strengths as a player to myself, or reminding myself of the mindset I should bring to these things as a Muslim. For example, midway through 2019, I wrote to myself:

> Whatever happens, win, lose, you don't play well, this is Allah's will as He is the best of planners. *Alhamdulillah*[4] for everything, you are so blessed with what Allah has given you from all avenues. Remember what Mufti Menk said: 'When something goes your way, say *alhamdulillah*. And when something doesn't go your way, say *alhamdulillah* twice.' Allah has planned something better for you, little did you know.

I wish I'd written that before Round 17, 2015. On that day at the MCG we played Fremantle, who were on top of the ladder – a position they'd hold until the end of the season. We needed the win to keep pace with the top four. And we played really well. With a minute and 22 seconds left in the game, we were leading by two points. All we had to do was kill the game, either by keeping the ball or by forcing stoppages, and then watch the time run out. It was basic stuff. *Alhamdulillah*.

---

4   Literally 'all praise to Allah', but it also carries the sense of thanking God.

Fremantle had just scored a behind, and I was taking the kick-in. In this scenario, there are really only two options. You find a free teammate nearby and kick short to him, or you kick the ball as far as you can towards the boundary line, and hope either that one of your tall players can mark it or that your teammates can force a stoppage.

On this particular occasion, the equation was even simpler than that. Just about every player on the ground had gathered about 60 metres away from me near the boundary line to my right. Kick it there and it was very unlikely the ball was coming back my way in a hurry – there was just too much congestion. As long as Fremantle didn't mark it, we should be able to kill some time.

But as I looked up, I saw a gaping hole straight in front of me. The centre square was wide open, and standing on his own in plenty of space was Kane Lambert, waving his arms, calling for the ball. There wouldn't have been a Fremantle player within 20 metres of him. My eyes lit up. *This looks juicy!* I thought. I kicked it hard in his direction about 55 metres. I didn't get it cleanly.

It takes a ball about three seconds to travel that far off the boot. I knew as soon as I kicked it that I was in trouble, and within about a second and a half everyone else could tell this kick was a terrible idea too. By the time the ball reached Kane, opponents had come from everywhere. He was surrounded by three Fremantle players, without a single Richmond player there to help. He stood no chance. Had he been a taller player, maybe. But Kane was one of our shorter players – a fact which was as true when I kicked it as it was when the ball reached him.

Within four seconds, Garrick Ibbotson had taken the mark for Fremantle, then passed the ball to David Mundy, who marked it about 40 metres from goal. Mundy took his time, went back and kicked truly. The game was over. We'd lost by four points.

It was a significant loss too, since at the end of the home-and-away season we narrowly missed the top four. If we'd won – and the other results had stayed the same – we would have made the top four and had a double chance in the finals. Instead, we finished fifth and went out in the first week. Freo, on the other hand, ended up on top of the ladder; they'd have been fifth if we'd beaten them.

Alhamdulillah. Alhamdulillah.

You know when people say they wish the ground would open up and swallow them? I'd always thought that was just an amusing expression. It's not. It was literally what I wanted to happen at that moment, and if I'd had a shovel on hand I would have started digging straightaway. It's a unique feeling when you think you've cost your team the game, especially one as important as this one. You feel like you're the only person anyone in the world can see, and it's like you can hear all their thoughts. Probably the worst bit is that you feel ashamed in front of your teammates.

True to style, Dimma didn't criticise me in the press conference afterwards. 'You can look at, you know, the last mistake, Bachar knows ... or you can look at the ten goals 18 [we kicked for the game]. We hit the post six times,' he said. 'At the end of the day, we had our chances to win the game and we didn't take it. It's easy to focus just on the last mistake of the day, but you know, our game was littered with mistakes. We had more than ample opportunities to win the game – we didn't.' He made the same point in our team meeting. I appreciated that massively, and factually he was probably right. But still I didn't feel it.

What do I do now? I wondered. *Do I just avoid the club for as long as possible?* I can tell you it's tempting, because the last thing you want to do at a time like that is see or talk to anyone, especially the media. And you can be guaranteed they'll be milling around the club waiting for you to arrive so they can stick a microphone in your face. I could have done my recovery somewhere private, trying to isolate myself. But avoiding it wouldn't have meant I was being the type of person I want to be, and I knew I'd have to face the world eventually. *Sabr.* Persevere. Keep doing what needs to be done in the face of what's coming. Don't shy away. Front up. And do it now.

The media were waiting for me in the carpark. 'I can't wait for next week because I'm going to take the first kick-in,' I told them. Then, having had a run at it, I went on Channel 7's Sunday morning *Game Day* show and reiterated my aim: 'I will take the first one, I guarantee you on that one.'

Now that I'd said it, I had to live it. And that meant fully accepting what had happened within myself, and with my teammates. I had help on that front, because all week at training the boys found my mistake hilarious. When we were practising kick-ins midweek, Jack Riewoldt shouted out to Kane Lambert, 'Go into the middle and wave your hands!' Everyone roared with laughter. Needless to say, I knew exactly where to kick it the next time I was in that situation.

We were playing Hawthorn on Friday night that week. These were the 2015 Hawks, too. Not just the best team in the competition but one of the best we've ever seen, which they proved that season by winning their third straight premiership. Home-and-away stages don't come much bigger than that, and it was on that stage where I'd take my next kick-in.

Hawthorn didn't score until nearly halfway through the first quarter, when Jack Gunston hit the post from 20 metres out. I'd been thinking about this moment all week, contemplating every scenario, every disaster that could possibly eventuate, and reassuring myself that I was a good kick. Now, finally, the moment was here. I didn't hesitate. I went straight for the ball to take the kick-in. No one else was ever going to take it.

I stood in the goal square, surveying the field to figure out my options, convincing myself not to be nervous, forcing myself to be confident. I scanned right, then left, then right again. Nothing obvious was on.

I don't often notice the crowd in games, but I could really feel them this time. They weren't hissing or laughing at me. They were just tense and anxious, which might have been worse. The Richmond cheer squad was behind me, and they were noticeably quiet. The usual racket was replaced by a murmur, the sound of people turning to each other and talking, rather than shouting towards the players. I couldn't hear individual voices, but it was as though I knew what everyone was saying: 'He's going to do it again! He's going to stuff up this first kick!' This whole process couldn't have taken more than five seconds, but it felt like a year.

Eventually, I took the easy option. I played on out of the square, ran about five steps and kicked long towards the boundary line. Contest. The ball hit the ground. Hawthorn won it and the ball came straight back to the 'hot spot', about 20 metres from goal. We punched the ball towards the goal line and eventually forced it over. Another kick-in. Take two.

Dylan Grimes had the ball and shaped to take the kick-in. I was standing in the goal square and I turned towards him with my arms out, asking for the ball. I wasn't about to let him take this kick-in. He tossed me the ball and I was right back where I was, surveying the field, looking for an option. I moved to my left, about to pass the ball short to a teammate who wasn't there. I quickly thought better of it and stopped myself kicking the ball in the nick of time. I looked right. Then dead centre. Then I walked slowly backwards.

It was time to be confident. I did exactly the same as last time: play on out of the square and kick long towards the boundary line. Another contest. Another Hawthorn clearance, and then a shot at goal, which we just managed to touch before it crossed the line. It was another kick-in but this time I was nowhere nearby, and Nick Vlastuin took it. But it was done.

Late in the third quarter, I took a mark near the boundary line at the Punt Road end and kicked a goal to put us 12 points ahead. The ball did not deviate. Finally, all the tension was released, all the weight was lifted. My teammates came from all directions, swamping me in their celebrations. They knew what that moment meant. It felt just so good. We went on to record our best win of the year.

Alhamdulillah.

The Fremantle kick-in was buried as a public saga. But it's never left my mind completely. To this day, I hate it when people bring it up, even if it's in a light-hearted way. My friends do it all the time. I'll laugh along, pretending to be in on the joke, but inside I'm burning. Still.

Even so, I have to admit that it was a very worthwhile failure. I'd been forced to look my fears and insecurities in the face and choose to confront them, to put myself in the position of discomfort that's necessary for growth. I'd owned up to my mistake, and subordinated my ego to do what needed to be done. That's one of the things that makes sport so great: it always has the ability to humble you.

Perhaps the biggest cultural change that happened at Richmond in 2017, and which played a huge role in turning us from a poor side into a premiership team, was that we came to accept our flaws. We didn't need to be superheroes, flawless and immune to life's difficulties. We began to address each other in our full imperfections, celebrating each other's strengths and supporting each other in weakness. It was a new culture of honesty and vulnerability, which created the secret weapon that we kept referring to throughout the season: *connection*.

It began at the top, with the captain and the coach. Damien Hardwick addressed the playing group at the start of preseason and completely bared his soul, telling us how he'd shut us out as players and tried to micromanage us. He even told us he'd become a worse person, and that his wife – who Richmond supporters would soon come to know affectionately as Mrs Hardwick – had told him as much.

This was a man who had won two premierships as a player and one as an assistant coach, and who had been coaching his own AFL team for seven years, and he was telling us that he'd got it wrong – that he should have trusted us more. It was an incredibly brave, vulnerable thing to do; he was potentially undermining his own authority. But the result was that it increased his standing with us massively. Immediately, you knew the whole environment had changed.

Then Trent Cotchin followed suit. To see this man, who I'd become so close to over the years, begin the season by standing in front of his teammates and explaining to them all the ways in which he'd let himself, his family and his teammates down, and failed as our captain, was moving in ways I could never have anticipated. Trent and Dimma were still our leaders, but now they'd lead us as friends, even family.

On our preseason training camp in Mooloolaba, we all went through a similar experience: the now much-publicised 'Triple H' sessions. Every player would stand in front of his peers and tell them about a hero, a hardship and a highlight in his life. We were all scared of doing this. We're footballers, not public speakers, and we'd spent our lives in an environment that celebrated toughness. Football had always been a world in which showing a weakness to anyone was basically asking for it to be exploited. We were people who, for as long as we could remember, went into the world wearing full suits of armour – and now we were being asked to take them off.

Brandon Ellis went first, and blew us away. He told us of the time he came home from school in Year 10 to find his parents crying on the floor. When he asked what was wrong, they gave him the terrible news: his dad had been diagnosed with throat cancer. 'You don't have long to live,' he was told. 'It's too far gone. We can't cure it. Start saying your goodbyes and cherish the time you have left with your kids and wife.' Brandon ran straight to his room, quickly followed by his dad, and they hugged for hours.

Brandon was so distraught that he gave up football and stopped going to school, wanting to spend every spare minute with his father. Over the next few months, his dad lost a lot of weight and all his hair, until, as Brandon put it, 'he looked like he was dead'. Then his dad told him these powerful words: 'Whatever you do, Brandon, go back and play footy. Do it for me.' So, Brandon did.

'Six months later,' Brandon told us, 'the lump was gone and he's still here today ... He's taught me never to give up ... I play AFL for my dad.'

We sat there stunned, most of us with tears in our eyes. And that was Brando's hero story. What was his hardship going to be?

It lived up to the billing. He told us about growing up in a Housing Commission flat, being bullied and called 'scum' at school for being poor, walking an extra kilometre home from school each day so his friends wouldn't know where he lived because he was so embarrassed. He spoke about his rough childhood, about the mates he saw stabbed in front of his eyes, about the way people would steal his family's clothes from their clothesline, so he'd go to a shopping mall and steal some new ones. He'd done it tough, and so had his family.

Brandon had promised his parents, and especially his father, that as soon as he started earning money in the AFL, he'd look after them. And he's delivered. Now they live in a rental property in the suburbs, with Brandon paying half their rent. 'It's the first time my mum and dad and brother and sister have had a backyard in their life,' he told us.

Now everyone was crying, especially me. I felt really proud of Brandon because I knew how much courage it took for him to tell us these things, which he'd been keeping to himself for so long. But I also felt ashamed that I didn't know all this, because I'd always considered Brandon such a close friend.

One reason he and I had bonded quickly was that he'd grown up playing footy with a lot of Lebanese kids at West Coburg, so he immediately related to me in a way no one else really did. He'd just bowl up and say something like, 'How are you going, *habibi*?' Or he'd drop a few Lebanese insults or swear words into a conversation and we'd be away. I knew from those chats that he'd grown up with some rough people who got into trouble occasionally, because he often told me he couldn't believe how I was the exact opposite of so many of the Lebs he'd grown up with, guys who'd often drink, party and smoke.

But I had no idea just how tough his life had been from such an early age. How could we not have spoken about this before? Was he not comfortable enough to tell me? Was I not a good enough friend to have asked about it?

Afterwards, in the hallway on the way to dinner, I gave him a massive hug. 'Bro, you know you can always open up to me. I'm never going to judge. I just wish I'd known that stuff earlier,' I told him. Far from judging him, I felt a new respect for Brandon and his approach to footy. Success for him had a whole extra meaning it didn't have for the rest of us. It was about the survival of his family. Suddenly this kid, still a relatively junior player at our club, appeared to me as a leader. Now I understood what motivated him.

When Brandon left Richmond after the 2019 season to take up a lucrative offer at the Gold Coast Suns, after Richmond's salary cap situation meant there were limits to what they could give him, I didn't begrudge him it at all, or feel like he'd betrayed us. *Good on you, Brando*, I thought. *You deserve this*.

Over the next little while at the Triple H sessions, player after player got up and did the same thing. And after each player had done it, you could see the difference it made to them on the training track. It was like they were a new person. They'd bounce around with the confidence of someone who felt completely accepted by their peers and comfortable being themselves. They were just . . . lighter. We'd never realised just how heavy that armour was, and how much it slowed us down.

Some of us – like Jack Riewoldt, who'd lost his cousin Maddie in 2015 to a bone marrow condition – had some really harrowing things to say. Others spoke about far less dramatic things. But there were some common themes, particularly around family. It turns out that, for AFL players, fathers and mothers seem to make the best heroes. The fact that so many of our stories were similar only helped us recognise that no matter how different we were, there was a part of us in everyone else.

I don't know how sessions like these sound to people who weren't there. But as someone who was, I can tell you that they were special, charged with a rich spiritual energy that didn't just dissipate when it was over. From the moment we left that first session to the moment we lifted that season's premiership cup, we lived with those stories. We had countless conversations with each other about all aspects of our lives – the kinds of conversations we'd never had before. We were so tightly bonded and we trusted each other so completely that we became a single unit, each of the component parts different but complementary. That's about the most valuable thing a football team can have. No longer were we invested in ourselves alone – we were invested in each other. We were brothers now.

My contribution was entirely focused on my parents. I spoke of the sacrifices my father, Malek, had made for me and my football: how he would accompany me interstate for my football carnivals before I was drafted, and how that required him to halt his taxi business at great financial cost to himself. Malek means 'king' in Arabic, and that's exactly what he is to me.

I also spoke of the way my life changed when my first child was born, how in awe of my wife I was, and how it made me see my mother in a completely new light. Finally I had come to understand two very famous things the prophet Muhammad had said. The first was 'Paradise lies at the feet of your mother', which gives us a sense of what kind of service is owed to the one who gave birth to you.

The second came in response to a man who asked the Prophet, 'Who among people is most deserving of my good treatment?'

'Your mother,' said the Prophet.

'Who next?' asked the man.

'Your mother,' said the Prophet again.

'Who next?'

'Your mother.'

Then who?'

'Your father.'

Being a father changed me as a person and my relationship with my parents. I had always made a point of visiting Mum and Dad as a way of according them the respect they deserve, but now it felt more like an act of love.

And saying all this in front of other people allowed me to understand the depth of my own feelings. I made a pledge to myself that day that every time I saw my parents, I would kiss them. And I'd kiss Mum on her forehead. I haven't let it slip.

On the morning of the 2019 Grand Final, I called Mum to see how she was doing, but more importantly to get her blessing for what I was about to do. I asked her to make *du'a* for me, which is a request Muslims will often make of other people they respect.

She replied that she had never stopped.

I fell silent. I couldn't talk because I was choking on my emotions, breaking down like I used to when I was a little kid. My wife, who couldn't hear the conversation, could tell from watching me what was happening, and that was enough for her to be overcome with emotion too. I don't know exactly why I was so affected, but it must have had something to do with the belief that mothers have the highest status in Islam, and that God accepts the prayers of a mother. Mum knew exactly what my silence meant. We quietly said our goodbyes.

I went to my phone and wrote myself a note:

> Ya Allah,[5] I have prepared for the game in the best possible
> manner, physically, mentally and spiritually, now You decide
> the result. Whatever the result is at the end of the day,
> ya Allah, make me among the thankful ones. *Alhamdulillah*.
> Play to your strengths. Have fun, buddy, and smile.

And I really did.

Back in the Triple H sessions, I didn't offer the group any particular hardship from my life, although maybe I should have spoken about that kick-in against Freo. Instead, I approached the topic by saying that instead of hardship, I chose to see lessons. Then I shared two very widely quoted Qur'anic verses that reverberate around my head any time I feel like something is getting on top of me: 'For truly, after hardship comes ease. Truly after hardship comes ease' (94:5–6). There's something about the way the statement is repeated, like hearing it once isn't enough for it to sink in. It's as if the text wants you to pause, take a deep breath and receive the message again, in the same way a parent might repeat their reassuring advice to their child who is having a rough time at school.

The irony was that I was going to need that advice more than ever in 2017. That year would contain some of the greatest weeks of my life, but also what was undoubtedly the worst week I've ever had in football.

---

5   'Ya' is just a way of calling on someone in Arabic. If I wanted to get
    Jack Riewoldt's attention in Arabic, I might say 'ya Jack'.

9

CHARACTER

EID AL-FITR IS ONE OF the best days of the year for me. It's the festival that celebrates the end of Ramadan, which makes it doubly great: it's a religious holiday like Christmas, but it's also the reward at the end of a month of sacrifice.

It's hard to explain the magical feeling of having your first breakfast after 30 days of fasting. Everyone's in an excited mood when you go to the Eid prayer in the morning, and then the day is filled with people exchanging gifts. In 2017 I spent the morning at my parents' house, but I had to leave early because we were playing Carlton in a twilight game at the MCG. It's fair to say I was in a good mood, but the joy of that day would be short-lived.

About halfway through the first quarter, the play was near the Members' wing. We'd won the ball and started breaking forward in waves. As my teammates handballed forward,

I ran on the inside, arcing towards our goal via the centre square, while other players ran on the outside, closer to the boundary line.

I'd had a quiet start to the game, partly because of the close attention I'd received from my opponent, Jed Lamb. As I ran past and called for the ball, Jed, running behind me, tried to slow me down by wrapping his arms around my waist. I spread my arms wide, appealing to the umpire for a free kick, but nothing came. Jed kept impeding me, so I decided to try to break free. I swung my left arm backwards to hack away the arm that had hold of me, trying to break his grip. But I got it wrong. Very wrong. My arm accidentally swung high, skimming his shoulder before my fist caught him flush on the side of the head.

Whack! Jed collapsed instantly, going face-first into the turf. He didn't move.

Initially, I had no idea what had happened and kept running forward to join in the play. But I knew soon enough that something was wrong.

The umpire blew his whistle and stopped the game. A group of Carlton players rushed towards me, trying to stand up for their teammate, who I'd just knocked unconscious. The umpire told them to back off, reassuring them that I'd been reported.

Looking at Jed, I felt ill. I'd never injured anyone like this before. I'd never even been reported in any level of football, from the under-12s at Spotswood through to the AFL. I'd played in plenty of games where there were scuffles, and where players antagonised the other team. But I'd never been involved in any serious push and shove, because I would always walk away. I'd grown up watching my brothers and cousins playing at Newport, where fights would break out every week until finally the club was banned from competition, and I rejected that approach to football from the depths of my soul. So this was completely alien to me.

How did I end up being the bad guy? I wondered. *I'm never the bad guy!* It was like being dumped suddenly into one of those weird nightmares that makes an unrealistic situation seem completely real. Only the situation was real, and I wasn't about to wake up from it.

I remember that moment of being rattled. And I remember the moment of clarity that jolted me out of it. I took a deep breath. *Whatever happens will happen*, I told myself. *I'll cop whatever I'm given. But I have to stay present in the moment. We still have three quarters to play.*

That mentality was a big focus at Richmond in 2017. Every player will make mistakes, even costly ones, and there's nothing you can do about that. But don't compound it by making another mistake because you're stuck in the past. Don't make new bad decisions in the game because you're consumed by that situation. Just live in the moment.

To be honest, I found it easy to adopt this mindset, because I've always been that kind of person. So I did it. I focused on the game. And after a terrible start, I turned it around: 28 disposals, nine marks, five tackles. Only Dusty and Bryce Gibbs got the ball more.

But once the game ended, the cloud returned to hang over me. I called Jed as soon as I could after the game to apologise because I knew that, whatever else happened from here, the most important thing was his health. And then I did what I'd so often done over the previous five years or so whenever I felt I needed to talk through something: I debriefed with Ali Fahour. Ali had long been central to the best things in my career, and to getting me through some of the worst things.

This was something different, though. We could talk this over all we liked, but we knew the Match Review Panel's charge was coming, and that I'd be missing games. It was a question of how many, and that depended on the details of the charge.

The next day, it arrived: striking, high contact, high impact, intentional.

Intentional? That was the part that hurt. That was the bit I couldn't live with. Obviously I didn't want to miss a lot of games, but the idea that anyone thought I had deliberately hit someone mattered more to me. That went to my character. I didn't deliberately hit people. I would never deliberately hit anyone. And I swear by God I didn't intend to hit Jed Lamb in the head – or anywhere near it – that day, which is as grave an oath as I can possibly give.

My intention was to shrug his hold on me, to hit his forearm so he'd let me go, just like you'd do anytime someone tries to tackle you. The fact that my arm went anywhere near Jed's head was a complete accident. You could call it careless. You could even call it reckless. But to call it deliberate pierced my heart.

I'm not a lawyer, but once upon a time the AFL had a scale for reportable offences that ran in exactly that way: 'careless' was the lowest category, 'reckless' was the next, and 'intentional' was the most serious. But at the start of the 2017 season, the AFL had got rid of the 'reckless' category. Everything became either 'careless' or 'intentional'. Given the seriousness of the injury Jed suffered, and the fact that I wasn't right near the ball, my actions were never going to be called careless, so that left intentional as the only available classification. I'm sure the aim of removing 'reckless' was to make the system simpler and clearer, but it seemed not so much simple as simplistic. It was misdescribing what had happened by removing the most suitable category.

For most reportable offences, the Match Review Panel assigns a penalty, which the player can either accept or appeal. But in this case the charge was deemed so serious that I had to go to the AFL Tribunal, which would determine the appropriate penalty. That meant every commentator in the country was free to state their hypothetical punishment, and I became the focus of the football industry's conversation for all the reasons that were furthest removed from my nature.

I always try to block out those sorts of conversations, but this was so intense that it became impossible. People were throwing around all kinds of penalties – some said I deserved a three-week suspension, others saying anything up to six. That was crushing to hear, because it meant the 'intentional' charge had lodged in people's minds and was beginning to be taken as fact. The matter was being compared to some of the most notorious striking incidents in recent football history. It was in this nauseating context that I would have to argue my case before the tribunal. And that was where it all spiralled horribly out of control.

A player in this position relies entirely on legal advice. I certainly wasn't about to do anything different. My lawyer advised that it would be helpful for me to get some character references. These are common in courts of law as a way of seeking a reduced sentence, and the AFL Tribunal was no stranger to them either. They aren't the main part of a defence, of course. They're the final thing you put forward, in the hope that if the tribunal members are uncertain about what penalty they will impose, they might lean towards the more lenient option.

So I agreed to contact some friends who had the kind of community standing that was appropriate for the situation. We wanted a good, diverse spread of people, so the tribunal would receive character evidence from multiple angles, which we hoped would make it more compelling.

First, I asked Ali Fahour. I figured he was best placed to do it because we'd worked so closely together for such a long time, and were close friends. He knew me as well as anyone did, and had an excellent reputation in AFL circles. What I didn't realise was that my request put Ali in a difficult situation, because he was an employee of the AFL, which of course was the organisation that was charging me with striking. CEO Gillon McLachlan spoke to Ali about the issue, telling him it wasn't appropriate for him to provide a character reference.

'Bullshit,' Ali said. 'He's my brother. I'm going to write him one if he wants one.' His reply gives you a sense of the strength of our relationship.

I also asked Mark 'Choco' Williams, who had been an assistant coach at Richmond for four years until the end of 2016. We often had good, in-depth conversations about things like faith and community. I'd asked him to speak at an AFL *iftar* one year, and he'd given a powerful speech about how working with me had led him to learn more about Islam and become a more rounded person. We'd really connected as people, which made him the perfect person to provide a character reference for me.

Next, I called Waleed Aly. It would have been about 5:30 pm when I called, so he was on the set of *The Project* at Channel Ten, getting ready to do the show. He must have known I was calling about something to do with the tribunal charge and that it was important, because he answered the call and ran backstage to speak to me. I'd known Waleed since just before I was drafted, when he came to my house to interview me for a Channel 31 show called *Salam Cafe*. Neither of us imagined that, more than a decade later, I'd be asking him for a favour on the advice of my lawyer, but he was once a lawyer himself and understood why I'd be asking. He asked to talk it over with my lawyer later that night, and then agreed to write a reference for me.

A lot of media reporting suggested I then got a character reference from the then prime minister, Malcolm Turnbull. That never happened. It's true my legal team considered it because I had a good relationship with him, and he had only just that week visited me at Punt Road for an Eid event, and to announce extra government funding for Bachar Houli Programs – a name we'd adopted in 2012 to cover the football academy as well as a range of other initiatives on leadership and employment. In fact, it was during that event that he spoke about me in a positive way:

It is very hard to think of a better example of the strength
and resilience of our great nation, our great multicultural
society, than the work that Bachar does. Bachar's skills on
the sporting field . . . are matched by his commitment to
his community and building a stronger and more cohesive
Australia. Bachar's mentoring program for Muslim youth
demonstrates the power of sport to foster multicultural
unity and develop teamwork and leadership skills . . .
So I want to congratulate the AFL, the Richmond Football
Club, Ali Fahour and Bachar Houli for building bridges
of understanding, through the AFL, this national game,
and serving the community in such an inspiring way . . .
Bachar, what wonderful leadership you're showing here
at your work here at Richmond, your work right across
the community.

In the end, my lawyer decided just to include those words
in our case at the tribunal. As much as I'd love to say I had
the power to get the prime minister to intervene in an AFL
hearing, I didn't. He didn't write anything for me.

In any case, the character references weren't the main part
of my case. Our main argument was that the contact wasn't
intentional, and should be graded as careless. But we thought
it might be hard to get the tribunal to accept that, so realistically we hoped for a sentence of three weeks. Unfortunately, as
it turned out, it went too well. The tribunal did rule that I'd
hit Jed intentionally, but then, making specific mention of the
character references, decided to give me a two-week suspension. I was delighted with the result, as you'd expect.

It had been an intense experience, one I never wanted to repeat. But it was over now. Even before the tribunal hearing, I knew I'd get suspended, and after the few days I'd had, I needed to clear my head and get away. I'd already asked the club for some time off, which they gave me, and I'd packed my trailer before the hearing so I'd be ready to leave straight afterwards. Then I called Ali Fahour.

'Man, I've got to get out of here – would you come with me? My family's gone up to Roto to go camping for a few days, and I'm going to join them for a bit. It's about an eight-hour drive away.' Roto is in the middle of nowhere, roughly in the centre of New South Wales. And by 'family' I meant a crew of around 30 people: Dad, Mohamed, Khaled, uncles, cousins, some friends. They'd rented a big private property there where you could camp, ride quad bikes, even hunt for goats. Aside from that, there was nothing there. No footy, no people and no phone reception.

'Yeah, no worries,' Ali said. 'Come pick me up.'

I went straight from the tribunal to meet Ali. There was no way we were going to get there that night, but I definitely wasn't going to stay in Melbourne. We ended up spending the night at a motel in Griffith, then continuing early in the morning. The mood in the car was light, full of chat. It wasn't happiness so much as huge relief that a difficult episode was over, and had ended well. Neither of us could believe I only got two weeks, and we laughed at how fortunate I was.

Once we arrived, I started setting up our tents. I take my camping seriously, so it took about two hours to set everything up, after which I spent another couple of hours hanging out with family and friends around the fire. Then, around 3:00 pm, Ali wanted to drive out a bit to get some phone reception so he could call his wife and family. As soon as our car moved into range, both our phones exploded.

'Bro, I got a missed call from Gillon McLachlan and the club,' I said.

'I got a missed call from Gil too,' replied Ali.

'You ring Gil and I'll ring the club,' I said. I had a hunch what was happening, and it wasn't good.

Ali got onto Gil. 'Are you with Bachar?' the CEO asked.

'Yeah,' Ali replied.

'Mate, I need you to speak to Simon Lethlean ASAP,' Gil told Ali. Simon was the AFL's football operations manager at the time, which meant tribunal charges came under his authority. Ali called him straightaway.

'Sorry, mate, but we're appealing Bach's ban,' said Simon. 'We just can't accept the two weeks. We know he's a ripper guy but the penalty's just too light. We need him to come back because the tribunal's going to be on Thursday.' That was tomorrow. 'Can I speak to Bach?' Simon asked, and Ali put me on. 'You can't take this personally,' Simon said to me. 'It's just the rules of the game.'

It was a sensitive moment because I'd been working with the AFL for five years on my academy. If Ali was in an awkward position just for providing me a reference, you can imagine how it was being the guy at the centre of something so unprecedented. To be suspended is one thing, but to have the AFL appeal the suspension because they wanted it to be longer? That had never happened before, in 120 years of the league's existence. I'd spent my career being the first of a kind, but there was no way to prepare for being the first of this kind.

It was a real sucker punch. That feeling of lightness and relief I'd experienced after the tribunal hearing suddenly became leaden. The world I'd tried so hard to escape had come rushing back, with even more chaos and intensity than before. Slowly it began to dawn on me just how out of control the story had become. My 'lenient' suspension was one of those stories that makes both the front and back pages. It had dominated the news that day, and the public reaction was nothing short of enraged. All hell had broken loose, while I was out of range and oblivious to the whole thing.

The media focused on the character evidence given by Waleed and the prime minister, I suppose because you wouldn't expect their names to turn up at an AFL Tribunal hearing. I guess people assumed that only people who worked in football could give character references. The media quickly leapt to the conclusion that having Waleed and Turnbull vouch for me was what turned it around. As far as the media were concerned, I had been given special treatment for having friends in high places. But the truth was we didn't know whether those comments had persuaded the tribunal. Maybe Ali's and Choco's references – coming from a highly valued AFL employee and a premiership coach – were just as significant, or even more so. We don't know for sure because the tribunal never said.

Every time I thought about heading back to Melbourne to go through it all again, I felt annoyed and emotionally exhausted.

I didn't have the reserves to keep going. To make things worse, I spoke to Richmond, who explained that the appeal wouldn't be like the original hearing. I wouldn't need to give evidence or say anything – the lawyers would handle it all, because it was really about the appeals panel deciding whether the original hearing had been conducted correctly. They didn't need me to be there for that. The AFL and the club were insisting I show up, but within myself I knew I just couldn't. And by the time we got back to the tent, I decided I wouldn't.

'No, don't worry about it, bro,' I said to Ali. 'We're not going back. Let them have the tribunal without me. What's the worst thing they can do? They're just going to give me more weeks, and me being there won't make a difference.'

'You can't,' Ali said. 'You've gotta go back.'

'No. I'm over it. I'm going to ring the club and just tell them to do it. I'll get whatever I get. I don't care anymore. I just drove eight hours. I'm here. I'm not leaving. Why should I stuff up my trip?' I meant it, too.

'We've got to go back,' Ali insisted. 'You've got to give yourself your best chance. If you don't show up, it's not going to be a good look.'

Ali kept on at me, and his words very slowly started to sink in. It was a strange feeling. I resented having to face this again, and I just wanted to be with my family and friends, but I knew that Ali was right. I can't remember how long it took, but eventually my head won out over my heart. Ali had convinced me.

The hearing was scheduled to start at 6:00 pm the following day. I started packing up, which took me at least another hour, then we left around 8:30 pm, staying overnight in Griffith again. Throughout the drive I was fielding calls from Richmond and my lawyers, as they went through the argument they would make and asked me questions.

I only really remember two things from those conversations. First, that Jed was going to be okay, which came as a massive relief to me. And second, I keep reiterating, over and over: 'It wasn't intentional. I didn't hit him intentionally. I was trying to shrug him. I've never had an incident before – why would I do that now? They know who I am.'

Ali noticed how rattled I was. He tried to talk to me, saying the final penalty wouldn't be too bad. Then he'd change the subject and talk about stuff that had nothing to do with football, but I wasn't a very good conversationalist at that point. I was vague, not really there. I couldn't engage with Ali's words because I was so in my own head that whatever he said just seemed like background noise.

I kept saying to him that I didn't care anymore. But the truth was I cared deeply. Not about the suspension, but about the way people now viewed me. All I had ever wanted was to be an example of fairness, humility, respect and good character. Throughout my whole time in football, I'd never heard anyone connected with the game speak badly about me, even the fans (some mindless racist insults aside). Now I was being painted as someone who had cheated the system, like I had pulled off some shifty manoeuvre.

I had never experienced anything like this, so I didn't know how to come to terms with it. In that moment, it felt like the whole world revolved around this story, and it felt like an injustice. I'd never been reported before at any level of football, I hadn't intended to hit Jed Lamb, and I'd simply followed the advice of my lawyer, who put forward the best case he could in a way that wasn't even unusual. The only thing that was strange was the way the tribunal decided the case, and that had nothing to do with me.

I'd been through some low points in my career, but this felt bigger than football because it was about me as a person. Character matters. Very little matters more. It's not a moral failing to be a bad footballer. But to have my character in question was like an assault on my soul. 'I have only been sent to perfect good moral character,' the Prophet once said, so you can imagine how seriously I took this. No doubt there were people defending my character in all this too, but at times like this you don't notice those things. You're so overwhelmed by the negativity.

I made the mistake of looking at a newspaper when we stopped for petrol in some little country town, and I saw how the media was treating the people whose words we had used as character evidence. That might have been the worst part of the whole thing: I had dragged other people – especially Waleed and Malcolm Turnbull – into my mess. They had done nothing wrong in this. All Waleed had done was agree to write a character reference for me, and the prime minister hadn't even done that! Now they were in the middle of a storm and being attacked for it. And I felt real guilt over that.

It was 3:00 pm by the time we got back to Melbourne, just three hours before the tribunal hearing. By that time I'd become sick. The emotional intensity of the episode had run me down physically. When the tribunal increased my suspension to four weeks, I was disappointed but I barely had any energy left for the matter. 'The decision has been made and I accept it,' I told the media after the hearing. 'My concern is and always has been for Jed, and I hope he recovers really quick. The other thing is we move on with life . . .'

I wanted nothing more desperately.

That Saturday night I arranged with Ali and another of my good mates, Maher, to get together and watch Richmond play Port Adelaide on TV.

Ali looked distraught when he arrived. 'Boys, I think I f★★★ed up,' he said.

'Oh, what happened?' I asked, with a tone that assumed it was nothing major.

'I punched a guy at footy today.'

Ali's version of events was that three guys on the other team had hold of one of Ali's teammates; one of them was choking him, and one of them was punching him in the head. Ali originally wanted to break up the fight but once he saw that, he said, he snapped and went straight at the guy who was doing the punching. I believed Ali was telling the truth, and what he said provided some context, but it didn't excuse what he'd done. Even Ali would tell you that.

But even though I knew it wasn't good, I didn't realise just how serious it was, and I never even considered it would become a public issue. I think that's because to me it seemed like the kind of thing I used to see at Newport every week. I hated it, but it never made the news. *It's suburban football — who cares?* I thought. In the coming days, video of the incident would become infamous, being shown repeatedly on the TV news. There's a melee involving about a dozen players when Ali comes screaming in from the left of the picture targeting one particular guy and punches him hard in the jaw. The guy hits the deck instantly and is unconscious for a moment. It really is hard to watch. But I hadn't seen that vision yet, and even if I had, I'm still not sure I would have understood what was coming.

As soon as Ali finished telling me what had happened, he called his boss at the AFL, general manager Andrew Dillon, to fill him in. Everyone except me realised it was going to come out sooner or later and that Ali's position as an AFL employee would probably complicate matters. Even when the matter became public on the Monday, I had no idea because I hadn't read the papers or watched TV at all. I rang Ali to talk to him about some Bachar Houli Programs stuff, completely unaware of what was going on.

'Have you been listening to what's been happening?' Ali asked me.

'No – what's happening?'

'The story about what happened on Saturday's gone public.'

'Oh really? Whatever,' I said. I still didn't get it. I just couldn't imagine the media would stay interested in a story from a suburban league.

It was only the next day, when I was at training at Richmond and my teammates started asking me about it, that I realised just how big this story was becoming.

I called Ali again. 'Is everything alright?'

Ali broke down. His bosses had reassured him that it would

all go away in 24 hours and it wouldn't have an impact on his work, but now it was becoming clear that it would have a major impact. The story was swallowing Ali's life in a way none of us had anticipated. After the week I'd just been through, I understood how he was feeling.

What was I to do? I couldn't defend Ali's actions because they were indefensible. I told Ali how I felt about what he'd done, but I also knew the vilification that was coming his way. Whatever his failings on the field, this was the guy who had given me so much support, attention, time and love through so much of my career. He'd talked me through my most difficult patches, and had stood up for me when it was risky for him to do so. He'd just spent the past week in my corner, hanging out with me to help distract me, then bringing me back into the real world when I needed to be convinced that was the right thing to do. He'd been my ally, my friend and my adviser, just like he'd been for years, for no benefit to himself.

Ali had done something terrible, but I knew better than most that off the field he remained a selfless, generous, kind-hearted person – the kind of person I was honoured to call my friend. I can't have been the only person to feel that way, because in his six years at the AFL Ali had built many great relationships with many (particularly multicultural and Indigenous) players, and was hugely respected by the AFL executive. As the storm was brewing, several of these people sent him texts and called him with messages of support, but none was prepared to say anything publicly. It looked to me like he was being left to fend for himself as the public formed a view of him that everyone who knew him knew wasn't true.

That simply wasn't an acceptable situation for me. I couldn't stand by while people who didn't know Ali went beyond criticising his actions and started attacking his character. He'd stuck his neck out for me, so surely that was the least I could do for him.

I took to Facebook:

> Ali Fahour made a mistake, an error of judgement, and knows full well that these actions, like mine, are not acceptable. I don't condone what he did although he is not alone, we have all made mistakes in our life and it's about owning it and how you use it to make you a better person.
>
> Let me tell you something, Ali Fahour is a person of highest character, a person who has done so much for so many people, and a person I would trust my life with. He's a caring, humble, honest person who I would give anything to. Don't let the people who have unfairly portrayed him or others who don't know him give you any other perception of a guy with incredible character.
>
> You will always be my brother, no matter what.
>
> Stay strong – we are with you!

The backlash was fierce. It turns out a lot of people wanted to define a man they didn't know by the worst of his actions, and wouldn't tolerate anyone supporting or even seeing the human being behind those actions.

'Bro, don't bring attention to yourself,' Ali had pleaded with me before I posted this. 'You don't need it. You've just come out the other end of the Jed Lamb saga.'

'I don't care if it costs me my career,' I said. 'I don't care if people say shit about me.' I was happy to wear it, because while I knew I was a people pleaser and I cared what people thought of me, I cared more about doing what I believed was the right thing, especially when it concerned my faith, my family or my friends. If that meant people attacked me, then so be it.

Richmond told me it was best I didn't comment, not because they didn't want me to support Ali, but because it would reignite the conversation. I understood their position, but the thing that mattered most to me was what Ali wanted. I told him what the club had said and asked what he wanted me to do. 'No, they're right,' he said. 'Don't say anything else.' That was the only reason I didn't say more.

But that didn't stop things from escalating. I made my post on the Tuesday, and by the Wednesday the police had charged Ali with assault. That changed everything. The AFL's support for Ali was suddenly hanging by a thread, and the best he could hope for was that he'd be suspended from his job for a few months, and seek professional help, before coming back in a different role.

Then, on the Thursday, Ali was banned for life from playing football. He lost his job at the AFL that night because the AFL felt the life ban made his situation untenable, even though no one at the organisation wanted to see him gone. Ali said he received about ten phone calls the next day telling him that Gillon McLachlan got very emotional as he told staff Ali was going. Ali understood that Gil had little choice, but it was obvious that the situation had been driven largely by media outrage.

It hit Ali hard because he was a creature of routine. Work and footy gave him that, and now it was gone in an instant, in the worst circumstances I could imagine, as a public villain receiving no sympathy. He had nothing, and seemed to have lost his purpose and his confidence, so that was when I figured he needed me most. I'd speak to him most days, either on the phone or in person, when I'd take my family to visit his. We'd go fishing as often as possible, and I'd give him as much time as I could just to chat.

But the best thing I could offer was to look after him spiritually. I'd always found that nothing makes as immediate a difference as going to the mosque for the dawn prayer every day. It's the hardest one to do, but it's also at the most tranquil time of the day, and that feeling really enters your heart. I pleaded with him to attend the prayer at his local mosque, and he did. I think it made a big difference for him.

I also texted Ali a graphic I found online with the Qur'anic verse that seemed most relevant to both his situation and mine: 'But perhaps you hate a thing and it is good for you; and perhaps you love a thing and it is bad for you. And Allah knows, while you know not' (2:216). Ali printed out the image and stuck it on his wall. It's still there, and he looks at it nearly every day.

All this had flow-on effects for Bachar Houli Programs. Without Ali there, we had less support at the AFL. The league didn't fill Ali's position, so the programs had no active management and quickly started running out of funding. I found myself talking to Gillon McLachlan and Andrew Dillon about it, as there was no one to approach in middle management anymore. They were huge supporters, but programs like this were well below their level and there was no way they could fill the hole Ali had left.

Behind the scenes, and without payment, Ali helped me keep the programs going, writing reports and funding proposals for me and lending me whatever expertise he could. He cared deeply about the programs and knew I had no one else to go to who would be hands-on. But there were some areas in which Ali couldn't help and I was on my own.

Because Ali could no longer come to meetings with government when we were seeking funding, that task fell to me, even though it's a million miles away from being my strength. Ali would guide me on the key points, and I'd go in there and do my best. It wasn't the same, but because of all the work Ali had done in previous years, and all the work he was now doing behind the scenes, we managed to secure the government funding we needed to go on. Here was Ali, forced to leave his job at the AFL, yet still bringing in funding for its programs.

Probably the most crushing blow came later in the year, as I was preparing for the Bachar Houli Academy's Elite Performance Camp. This is where we take the ten best kids, as voted by their peers, to New York University's sports facility in Abu Dhabi for an accelerated training, leadership and development program. It's an incredible facility – clubs such as Real Madrid use it when they're in the region – and the program, which runs for eight days, is the highlight of the academy's year. Ali had always been central to this event, and I couldn't imagine running it without him. So I told the AFL I wanted to bring him along for the camp, as a mentor or coach. The AFL shot that down immediately. 'I don't think that's a good idea,' said Andrew Dillon. 'Not for Ali, or the AFL. The controversy needs a bit of breathing space.'

I rang Ali to pass on the news. It cut Ali deeply, because he had put so much work into this program for so long. Privately, Ali's former colleagues at the AFL – and especially Andrew Dillon – were still extremely supportive of him, regularly checking in to see how he was going. They cared deeply about his wellbeing. But the fact they could have no public relationship with him was beginning to bite. It was the first time Ali was really upset about the way the AFL had handled the matter, especially as it came from someone we both respected so much. Ali felt like he was being separated from one of his children. The whole situation just seemed wrong.

'That's it, I don't want their money,' I told him. 'I'll pay for you to come along.' But I couldn't convince him to let me do that, no matter how much I insisted. 'Alright, then, I'm going to tell them we're not going anymore,' I said at last. 'None of us will go.'

'Nah, that's not fair on the kids, bro,' Ali replied.

He was right – and so was Andrew Dillon, who had made that call because he knew it was the best thing for all of us. I'd overreacted, but I was being sincere. I knew I'd feel Ali's absence deeply. This wasn't just a job – it was about our community and our lives. And it was about what we'd built together. It was personal. The academy *was* us. And the camp was everything.

In the end, Ali did come. He paid his own way, and was there for just the last couple of days. He had no official role, and no one at the AFL knew. Once he was there, we were careful to keep his presence secret. In every group photo we took, he'd stand out of frame or be the photographer. The kids were told to make sure that whenever they took a selfie or a video, Ali couldn't be seen. It quickly became a running joke among the group, but actually it saddened me. Ali had gone from being the second-in-command to being a ghost.

By the end of 2017, Ali had taken a job outside football as the general manager of the Islamic Museum of Australia. He enjoyed it well enough, but his passion was always to work in sport, and he wanted to get back to the AFL somehow. But Ali knew two things would have to happen to make that possible: first, he needed to deal with the assault charge, and second, he'd need to get his life ban from football overturned. He achieved the first of these in early 2018, when the court fined him and ordered him to do community service, but decided to record no conviction against him. But his life ban would take longer to deal with, so in the meantime he needed to find another path back into the industry. And in the middle of 2018, one opened up.

Richmond was trying to get government funding for a new education facility they wanted to build at the Punt Road Oval, to be called the William Cooper Centre. The club felt that the pitch would be stronger if it included the programs we were running, so they asked me if I'd consider basing them at Punt Road.

My response was emphatic. 'If this is going to happen, Ali Fahour's going to have to run it,' I said. 'You've gotta call him and speak to him about it.'

To Richmond's credit, they did, via Simon Matthews, the

club's chief marketing officer. 'We're thinking we want to base Bachar's programs at the club in the new centre,' Simon told Ali. 'We think that would help grow the programs, and we also really want to cement Bachar's legacy. We think this could do that. Would you like to be a part of it? Bachar trusts you and you know the programs better than anyone else. We'd need you to help drive the conversation with the AFL to make it happen, and then we'd need you to come on board as an employee of Richmond to lead it.'

You don't need me to tell you Ali's reply.

What no one knew was that Ali and I had been talking for a while about how we wanted to grow Bachar Houli Programs by broadening its social objective and purpose, and how that would require more autonomy and Muslim leadership. We'd been figuring out how we could set up a foundation with its own board so we could take control of the programs and make them a little more independent. Now Richmond was providing us with exactly that chance. It would give us a fantastic home base with all the office space we needed – but we still needed the AFL's support so we could maintain our position as a national organisation.

I arranged a meeting with Andrew Dillon at the AFL's Docklands headquarters to see if he'd support the move. But I didn't go alone. A year on from the phone call that had broken his heart, and even though he had no official role with the programs or with Richmond, I took Ali with me.

He felt sick with nerves about it. Since losing his job, he'd never set foot in the building. If Ali was meeting Gil or Andrew Dillon for a chat, he'd always do it at a cafe nearby because he

I've been number 14 ever since I got to Richmond. Management has fostered a culture of respect and connection, and I think the results speak for themselves.

(Cameron Spencer / AFL Photos)

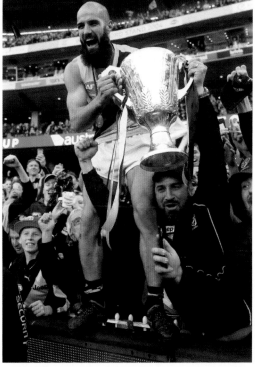

(Michael Willson / AFL Photos)

The 2017 finals series remains the most magical and unbelievable experience of my career. *Left, above and right:* The goal; the siren; the victory lap. My brother Khaled is underneath the cup. Talk about things coming full circle: having introduced me to the game all those years ago, he was there with me on football's biggest day.

(Adam Trafford / AFL Photos)

(Adam Trafford / AFL Photos)

I knew from my own childhood experience that there are so many Muslim kids who love footy to bits, so *(top)* it was a thrill to launch the Bachar Houli Academy, and later be supported in our endeavours by Prime Minister Malcolm Turnbull. *Bottom:* At our 2017 Eid celebration at the Punt Road Oval. The sense of purpose the academy gave me actually helped my football.

We'd learnt in 2018 that being the best team doesn't guarantee you anything. Here I am *(top)* with Alex Rance at the end of our Round 3 Hawthorn match, and *(bottom)* vs Essendon in Round 22 at the coin toss with Jack Riewoldt. Being able to recognise and celebrate what we achieved as Tigers that year set us on the path to success in 2019.

(Quinn Rooney/AFL Photos)

(Dylan Burns/AFL Photos)

(Kelly Defina / AFL Photos)

(Daniel Carson / AFL Photos)

We crushed GWS by 89 points in the 2019 Grand Final. I'd never been more aware of the crowd than at the MCG that afternoon. *Bottom left:* Celebrating with Ryan Garthwaite, Liam Baker and Nick Vlastuin. *Top:* Post-match celebrations with (left to right) Daniel Rioli, Jayden Short and David Astbury. *Bottom:* At the presentation party that evening.

(Brook Mitchell/AFL Photos)

Reciting from the Qur'an at the GWS *iftar* in May 2019. Throughout my career I have seen how events such as these can foster understanding of our differences and similarities.

(Dylan Burns/AFL Photos)

Funds raised at the 2020 Bushfire State of Origin between Victoria and the All Stars helped to rebuild football facilities affected by the national bushfire crisis.

(Ryan Pierse/AFL Photos)

(Chris Hyde/AFL Photos)

It's not uncommon that people become better players once they become parents, playing with greater freedom and less pressure.

(Darrian Traynor/AFL Photos)

With Sarah *(top left)* in May 2014 after the Round 10 Tigers–GWS game; celebrating beating the Lions at the Gabba the following April *(top right)*; and *(bottom)* with Sarah and Maryam at the 2019 Grand Final parade.

Everything about my life involves my family. Playing your 200th AFL game is a major milestone for any player, so I had to share it with (left to right) Mohamed, Khaled, my nephew Nezor in the beanie, Rouba, Sarah, Maryam, my dad Malek, brother Dr. Nezor, and nephew Malek. *Right:* Chaired from the field by members of my other family, Brandon Ellis (left) and Trent Cotchin (right).

(Michael Willson/AFL Photos)

Doing the right thing and being proud of your identity and beliefs will bring you real success.

couldn't face going inside. He'd even tried to get this meeting moved somewhere else, but without success.

As I drove in to Docklands, he called me. 'I don't want to go in, man. It's weird,' he told me.

'I find it weird too,' I replied. It was true, because I'd worked in that building every Wednesday when Ali was there, but I'd stopped going in once he left. In these circumstances, going back felt off. But we took a deep breath and went in.

It went brilliantly. The AFL was entirely on board. Andrew Dillon was always a big supporter of the programs and of Ali, and he could see this would be good for both. It would also give Ali a way back into the industry without coming back to the AFL itself.

It was a big moment for both of us, but especially for Ali. He was being offered a way back to work that he loved, but he'd also spent more than a year getting used to life outside footy. To dive back in was a big deal, and he called me to talk it over. 'Bro, I'm unsure whether or not I should do this,' he said. 'I just escaped the bubble and now I'm going back in. What's the club like?'

Now it was my turn to reassure him. 'Man, you'll love it here. Richmond's an awesome club. Everyone's welcoming. Trust me, it's a good culture.'

'Would I be getting in your personal space by working at the same club as you? I don't want to get between you and your teammates. We're best mates, and I don't want to ruin that. How do you feel about that?'

'Bro, are you serious? I want to do this together! I need you. Let's just start this!'

A while later he called me again. 'Bro, I'm about to sign this contract. You sure you're good with this? Are you sure you want to do it this way?'

'Stop being stupid!'

Ali started at Richmond in 2019. We were flying again. A year later, he went to the AFL Victoria Tribunal and got his life ban overturned. Now, if he wants, he's clear now to return to the AFL job he loved so much. But with what we're building, he seems to have other priorities at the moment.

It took Bachar Houli Programs twelve months to recover fully after Ali lost his job. But now the whole project is stronger than ever. Ali and I are colleagues at a club I love, and which takes this work seriously. And I'm probably better at running things than I might have been if I hadn't gone through that period of struggle without him. Who knows? Maybe, without all this, the programs might have stagnated or even died away.

Back in 2017, when Richmond made the Grand Final, we were given four tickets to share with family or friends. After all that had happened that year, I did not hesitate in giving one of them to Ali. After the game, as I headed towards the race, a newly minted premiership player, there he was. We were ecstatic. We'd both been through some awful stuff in the past few months, but there we were on the final day as brothers, him sharing my success as his own.

It was an emotional moment for both of us, and brought an unexpected feeling of redemption, especially for Ali. After what he'd been through, he'd fallen out of love with football. That day, in that moment, he fell in love with it again. After hardship comes ease.

10

SUCCESS

PLAYING YOUR 200TH AFL game is a major milestone for any player. Fewer than five per cent of players get there, and given that well under one per cent ever make it to 300, the chances are it will be the last milestone you celebrate in your career. And it was something I'd always wanted, even before I was drafted. So the fact that mine came on a wet, freezing July Friday night wasn't enough to devalue the occasion for me.

Especially because it turned out to be a massive game in the context of our 2019 season. We were playing Collingwood at the MCG, who had beaten us the last two times, including in the 2018 Preliminary Final. As if that didn't make it loaded enough, they were sitting fourth on the ladder, with us in fifth, behind them only on percentage. We'd spent the first 13 weeks of the season destroyed by injuries, just eking out enough wins to keep in touch with the top eight, which meant we had hardly any room for error for the rest of the season. Since then we'd won four in a row, but lose to Collingwood and we'd be pretty likely to finish outside the top four. And winning the premiership from there is extremely rare.

Collingwood kicked the first goal, but after that it could hardly have gone any better. We kicked the next nine, and were leading by 50 points in the middle of the second quarter. It was apparently around then that we officially became premiership favourites, a status we rode all the way to the 2019 premiership. Everyone knew the magnitude of that game at the time. The fact that it was Collingwood versus Richmond only heightened it. This was undoubtedly one of the most important games of the season purely on its own terms.

So although the milestone meant a lot to me personally, I found it odd – and a little uncomfortable – that in the lead-up to the game so much was centred on me. Sometimes that would be in the form of media interviews, or in the way the coaches talked about my 200th at training in front of my teammates, or even in suddenly having to be some kind of ticketing agent, figuring out how many tickets my family would get and how they'd be divided up.

I suppose the common thread in my responses to all these things was to deflect them to other people. So I set aside two tickets for my wife and daughter, and gave the remaining ten to my family and told them to sort out who would get them and who would have to miss out. In interviews I spoke constantly about the team, about how team success was far more important than any milestone of mine, and about how much I loved being part of this Richmond group.

Justin Leppitsch taught me a lot about that. He's been our backline coach at Richmond for a significant part of my career, so I go to him a lot for advice. This game came during my best season of football, which delivered new successes I'd not encountered before, and which had the potential to distract me.

I'd started to hear people talk about me being a chance for the All-Australian team, for instance, which made me conscious of my performance in a way I'd never been before. I'd always limited my social media use and rarely looked at AFL news. Suddenly I found myself checking Instagram to see if I'd made Campbell Brown's team of the week, refreshing the screen every few minutes around the time it was due. Then the next day I'd check the AFL website to look at their team of the week. I began to worry that I had to get 30 disposals every time I walked out onto the field to make sure my season average didn't slip.

I could hear my own voice in my head reprimanding me: *Bachar, what are you doing?* There's nothing particularly wrong with wanting personal satisfaction and peer recognition, but this felt different. I knew I was thinking about myself far too much. I knew that wasn't who I am, and I knew I needed to get out of that mindset.

About a month before the Collingwood game, Leppa told me what I'd always known but needed so desperately to hear: 'The best thing you can possibly do is think about how you can help someone else. Watch someone like Jayden Short or Derek Eggmolesse-Smith – the younger guys who play in your position. Look at their videos and give them some feedback. Shift the focus away from yourself.'

It was excellent advice. But it might have been nice if Leppa had given it to the club during that milestone week. There was no chance they were going to shift the focus. It began with a meeting about how I wanted game night to work: whether I wanted my family there, and whether I'd take my kids through the banner.

Immediately I thought about my eldest daughter, who'd been in the changerooms with me after the game the previous week. She had spotted some grass on the floor and rushed over to pick it up. 'Yes! Finally, I get to touch the ground!' she shouted.

'Well, next week you're going to get the chance to run through the big banner!' I had told her. 'It's going to be so much fun!'

'Really?' She couldn't contain her excitement. All week at school she was telling her friends about it.

So that was an easy enough conversation to manage with the club. The harder part for me came the day before the game, when the coaches showed the players a seven-minute video package of highlights from my career and messages from people who had been really important throughout – in my case, Trent Cotchin, Ivan Maric and Brandon Ellis. Then Damien Hardwick addressed the group about what I meant to him.

'As a footballer, we sometimes take for granted what Bachar brings to this football club,' he said. 'Watching those highlights, you realise it's special, but you forget because he does it week in, week out. He's just so consistent. His impact on the game goes way beyond what happens on the field. I've learnt so much from this man, and I'm proud to have him as part of the family. To start with, I didn't know what Islam was about or what being a Muslim meant. I'd never met one. But now I know that, because the character that this man displays is mind-blowing. I'm so honoured to have met someone like Bachar.'

I'm not really an emotional person, but Dimma is, especially when he's speaking like that. And this one got me, because I heard him describing someone I wanted to be, and someone who had the kind of effect I wanted to have.

The Prophet once said that 'a believer is the mirror of his brother' – meaning that the greatest service you can do someone is to reflect them back to themselves, so they can see what their best and worst qualities are. At moments like these, people do reflect your character back at you, and it's a nerve-racking experience. I understood that before a milestone game people would say nice things, but it was what Dimma chose to say that mattered, and that's what I took as the image in the mirror: that he chose to focus on character and my contribution as a person was the most meaningful thing he could have done.

So I was pleased, but still uncomfortable. I don't like things being about me, and I don't feel comfortable being the centre of attention, having people heap praise on me in front of others. Yes, it feels lovely to hear people say nice things about you, but there's something about it being done with an audience that makes me shrink into my shell. I put my head down and stared at the ground, avoiding eye contact with everyone. For me, the best praise, the best celebration, is brief, and comes in private from people I respect.

Probably my favourite moment of the week came early on, when my two best mates organised a dinner with my brothers, my father and a few friends at a pizza joint in the western suburbs of Melbourne. These were the people who mattered most in my life, who were closest to me for the longest time. And it was extremely rare to have all my brothers there at once. I couldn't have asked for anything more. Even then, I really felt uneasy about the celebration until it was underway.

So you can imagine how I felt after the game, when Brandon Ellis and Trent Cotchin insisted on chairing me off the ground, even though Trent had injured his hamstring that night. I did my best to talk him out of it, but he made it clear that wasn't an option.

I think I've been this reluctant to accept praise ever since I was a child, so it must be innate to some degree. Part of it is that I genuinely fear becoming arrogant, and I have to guard against that. It's a serious matter for me. 'Do not walk on the earth arrogantly. You can neither tear the earth apart, nor can you match the mountains in height,' says the Qur'an (17:37), reminding us of our smallness, which we so often forget.

It's hard to overstate the importance Islam places on humility, and just how keen the prophet Muhammad was to warn us against losing sight of that. Maybe the easiest way to illustrate it is to quote a small sample of his statements on it:

'No one who has the weight of a seed of arrogance in his heart will enter Paradise.'

'There is no human being except that the wisdom of his mind is in the hands of an angel. When he shows humility, the angel is ordered to increase his wisdom. When he shows arrogance, the angel is ordered to decrease his wisdom.'

'Allah has revealed to me that you must be humble towards one another, so that no one wrongs another or boasts to another.'

'When you think to mention the faults of your companion, then remember your own faults.'

The thing about humility, though, is that it's not something you can ever believe you've achieved, because as the famous mystic scholar Ibn Ata'illah said, 'The one who sees his humility has lost humility.' Pride can be one of the hardest things in the world to spot in yourself, and it's especially a challenge when your work is public. People can attack you mercilessly when you're a footballer, but they can also go overboard in their praise. Sometimes it feels like those are the only two options.

Which brings me to my teammates' comments in that milestone video. The general theme of their words was that the biggest thing they'd learned from me was to be grateful for every opportunity, for everything that we have in life; to understand that whatever we're going through and whatever frustrations or difficulties we have, we're blessed with all we've been given and what we get to do, and that there are countless people in worse positions than us. Football is just a game. We win, we lose – either way, we're blessed. And the best way to show gratitude for our blessings is to serve others: to devote ourselves to helping other people achieve their potential, and to ask ourselves constantly, 'What can I do to make someone else's life better?'

That approach to football and life – the idea that it's ultimately about gratitude and service – is something Ivan, Trent, Brandon and I talked about a lot. It meant so much to me that they seemed to feel this was as important as I did, and that they saw me as helping them realise that. As well as showing the kind of values we share, that approach has become pretty important to the way our club operates.

Our motto at Richmond in 2019 was 'Hungry and Humble'. We knew we were in a period of success, but also that it would disappear quickly if we ever became satisfied with ourselves or got ahead of things. We would be grateful for everything we had achieved, and we would celebrate the journey of the season irrespective of the result, because there was so much to be thankful for, so much to celebrate even in defeat, and so much to appreciate about each other.

We would be hungry for success, of course, but the best way to stay hungry after having won a premiership is to recognise that you aren't entitled to it – that you have to work tirelessly for it – after which it is a blessing, and there are many other people who were equally deserving of it. We'd learnt in 2018 that being the best team didn't guarantee you anything. If anything, we were a better team then than in 2017, but history will only record us as premiers in one of those years. That's sport, and that's life. Sometimes it's not your time. When it's not, be patient. When it is, be humbled that you were chosen for that success, and be grateful for it.

It's a philosophy that's very easy for me to accept because it chimes so clearly with Islamic teachings. Gratitude is one of the most frequently occurring themes in the Qur'an: gratitude to God, obviously, but also to everyone who's helped you along the way. 'Whoever does not thank people has not thanked Allah,' said the Prophet. So when I pointed to the sky on the premiership dais as I received my medal, or as I deflected praise away from myself and towards others in interviews about my milestone match, I wasn't doing something tokenistic or false – or at least I hope I wasn't. I was simply recognising the truth of the situation. Whatever success you've had, you owe to others. And the moment I don't really believe that, I have a problem.

That's the difference between humility and self-loathing. As Muslims, we don't have to deny our talents in order to be humble. In fact, the danger of that kind of denial is that it risks becoming ingratitude, because you can't be grateful for something you don't accept exists. You can be optimistic about your ability and confident in yourself without tipping over into arrogance. You can enjoy your successes without bloating your ego. The trick is to understand that none of it is down to you.

Two days before my 200th match, I wrote myself a note trying to strike that balance between gratitude, humility, nerves and confidence:

> Enjoy the moment, it only comes once. Be very grateful
> to Allah for it. Of course you can enjoy it because Allah
> wants us to be happy within the boundaries of Islam. Every
> moment you start to overthink, think about the star player
> you are and have been throughout your career. You don't
> reach 200 games by luck. It's all from Allah, and then hard
> work with quality talent. You don't have to do anything

out of the ordinary because it's your 200th game. You do your best and approach the game as normal. Put your trust and have *tawakkul* in Allah. Allah is the best of planners and knows what's best for you.

Reminding myself in this way helped me realise that, for all the hype of milestones, and all the pressure of a must-win game against a seriously good team, this was just another game of footy, and would be played by the same rules and based on the same principles as the other 199 I'd played, and even the ones in juniors or in the VFL before that.

Earlier in the week I'd been fretting about something going wrong. I'd known too many players whose milestone games had ended with a loss, or even in injury: Trent Cotchin, Troy Chaplin, Chris Newman, Jack Riewoldt, Alex Rance. But by the time the game arrived, I felt completely relaxed about it because I had processed the idea of it properly. And I did enjoy the moment, especially taking my kids out onto the ground. In fact, I got so completely preoccupied with trying to herd them, I didn't even notice the cheer squad had put me on the banner.

For me, a lot of 2019 seemed to follow that pattern: tension, self-obsession, shifting focus to others, then release. I think I only got through it because I put extra work into what you could call my 'spiritual preparation'.

One major change was that on the day of every game, I performed a special 'night prayer' the Prophet used to do, known as *tahajjud*. Its mechanics are the same as any other prayer, but the difference is that *tahajjud* occurs in the last third of the night, which makes it highly regarded for two reasons: first, it's often difficult for people to sacrifice their sleep at that point; and second, Muslims believe that is a particularly blessed time of the night. The Prophet told us that God 'descends to the nearest heaven to us' at this hour, 'saying "Is there anyone to invoke Me, so that I may respond to invocation? Is there anyone to ask Me, so that I may grant him his request? Is there anyone seeking My forgiveness, so that I may forgive him?"'

My commitment to doing this meant that my match-day routine looked like this: I would wake up around 3:30 am to pray, then I'd go back to sleep and wake again at about 5:30 am, when I'd head to the mosque to pray *fajr*. Within these prayers I'd be asking God for success, for me to play well and be influential in the game, but I'd also be reinforcing to myself that whatever I achieved was spiritually and psychologically anchored outside of myself. And with how I was playing, it certainly felt like my prayers were being answered.

Ultimately, I had realised that whatever skill or ability I possessed was only possible because it had been given to me, and because so many people had helped me nurture and hone it, and given me the opportunity to express it. Whatever natural talent I had could easily have been given to somebody else, and there was nothing to say they'd have been any less deserving of it.

And there were undoubtedly people who had more talent than me but, for whatever reason, never had the chance to do anything with it. Every now and then you get a glimpse of it. Take the incredible example of Marlion Pickett, who completed one of the greatest stories in football by making his AFL debut in the 2019 Grand Final at the age of 27. At the start of that season, he was playing state league footy in Perth, and he only came to Richmond in the middle of the season to replace Shaun Grigg, who had retired. About a decade before all that Marlion was in prison, and it looked like he'd never make it anywhere near the AFL. And had he not made it – like just about everyone else in his position – he'd have been an incredible talent none of us ever would have seen.

Once I saw things that way, I came to see success as a gift rather than my own just reward. The Islamic saying goes that 'there is no might or power except in God', so Islam warns severely against pride and arrogance. It's not just that they are bad personality traits; it's much more serious than that. If you're prideful, you're taking God's power and blessings and attributing them to yourself. To put it strongly, it's a form of self-worship.

And that means that whatever you've been given might turn out to be a test of your character. If you're unusually intelligent, do you use this for the benefit of others, or do you use it to take advantage of them? Do you use your strength to harm other people or to help them? What about your wealth? Do you forget yourself in success, or do you remember who granted it to you?

To an extent, that's how I understood the disruption of COVID-19. It showed just how quickly the gift of my football career could be taken away from me, and how powerless I am to stop that. That was an invitation to be grateful for all the blessings I'd enjoyed up to that point. 'Look at those below you and not those above, as it is more suitable to remember the blessings of Allah granted to you,' advised the Prophet. And during COVID-19 there were so many whose situation was worse than mine – and worse than ours generally in Australia – to look at.

When we returned to the changerooms after winning the premiership in both 2017 and 2019, the first thing I did was head to a quiet corner, sit and reflect until I'd calmed down. Then I went and got a towel, made *wudu* and prayed *asr*, the midafternoon prayer. A while later the coaches gathered us together to walk out into the middle of the MCG and sing the club song. It's one of the sweetest moments you can have as a footballer, standing in the middle of this great stadium where you've just won the ultimate prize. Only an hour before it had been vibrating with unbelievable noise and bursting with people. Now it was empty, still, silent. It was all ours. We belted out the song that symbolises us as a group and has been sung by so many Richmond premiership sides before, and which is so widely accepted as the best song in the league. But as we finished, I noticed the sun had set, so I returned inside to the changerooms on my own to pray *maghrib*, then I went back outside to join my teammates. It wasn't a time to forget myself and my greater obligations. It was exactly the time to remember them. It's so easy to forget that you can be tested in prosperity and triumph just as easily as in hardship and defeat.

I never thought we'd win a flag. And if you'd told me we'd win two, I'd simply never have believed you. If I'm honest, I never thought we'd even become a consistent finals team. In our quieter moments as players, when we talk honestly to each other, we'd even admit this; at least, Trent Cotchin and I would, reflecting on how quickly belief can grow and the world can change for you. Sometimes this happens in unforeseen ways, only emphasising that whatever planning or modelling we do, and however much we think we know about how the world (or even just football) works, we're not in control.

That was definitely the story of the 2017 finals series, which remains the most magical and unbelievable experience of my career. It was remarkable enough, after the way we'd finished 2016 in the doldrums, that we managed to end 2017 in the top four, and I suppose on some level I knew that once you were there, anything could happen. We'd even had the example of the Bulldogs the previous year winning from seventh after 62 years of trying. But surely not this. To put it in context, our first task was to get past Geelong, a team we hadn't beaten in more than a decade. And to put *that* in context, Richmond hadn't beaten Geelong in the whole time I'd been playing in the AFL, even when I was at Essendon.

That Qualifying Final was the night our world was turned upside down. I vividly remember running out onto the ground and feeling that whatever was happening in that moment, it wasn't normal. We couldn't hear the Geelong theme song because of the Richmond crowd. Often in football they talk about the crowd as a '19th man'. This time the whole stadium was heaving with yellow and black, as though it was screaming at us in a single voice, 'Bring the heat, bring the pressure' – and that's what we did.

We played with a brutal, manic intensity that night, but even so we struggled to take control on the scoreboard. We managed to keep the Cats goalless for nearly an hour and build a 21-point lead, then suddenly they kicked two in three minutes and the margin was just nine. By three-quarter time, the game was still in the balance. Then suddenly all that pressure we'd been applying blasted the dam wall to pieces. We kicked seven goals to one in that last quarter, having only kicked six before then. Geelong would only kick five for the game.

Even while we were playing it was hard to believe what was happening – it was like we were in a parallel dimension where none of the normal rules applied. We were living in a world where Richmond beat Geelong by 51 points in a final. Surely that meant anything was possible.

After that, everything around the whole club felt special. These were the biggest games of our lives, but there wasn't any pressure, just happiness. We were like a group of kids playing under-12s footy on the biggest stage there is. We didn't have a care in the world – our aim was to have fun. We weren't worried about results, and so we just rode the wave. I remember the whole MCG shaking when we kicked the first two goals in the opening minute of the Preliminary Final against GWS. I could see it. I could feel it. And I hadn't felt that since we ran out to warm up before the 2013 Elimination Final against Carlton, when Richmond hadn't been in the finals for 12 years.

We went into the 2017 Grand Final with no expecta-tions and nothing to lose. None of us had been there before, and Adelaide had been the top team all year, so we went in with the freedom of underdogs. We drank in the week – the crammed open training sessions, the parade the day before the game – deliberately choosing to immerse ourselves in the excitement rather than shield ourselves from it. We stayed childlike through the whole process, ecstatically living out our dreams. For us, that whole 2017 campaign is best remembered as a carnival, the moment footy stopped being a job and started being fun again. The success was a result of the fun we were having, not the other way around.

But 2019 was different. We carried expectation: we were favourites well ahead of the finals and we had plenty to lose, especially after the way 2018 had ended. And there's no doubt that it was emotionally exhausting. After the Grand Final, I felt destroyed for a week or two. I didn't want to celebrate, I didn't want to see anyone, I just wanted to go home. And I know people like Trent Cotchin and Jack Riewoldt felt the same. We were spent – and in their cases it can't have been physical, because they'd missed big chunks of the season.

But the upside of all that expectation was that everything around the club in that month had an air of calmness. We had two weeks between beating Brisbane in the Qualifying Final and facing Geelong in the Preliminary Final, and for the first week and a half I didn't hear any of the players speak about the approaching game. Geelong wasn't mentioned until we did our opposition analysis a couple of nights before the bounce. We weren't the same group of supercharged, excitable kids we had been in 2017. This time we were much more in control: we knew when to relax and when to switch on.

Personally, I felt the desire to win more strongly than at any other time in my career. In 2017 I just enjoyed the ride, really, taking everything as it came. But in 2019 I was chasing a feeling I already knew, and was desperate to crown my best individual year with the highest team prize our game has. And probably because I wanted it so much, I had spent a significant amount of time contemplating the possibility we'd fall short, or that I wouldn't perform. That was especially a problem after the final against Brisbane, when I felt I'd had possibly my worst game for the year. The next day I wrote a note to myself:

> Your performance is truly a test from Allah. He has given you victory so be grateful and, above all, be patient. It's not all about you. You can be a little hard on yourself but the more you think you are a failure, the more you will believe you are a failure. You're a star by the will of Allah, and the evidence is there. They focused on me because they respect the player I am, so believe you are a big asset to the team and always say *alhamdulillah* for everything.

Even after writing that, the game stayed in my mind for days. I spoke with Justin Leppitsch, who explained that the way the Brisbane game had unfolded meant it was never going to be a high-possession game for me; instead, it had required me to do my job defensively. I also took the reluctant step of burdening my wife with football because I needed some reassurance. Maybe I should do that more often, because she was wonderful at reminding me what I'd achieved that year and giving me the shot of confidence I needed.

It helped, but strange as it might seem, the fact that I'd had such a successful season, capped with All-Australian selection, was exactly why I was finding this moment hard to cope with.

Certainly it's one of the biggest achievements of my career. I'd had All-Australian as a goal for years, but the truth is I was never seriously in the frame until 2019. Then suddenly I was on stage, looking at the players around me – Bontempelli, Cripps, Dangerfield, Grundy, Fyfe, Pendlebury – and trying to come to terms with the idea that I belonged in their company. Then I thought about the players who hadn't made it – Ablett and Dusty, for instance, who had three Brownlows and a Norm Smith between them (with another Norm Smith soon to come) – and it began to feel like a dream. I'm someone who values peer recognition, and there aren't many greater forms of that than having a panel of experts declare you to be the best player in your position in the league.

But the inherent problem with valuing such things is that you're allowing yourself to be affected by something that's beyond your control. As esteemed as it is, selection for the All-Australian team is still a subjective judgement, which is why it creates so many debates each year. You could have an incredible season only for the selection panel to prefer someone else. That doesn't make your season any worse, just as having them select you doesn't make it any better. I can't pretend such accolades are insignificant, or that I'm above them, but you can't give them a meaning beyond what they have.

This combination of really wanting something, but not so much that it becomes about your ego – of valuing something a lot but keeping it in perspective – is one of footy's hardest highwire acts. And when you get the balance wrong, success can become a burden.

In my case, it was as though the heightened personal success of the season led me to a heightened fear of failure when there was no need for it. Success can lead you to more misery if you let it create a thirst in you that can never be quenched. Just as failure can distort your perspective and overcome you, so can success. Perspective doesn't become less important just because you're winning.

I really struggled in the week of the 2019 Grand Final for that reason. In 2017 I loved the Grand Final Parade, the colour, the excitement, the fact I could bring my daughter with me in the car. In 2019, all I could hear was Richmond fans in the crowd yelling out at me: 'Norm Smith this year, Bachar!' Of course, that was lovely. And it was probably a reflection of the fact that I was close to winning it in 2017, I'd just had my best season of football, and I was coming off a good Preliminary Final. But it wasn't a form of expectation I was ready to handle. I know it was meant as support, but I experienced it as pressure, and this was the culmination of a whole week of noise that had been coming my way. People were telling me they'd put bets on me winning it, which, as someone who detests gambling, I have to admit made me feel extremely uneasy. I'd never really encountered anything like that before.

I have to win the Norm Smith Medal or else I'm a failure, I thought, which was clearly ridiculous, but seemed accurate at the time. And once that started, other thoughts flowed: *What if I don't play well? What if we lose? What if I fail again?* I'd managed to put the disappointment of the Brisbane game behind me, because I'd gone into the Preliminary Final convinced that I cared only about winning, whether I touched the ball or not. Now, experiences like this were dragging me back. By the end of the parade I just wanted to go home and get away from everyone.

A handful of the people who really knew me could tell. Ali Fahour front-footed it straightaway and made me confess: I was distracted and edgy, I was emotionally exhausted and I couldn't sleep. Nerves were getting the better of me in a way they hadn't in 2017, and the more I thought about my own performance, the more doubts began to creep in. 'Houli, you've got to snap out of it,' Ali said to me on the phone the night before the Grand Final.

The next morning he sent me a long text message separated into headings: Bachar Houli the person, Bachar Houli the football player, and Bachar Houli the Muslim. The contents were nothing that wouldn't be familiar to you by now, focusing on things like my strengths as a player, and emphasising humility, gratitude and *tawakkul*, but it had a big impact because Ali wasn't telling me what to do: he was reminding me who I was.

Ali had accompanied me all that week, working on the one project that was most responsible for keeping me relaxed and sane: the Bachar Houli Academy. Every year culminates with an intensive program in Grand Final week: six full days of training and education sessions for the academy kids, beginning each day at around 7:00 am and finishing at 9:00 pm. It might seem like a crazy thing to try to squeeze into the week if you're actually playing in the Grand Final, but for me it was the best thing I could do – firstly because I believed in our mission so strongly, but also because, in this psychologically thorniest of weeks, it forced me to live out the idea I'd discussed with Justin Leppitsch of shifting the focus away from myself and onto other people: to help them, but also to help myself be better as a person.

In 2019 the academy staff tried to convince me to stay away, but I couldn't help myself being there. Of course, I still did all the relevant meetings and training at Richmond that week, but the academy sessions I participated in – talking to young Muslim footballers about team values, giving a presentation about what it means to have an Australian Muslim identity, running a one-hour session on gratitude – served as a powerful reminder to myself of who I am and what my greater purpose is. I couldn't get too absorbed in the idea of being the next Norm Smith medallist because I had to focus on being a role model right there and then. It meant I didn't have a lot of time to think about the game, and instead I was thinking about those very things that were bigger than football, but also made success in football possible: gratitude and service.

On Grand Final Day, I got to the ground around 12:30 pm and made my way to the locker room. I opened my locker and saw all the usual stuff – food, my strip – and, sitting next to it, a rock. Dimma had left a lot of things in our lockers over the past few years: a CD or a T-shirt from a band he'd been telling us about that week, or a hammer to remind us to 'bring our tool bag' (or our strengths) to the game. Before the Preliminary Final, he'd written each of us a letter telling us why he loved us. But a rock?

Fifteen years earlier, Dimma and our strength and conditioning coach, Peter Burge, had walked the Kokoda Track together when they were working at Hawthorn. People have died trying to do that trek, or sustained bad injuries. Others have had to deal with dehydration and heat exhaustion. It doesn't matter how fit you are, walking nearly 100 kilometres through the mountains in the tropical heat, carrying supplies to last you for days, dealing with the rain, the mosquitoes, the stinging plants and of course the blisters, is a brutal experience, especially if you're trying to complete it quickly by doing around 12 hours of hiking for five or six days. By the last day, they were really struggling. Burge stopped and picked up a rock and wrote a message on it: 'I love you, Dad,' it said, in honour of his father, who had passed away a few years before. He was dedicating that last gruelling day to his father, to inspire his final push to the finish. They made it.

'Today, I want you to dedicate this game to someone else who means a lot to you,' said Dimma, addressing the team.

We all went to our quiet corners and started writing. 'Rouba, Sarah and Maryam,' I wrote on one side of my rock, then, 'I ❤ you. 2019 GF,' on the other. It couldn't have been more appropriate, because in this year of peaks and troughs, when Rouba had been through all of them with me, the day of the Grand Final happened to land on our tenth wedding anniversary. She had ridden the bumps with me, although I could see her determination to hide it from me because she didn't want me to take on her own worries as well as my own. She felt her role was to balance my anxiety, which she always did with unbelievable strength and poise. As I'd sat anxiously on the couch the night before the Grand Final, she was the one calling me to be my better self. 'You're worrying about the Norm Smith Medal, but that's selfish,' she told me. 'That's not

you. You never think about yourself. You're a selfless person.'
She was right.

She'd devoted her whole year to me. Now I was going to do this for her.

I put the rock at the back of my locker, but I took the message that was on it everywhere with me that day. No one else saw what we wrote. They didn't need to, because the point was the inspiration it sparked in each of us. One last time I'd shifted my focus, this time to the person who, alongside my parents, deserved it more than anyone else in the world. Giving everything on this day would be my act of gratitude. By game time I felt completely sorted: relaxed, calm, ready to deliver.

Enjoy it, Bach. Enjoy it. That can be harder than it sounds, which is why I have to remind myself of it occasionally. Every game, I write the same words on the strapping on my wrist: 'Work rate. Enjoy.' Reading back through my notes, I see that I often wrote on similar themes before the finals matches in 2019. Before the Qualifying Final: 'If you stuff up, smile and carry on.' During Grand Final week: 'Smile and enjoy the moment. It might not ever come again.' On the morning of the Grand Final: 'Have fun, buddy, and smile.'

In the changerooms before the Grand Final we broke up into our line meetings: me with my fellow defenders discussing how we'd approach it. 'Today is the day we celebrate every single little thing,' I said. 'I don't care if it's a spoil, or a tackle, winning a contest or just forcing the ball out of bounds. Whatever it is, and whatever the score, we just celebrate it. And I want you to be loud about it, because I want the opposition to hear it and see it and envy it.'

And we did. At every available opportunity, we sought out our teammates and gave them a high five or a pat on the back. We wanted to make all those moments significant – to walk taller after even the small victories. Early in the first quarter I laid a big tackle on Tim Taranto that set the tone for us. It was especially significant because my game is based around running and creating, and tackling isn't usually a big feature. Dylan Grimes rushed over to me as soon as he could: 'I'm so proud of you. What an effort!' he said. Immediately, I felt inspired to do it again, because that kind of enthusiasm and celebration quickly becomes infectious.

My favourite personal moment in the whole game came early in the second quarter. On the outer wing, I spoiled the ball in a contest with Josh Kelly, then jumped to my feet and sprinted to tackle Adam Tomlinson, who had gathered the ball. I got the free kick, but the ball spilled free to Dan Rioli, who played on and passed it to Tom Lynch, who kicked the goal. I barely touched the ball in that passage of play, but it was more rewarding than all the times I did. I felt like the greatest player in the world in that moment. Teammates were high-fiving me and I was hitting them so hard with excitement I felt like I was breaking their hands.

We celebrated all game. I think it probably intimidated the opposition, because when they saw us getting so much motivation from our small victories, they could tell something special was happening. In the last five minutes, with the game well and truly won, I was still desperate to lay another tackle, to impose myself physically on a contest. That's not how I usually play. But I'd been inspired to take that approach because of our determination to enjoy and celebrate every moment.

Actually, it's an aspect of gratitude. To play a game of this scale was nerve-racking, but it was also a monumental blessing to be there, and forgetting to enjoy it would have been an act of ingratitude for what I'd been given. One of the greatest mindset changes at Richmond when we began our era of success was that we learned to love the journey we were on, rather than be focused on the destination. It helped us win the premiership in 2017, when we had hardly any finals experience. It definitely helped us recover from the crushing loss in 2018, because despite losing the Preliminary Final, we were able to recognise and celebrate what we'd achieved in being the best team all year. And it made the 2019 premiership possible, because our sense of enjoyment and optimism held us together in the first half of the year when we had an incredible injury toll and lost plenty of games – some quite badly. We were able to see the blessing in everything that was being thrown at us: how being forced to give games to young players who'd never have had the chance would fast-track their development, but also make us a much stronger team in a few years' time.

There were times that resolve was tested, though. When we lost three games in a row midway through the season, I began to doubt we'd be able to recover. And when we were 21 points down at half time in the Preliminary Final against Geelong, it's fair to say we were aware of the ghost of our Preliminary Final loss to Collingwood a year earlier. But our humility, our gratitude and our ability to stay in the moment was strong enough for us to put all that behind us. We didn't foresee it was going to lead us to another premiership, but the attitude we had cultivated all year made it possible.

It's true that the 2019 flag wasn't as exciting as 2017. Maybe that was because it was our second premiership, or maybe it was because the Grand Final itself was so one-sided. But the 2019 Grand Final definitely allowed me the rarest moment you can have in football: the feeling of knowing you've won the premiership when there's still plenty of time left to play.

For me, reality hit about halfway through the third quarter, when we were up by about ten goals. That last quarter was as close as you can get to a victory lap in football: a full half an hour of soaking it all in, looking around at your teammates and feeling the vibrations of the stadium, which was bursting at the seams. I am rarely conscious of the atmosphere of a game I'm playing in, because there's always so much to concentrate on, but on this day I experienced it totally.

There's a unique joy in being so fully in tune with a moment like this. To know that every contest would go our way, that whenever the ball came into our defence we'd catapult it back towards our goal, and that whenever it entered our forward line there was a big chance we'd score. To choose to experience the moment without there being any danger our play would suffer. It was like watching and playing the game at the same time.

And for me as a spectator, there was no greater moment than when my mate Trent Cotchin marked the ball in the middle of the MCG with about a minute to go, played on and ran directly at goal, took a bounce and then put it through

from 50. His raw, unrestrained and hilariously ungainly celebration expressed everything that made this day so special:
the difficulties, the failure, the hunger, the celebration of
each other.

After the game we spoke about that goal, about the season,
about how proud we were of all our teammates who'd managed
to do it again. As we spoke, Trent broke down quietly. It wasn't
a time for us to shout in triumph or lose control. It was a
moment to be absorbed and appreciated, because, after all,
there was so much to be grateful for.

11

PERSPECTIVE

ABOUT THE WORST THING you can hear when you answer the phone is someone you love bawling, unable to speak. You know immediately something very serious has happened, but in the absence of concrete information all your mind can do is race through all the gravest possibilities. You can feel the rush of adrenaline as you go on high alert. It might only be a few moments before the caller speaks, but it feels like years.

On this occasion it was my sister Marwa.

'Bach, Mum's going into intensive care,' she cried.

My mind immediately conjured up images of Mum smothered in tubes, surrounded by machines, lying there in a coma. The thought of it hit me like a train.

'What? What do you mean?' I replied quickly.

'She just called me to tell me,' explained Marwa. 'She said they were about to take her in, and that she thinks once you go into intensive care, you don't come out. Then she told me where she'd been keeping some money in the house and asked me to give it charity so it counts as one of her good deeds. She called to say goodbye, Bach.'

About a thousand emotions collide in a moment like that. There's the thud you feel in your heart almost before you even comprehend what you've just heard. Then there's a combination of urgency and confusion as your brain scrambles to piece everything together.

Mum had been sick for a few days, but that wasn't why she'd gone to hospital. She went because she'd had a fall, hurt her ribs and needed some scans. While she was there they diagnosed her with pneumonia and admitted her, but there was no sign that her condition was even especially serious, let alone life-threatening. How was Marwa suddenly telling me she was about to die? I could only assume that everything had happened instantly – that Mum had just collapsed or something.

Marwa was breaking down completely, so distraught she could barely talk. The only other time I'd heard her like this was when one of our uncles died, so there was no doubting how certain she was. But it just didn't make sense to me.

I immediately called my brother Nezor. Because he's a surgeon, and also the eldest, we all turned to him as the leader of the family during this time. He understood better than anyone what was happening at every stage of Mum's illness, so he updated us frequently, and we hung on his every word. Sometimes he sent a message to our family WhatsApp group, or if it was more complicated he called each of the siblings individually. At this moment, though, I wasn't about to wait for his call – I needed answers.

Nezor didn't pick up, which only made me worry more, as though the situation was such an emergency that he didn't have time to take the call. By now I had so much pent-up anxiety, emotion and confusion, but nowhere to direct it. There was nothing I could do, and I had no way of even understanding the situation. I asked Rouba to get the kids ready in case we needed to go to the hospital to farewell Mum.

Then I called Mohamed and Khaled.

'What are you talking about?' said Khaled. 'I just spoke to Mum 20 minutes ago, and she said it was all good and the doctors had a plan.'

All of that was true. That's how quickly Mum's health had turned. Later, the doctors explained to us that her oxygen levels had suddenly dropped, and that they'd decided to admit her to intensive care as a precaution. Nezor reassured us that this was the right thing to do. Mum's health was only going one way, and it was better to get treatment started early rather than waiting and then having to rush everything.

We didn't know it was COVID-19 at the time. Mum had been tested but hadn't had the result yet, and by the time it came back positive, the news didn't have much emotional impact. Mum was already fighting for her life, and we weren't especially concerned about which disease was doing the damage.

But the positive diagnosis did make one extremely signifi-cant difference to everyone in the family. It meant none of us was allowed to see Mum. At all. Even Nezor, who worked at the same hospital and knew all the relevant people personally, was barred from seeing her. There were absolutely no exceptions, as it should be. You might think the worst thing in life is coming face-to-face with a dying loved one. We had just discovered something even worse: not being able to come face-to-face with them at all.

That hit Dad extremely hard. This was the first time in their marriage that he'd been separated from Mum, and the circumstances couldn't really have been worse. His wife of 48 years was on the brink of death and he was at home on his own, completely helpless to do anything about it. Imagine if it ended this way.

Dad's a rock, and his faith is extremely strong. But now he was vulnerable in a way we hadn't seen before. He needed support, and soon enough it came in the form of my other sister, Safa. She is probably the closest thing in our family to being Mum's carer. Unfortunately, that made it inevitable that she and her family tested positive as well, and of course, so had Dad. But at least that meant Dad could stay with Safa's family and they could get through it together. It was the best place for him to be, surrounded by his daughter, son-in-law and grandkids. The only trouble was, Dad wasn't fully there. Safa often saw him pacing around the house, not responding to conversation.

Rouba and I experienced this isolation too when, just a few days after Mum first started showing some mild symptoms, Rouba gave birth to our third child, Mohamed – named after the Prophet, not my brother! As with our other kids, we thought carefully about the name, because the Prophet explained that being given a good name with a good meaning is one of the rights children have of their parents, on a par with their right to education. For our baby son we also considered Bilal, Omar and Ibrahim, all of which belong to important figures in Islam, but in the end we couldn't go past naming him after the man Muslims believe is the best of creation. It's the most popular name in the world for a reason.

In some ways, his birth went perfectly. The labour lasted only 50 minutes, he arrived without complications, and of course we were overjoyed. He was calm from the moment he was born, and didn't even cry straightaway – though I have to say he's making up for it now. I took hold of him as soon as I could and quietly sang the call to prayer (the *adhan*) into his right ear, and a slightly different version of it (called the *iqamah*) in his left. This is a common practice among Muslims based on reports of the Prophet's life, so that the first words the child hears are anchored in faith. It really is a lovely moment.

But the occasion was tinged with the fact that so many important people were missing. That made it completely different to what we'd experienced before. When our two girls, Sarah and Maryam, were born, both Rouba's mum and mine were in the room with us, giving Rouba all the support she needed, helping her through every moment. Then, within an hour or two of the birth, both our fathers were there too. Not long after that it felt like all of Mish Mish was there.

This time, COVID-19 made that impossible. I had to take a more active role, encouraging Rouba and keeping her calm in the way our mothers normally would. No one at all could come to see us, and even I wasn't allowed to stay. Mohamed was born around 7:45 pm and I was sent home by about 10:00 pm. I wasn't even allowed to return the next morning because they needed to keep my presence at the hospital to a minimum. So I went off to training; there was nothing else for me to do.

Later that day, Rouba was discharged. I called Mum to let her know all was well and we were coming home.

'Bring him over, I want to see him,' she said.

Mum's name, Yamama, means 'dove' in Arabic, but in truth she's always been a warrior. She's the staunch one of our parents, the one who has firm views on things, who won't be pushed around or told what to do. She's the kind of person who never admits to being sick, and just powers on through whatever affliction she has. 'Nothing's wrong with me,' she insisted in the early stages of her illness. Now she was desperate to see her newest grandchild.

I hesitated. 'No, I can't, Mum,' I said. 'You're sick.'

Then I heard a pause. Not like the one I would hear later from Marwa. This was the silence of a mother, where nothing is said but everything is communicated. It felt the worst kind of awful.

'Oh . . . okay,' she said at last.

That didn't make me feel any better. It was the first time I could remember where I'd directly said no to Mum. I felt like I had disobeyed her. And for me as a Muslim, that was a heavy thing to do. Again and again, in both the Qur'an and the statements of the prophet Muhammad, being kind and dutiful towards one's parents is mentioned immediately after obedience to God. As I found myself defying Mum's wishes, one passage in particular was thundering away in my mind:

> And your Lord has decreed that you worship none except Him, and treat your parents with goodness. Whether one or both of them reach old age while with you, say not to them so much as '*uff*' nor chide them but address them in terms of honour. And lower to them the wing of humility out of mercy and say, 'My Lord, have mercy upon them as they brought me up when I was little'.

That word *uff* is famous among Muslims because it's meant to express something we would think of as being so small. It has no particular meaning, really. Probably the closest equivalent in English would be to say 'ugh' or make some kind of exasperated noise. The point is the Qur'an says that even this is an unacceptable level of disrespect towards your parents.

Yet I knew refusing to take Mohamed to see Mum was the right decision. In fact, it was the only decision. And, looking back now, so much was riding on me making it. Mohamed, Rouba and I might all have become infected – and who knows what might have flowed from that? But as Mum's condition got worse, that decision, and those Qur'anic verses, tortured me. Now I was the one pacing around my house. *Could my last words to my mother really be, 'No, you can't see your grandson'?* The thought repeated over and over in my mind. Then I'd make *du'a* for Mum's recovery, adding, 'Please, ya Allah, don't let these be the last words I left with Mum.' That would have haunted me for the rest of my life.

In moments like these, every slight change in your loved one's condition becomes amplified. Every improvement is a source of hope, and every deterioration a cause for despair. In Mum's case, it felt like a roller-coaster. Like so many COVID-19 patients, she would improve very slightly, then get worse, then improve slightly again. This went on for weeks. I tried really hard not to let my mind run ahead of me, not even to think about what would happen if Mum died, but when I was alone I couldn't stop those thoughts coming in. I ended up thinking quite a lot about that moment I would say the words Muslims traditionally do when they hear of someone's death. *Inna lillahi wa inna ilayhi raji'un* – to God we belong and to Him we return.

Our group conversations with the treating doctor became extremely emotional. My siblings regularly found themselves unable to speak, and when they gained enough control to start talking, they could hardly think of anything to say. What do you say in a situation that is so far beyond your knowledge, experience and control? Usually it fell to me to fill the silence, but all I could do was tell the doctor how much we appreciated her work, how much we trusted her expertise, and that we felt confident with the situation being in her hands.

In the meantime, it was placing enormous stress on Nezor. As word about Mum spread in the community, it wasn't just family asking him for answers about what was happening and why, but countless other concerned people. I did my best to leave him alone so I didn't add to his burden, waiting instead for him to contact me.

Often when he did, it was to update me, but other times he'd call, stressed and exhausted, asking me for advice. He was finding himself waking up in the middle of the night in tears, and his stress became obvious whenever he started talking about Mum's condition. He shared with me how serious it was, explaining that Mum's kidneys were failing, for example, then he'd ask me whether or not he should tell Dad, and whether I thought he'd be able to cope. I'd offer my view where I could, but really I felt like I was in no position to help him; after all, he was the doctor, not me, and I knew nothing that he didn't already know. In truth, I think Nezor just needed to unload. He did almost all the talking when he called. Then he'd say he had to go.

The one thing we all had to help us get through this was our faith. One of the literal meanings of the word *Islam* is 'surrender'. And through our discussions as a family, that's exactly what we did: surrender to the fact that we had no control over this situation, and that we were at the mercy of whatever God had planned. We tried to find the most positive way of looking at this. *Tawakkul. Sabr.* Death comes to us all, and if it was God's will that this was how Mum died, then we had to accept that it was the best plan. Our task was to be patient, because God is with the patient. Those ideas, which had proven so useful to me throughout my football career, were invaluable to me now. They helped me get off the roller-coaster.

It's hard to understand just how serious COVID-19 can be until you've seen it up close. When it's just a news item, you can wonder how bad it really is – I know I did. I got a sense of the illness it could cause when Safa first got infected, because she became quite sick. But Mum's situation brought its severity home with brutal force. And I knew that if I had to be jolted into recognising this, others might too.

I was probably fortunate that, as an AFL player, I was living under stricter protocols than the rest of society at the time. Everyone else was free to see their families, and in normal times we would usually do that twice a week. But the new AFL rules meant I could only see my parents if there was a real need. So I did see them occasionally, but nowhere near as often as I usually would have. And because the importance of maintaining distance was being drummed into us as AFL players, I was probably more vigilant about that than most people. No doubt the fact that Rouba was pregnant at the time played a part too, but I don't think it's a stretch to say that had I not been an AFL player, I would have been infected.

I was particularly concerned about people in the Muslim community, because I know many have large extended families like mine that are quite tight, and that many live in areas of Melbourne that had been identified as virus hotspots. If these families failed to take the risk seriously, the results could be devastating. I figured that maybe, given my profile and what my family was now experiencing, they might listen to me.

The idea that I could say something publicly was first planted in my mind before Mum got sick, when the Victorian government approached me to see if I'd be prepared to record a video message in both Arabic and English encouraging people to get tested if they had symptoms. The government soon called it off because they were on the verge of announcing new restrictions, which I assume meant any video from me might become either redundant or a distraction. But now, with Mum suffering so badly, that idea came flooding back to me. I could see – and, perhaps more importantly, feel – the urgency and seriousness of the situation.

But it was a hard thing to talk about. It was intensely personal for me, and for the rest of my family, but it was also sensitive because testing positive for COVID-19 seemed to have some kind of stigma, as though contracting the virus was proof that you'd done something wrong. That might be true sometimes, but so often it's not. You could walk into an elevator after someone has sneezed and catch it. You can follow every rule the authorities lay down and still catch it. The virus is extremely infectious – that's why it became a pandemic.

In the end, I decided that, however uncomfortable it might be, the message I wanted to share was too important for me to remain silent. I posted a video on Instagram, completely off my own bat, without any authorisation from, or even discussion with, the Victorian government. I told it as straight as I could. That my family had been affected. That Mum's condition was so serious that only God knew how it would turn out. That the fact we were isolated from her at a time like this was extremely painful. Then I came to my main message:

> Change your mindset about COVID-19. The reality is it
> is out there, and I'm experiencing it right now within my
> family. Please, I urge you, for the sake of Allah, to go get
> tested if you are showing any forms of symptoms. If you're
> not showing any symptoms, please do your bit, for the
> sake of Allah.

The response from the outside world was immediate and overwhelming. I was flooded with texts from friends, colleagues, even social and political leaders. I also know that, on some level, the message worked. I could see that people needed to change their thinking about COVID-19. And some did. I know people who went to get tested who otherwise probably wouldn't have.

But probably the most special thing was hearing from so many Muslims who were now making *du'a* for Mum. That meant a lot, because as Muslims we don't necessarily know whose *du'a* will be accepted. Having so many people giving Mum their prayers gave me a confidence that someone's would be. I know that meant a lot to my family as well. I'd made the mistake of failing to seek their permission before I spoke publicly, which upset some of them. I accepted my fault in this, but as soon as I told them about the responses I was getting, they understood the benefits of what I'd done.

In the middle of all this, the AFL had decided to move all its Victorian teams out of the state, with Richmond being one of the clubs to head to Queensland, to keep the AFL season alive as infection rates in Victoria spiked and Melbourne moved inevitably towards a second lockdown. I've always maintained that football isn't the most important thing in life, but there has probably been no time in my life this has been truer. In theory, I now had a decision to make: would I go to Queensland with my teammates, or remain in Melbourne? In reality, there was never a question in my mind.

That was true even before Mum entered hospital. At the time Richmond relocated, Mohamed was three days old.

Mum was sick but her condition wasn't yet serious. With the COVID-19 restrictions in place, Rouba would have limited support from family to help her out with the new baby and our two daughters, and there was simply no way I was going to be anywhere else.

Rouba tried to convince me I should just go with the team – she didn't want to hold me back – but that was never going to go very far. 'No, it's me who doesn't want to go,' I told her. Anything else would have been extremely selfish. I can't say I was a huge amount of help with the baby, but just little things like being there and taking Sarah and Maryam off her hands made a big difference.

Our original plan was that I would join the team in Queensland in a couple of weeks, once things were settled at home and Rouba was in a better position to cope. The AFL's intention at that time was that Victorian clubs would be in Queensland only for about five weeks, so that meant I would be there for about three weeks before returning home. Rouba and I agreed that was doable. But as Mum's health got worse, all that changed. I wasn't going to leave while Mum was struggling for her life, and while the rest of the family were struggling to hold their emotional and spiritual state together.

In the meantime, the COVID-19 situation in Melbourne continued to deteriorate. Pretty quickly the rest of the country responded by closing their borders to Victorians, meaning Richmond were looking at staying away until the end of the season. That was a long stretch, and it wouldn't be feasible for me to return home regularly, then quarantine for two weeks every time I went back to Queensland. The good news was that the AFL would allow Rouba and the kids to come to Queensland with me, but that still left me with one very big conundrum: how could I leave for Queensland with my mother in an intensive care unit?

It was true that I couldn't help her even if I stayed. I couldn't even visit. And with Melbourne entering a second period of lockdown, I couldn't really even see Dad to lend him support. But the thought of being elsewhere felt wrong. It felt like I would be abandoning my family so I could go and play a game. It's a game I love, of course, and which provides my livelihood, but a game nonetheless.

Then, after all the ups and downs, all the tears, the stress and the anxiety, Nezor finally passed on the news we were so desperate to hear: Mum had begun improving. Not in the tiny ways we'd seen before, which were then quickly reversed. No, she was improving significantly in a way that looked like it would be sustainable. She was still in the ICU, but she was beginning to beat the virus.

I vividly remember when Nezor's message arrived in our WhatsApp group. The whole family's massive relief leapt off the screen. It was clear in Nezor's message, and even clearer in the explosion of messages that followed an instant later. It was as though everyone had been staring at their phones all day just waiting for this news to arrive. Clearly, there was nothing more important in our lives in that moment. Personally, I felt an overwhelming sense that God had answered someone's prayers – not necessarily mine or my siblings', but someone's. It was like the support of an entire family, community, even country landed in my heart in a single moment.

Without this news, I doubt I would have come close to heading to Queensland to resume my football career. Even with it, I felt some discomfort at the idea. But I needed to come to a decision, because there was a special AFL flight leaving the next week, and that would be my last chance to get there for a long time, possibly even the entire season. Richmond needed to know if I would be on it. I spent days thinking it over, and doing that same *istikhara* prayer for guidance I'd done when I was considering moving to GWS in 2016. Soon enough, it became clear to me that the only way I could do this with a clear conscience was to seek Nezor's advice, and above all the blessing of my father.

I spoke to Nezor first. I needed to be sure of Mum's condition, and since he'd been working directly with the ICU team, he would know how much Mum was improving and would be able to tell me when we'd be able to see her again. He reassured me that her improvement was real and sustained, but said it would still be a while before anyone could visit. He figured being in Queensland wouldn't keep me from seeing her for a while, at least.

Then Nezor said something I wasn't expecting: 'Going back to work was the best thing I did.' He'd been forced to quarantine for two weeks at the beginning of this ordeal, which he'd found extremely difficult because it meant he couldn't do much except think about Mum. 'It made me sane again,' he said. I hadn't really thought about the possibility that playing football might actually help me in some way.

I'd also sought out the opinions of an imam I knew, to make sure it wouldn't be wrong for me to leave my parents in this situation. And he reminded me the Prophet had said that 'the *du'as* of three people are answered: the traveller, parents and the oppressed'. His point was that if I went to Queensland, I would be a traveller. If anything, that meant I would be of more help to Mum there than I would be in Melbourne, because my *du'a* would carry extra strength.

With all this in mind, I was ready to speak to Dad. 'How are you feeling about Mum?' I asked him.

'*Alhamdulillah*, good. She's getting better,' he said.

A bit like me, Dad's a man of few words, but his demeanour said everything. His mood was transformed. He'd even gone back to work at Louay's fish-and-chip shop. I could tell all this made a huge difference to him, even in the way he did small talk. There were no pauses in his answers as he spoke, and he had an air of positivity. He'd become himself again.

'Dad, I need to decide if I'm going to Queensland to join the team,' I said. 'This could be the last flight I can take. I have to tell them tomorrow. Do you think—'

He didn't even allow me to finish. '*Tawakkul 'ala Allah*,[6] and go,' he said. 'There's nothing you can do here. The reality is all your brothers and sisters are here if I need anything.'

I could tell he wasn't just saying this – he wanted me to go and get back to football. He was even excited when I explained to him that Rouba and the kids could come with me. My decision was made.

I sent a message to my family to tell them:

---

6 This means 'Have *tawakkul* in God', which you might translate as 'Trust in God' or 'Rely on God'.

Salams family,

After consulting Allah through *du'a*, then Dad and
Dr Nezor, the family and I have decided to leave for
Queensland to join the team, *insha Allah*.[7] We will
quarantine for two weeks in a hotel then join the team,
so I won't play for another three weeks.

There is clearly nothing I can do for Mum by being
here other than *du'a*. But a more effective *du'a* is the *du'a*
of a traveller.

I hope everyone understands, *insha Allah*.

Within about half an hour every one of my siblings had replied,
as well as some of their spouses and children. Not only did
they understand, they were excited that I'd be playing again,
and were looking forward to seeing me out on the footy field.

Does football matter? An experience like this makes really
clear what's important and what isn't. And for me, throughout
so much of this ordeal, football wasn't even in the frame. But
there are times it does mean something, and it felt like that
time had arrived. For a while, football simply had no place
in my life, beyond the training I was doing to keep up my
fitness and do my duty by the club. Now that was beginning
to change.

Actually, as far as football was concerned, the hiatus was
good for me. If I'm completely honest, I entered 2020 with
little enthusiasm for the game. Maybe it was exhaustion after

---

7 Literally, 'if God wills'; this is an extremely common expression
among Muslims.

254

climbing the mountain in 2019; I can't say for sure. Whatever it was, I knew immediately that I was feeling the exact opposite of the 2019 preseason, when I was flying.

In 2020 I played terribly in my first preseason game, against GWS, and recognised within myself that I really wasn't ready to be back playing. I'd lost my passion for the game. I began asking myself questions like *Where am I going with this?* I wouldn't exactly say it was a relief when I got injured just before our season opener against Carlton, but I wasn't disappointed either. Then came the shutdown of the whole season, as states around the country closed their borders and we all headed into lockdown. For me as a player, that came at a good time. I needed a break and I took it as a chance to wind down.

I actually enjoyed the lockdown period. I was training a lot, which I like, but apart from that I felt I was rebalancing my life. I threw myself into all kind of mundane things like housework. I was cleaning the gutters, creating a veggie patch, going to Bunnings every day. After training I spent time with my daughter Sarah, going out for walks or bike rides.

Lockdown forced me to spend more time with my family, and that was the best thing that could have happened. It brought home to me that I hadn't been devoting as much time to my wife and kids as I should have. I'd been neglecting them a little. Lockdown took away all the distractions I normally put in the way – I couldn't go fishing, hunting, camping, anything really. Now I was giving them what was their right. The difference was profound. I could see my daughters becoming more attached to me. Even when I needed to go and train, they insisted on coming with me, just to sit in the park and watch so they could be with me.

Ramadan landed at this time too, which could have been a challenge. Usually it's a time of countless family and community gatherings in homes and in the mosques. But suddenly we couldn't do those things. Visits were banned and the mosques were shut. Heading into the month, it was a scary thought that the very things that make Ramadan what it is would be missing. But once it began, I couldn't believe how much I enjoyed it.

I missed going to the mosque, but instead it was like the mosque came into our home. I wasn't doing *taraweeh* prayers with hundreds of people every night, but with Rouba and the girls. It created a new kind of spirituality. And as there was no football, there was nothing complicated getting in the way. I've written a lot about how Ramadan affects my football. After going through 'iso-Ramadan', I now realise that the more important thing is how football affects my experience of Ramadan. Plenty of Muslims experience tension during Ramadan between worldly matters and spiritual ones. Iso-Ramadan removed that.

In my case, that meant throwing myself into my Qur'anic memorisation. I had been intending to memorise a particular chapter, called *Ya Sin*, which I'd promised myself I'd learn, but had been neglecting. It's a very famous chapter, partly because it briefly explores the whole Qur'an's main themes, but also because it is recommended for Muslims to read it over someone who is on their death bed. I had no idea at the time how close I might come to using it.

On my second day in Queensland, I was doing a weights session with some other Richmond players who were in quarantine when my phone rang. Given I was in the middle of training, I ignored it. Then it rang again, so I figured it might be important. I looked at the screen: 'Mum would like to FaceTime.'

What? I thought. *This can't be right . . . What's happening?*

I swiped my phone urgently to answer the call. And there on my screen was Mum. She was awake, with a nurse sitting next to her. After weeks of anguish, heartache and fear, weeks of talking about Mum's fight for life without actually seeing her, suddenly she was right in front of me, virtually at least. The combination of unfiltered joy and disbelief I felt is like nothing else I've ever experienced.

'Mum! How are you feeling?' I asked as I walked out of the gym.

She could barely talk. The nurse was trying to pass on what she wanted to say, but it was difficult for her to understand. It didn't matter. Nothing mattered except that Mum was okay.

'Have you called Nezor?' I asked.

'Yes, but he's not answering at the moment,' Mum just managed to say. I was familiar with that.

'Wait there,' I said. 'I'll go and get the kids and call you back!'

She agreed. Two minutes later I called back, but she didn't answer. I was left with only that short conversation, but it meant everything. The whole experience felt unreal.

I ran back into the gym. 'That was Mum!' I shouted.

All my teammates immediately got excited, because they'd watched me live this journey at training over the past weeks. Naturally, we'd spoken quite a lot about it.

'So, is she good?' they asked.

'Yeah! She couldn't talk, but she's okay!' I was like a little kid.

Now I felt I could attack football at full pelt. Football had found its place in my life again. I was excited to be training and looking forward to playing – for the club that had supported me, for myself, for my family. And I could attack this bizarre season with freedom. Even the insecurity I normally felt whenever I missed games through injury wasn't there this time. I wasn't worried about losing my spot in the team. I had no expectations of football. Now everything was a bonus.

Things were back in their proper place. Mostly. As I write these words, Mum still hasn't met Mohamed. I desperately hope that by the time you're reading them, she has.

12

KHALIFAH

LIKE SO MANY THINGS IN LIFE, football can be taken away from you at any moment. It might be a serious injury that does it, or – especially if you're an older player – a relatively ordinary but nagging one. You can go from being an automatic selection as a senior player to one whose position can't be recovered, and that can happen at lightning speed.

What then? There's a difference between caring about something and being dependent on it. You can't play elite sport without caring about it, but you can make sure that you're still whole once you're no longer able to do it. I realised a long time ago that I needed to reach a place where if Dimma called me to a meeting and told me it was over, I'd respond by shaking his hand and saying, 'Thank you very much for the opportunity, and for the belief you had in me when you recruited me. It's made me a better person and a better player, and I'm so grateful for it.'

That's not an easy destination for players. It's one thing to understand the end of your career intellectually, but facing it as a reality is something else entirely, because it disrupts many fundamental aspects of your life. You go from an environment where you get to do something you love every day as your job, to one where, at best, you'll be squeezing it in around another job you probably love a lot less. You go from having a clear, very public identity to having to answer the question: who are you if you're no longer a footballer? The world of sport moves quickly, and former players can be forgotten with alarming speed – even the great ones. No doubt that suits some people, if they were never comfortable with the limelight but just happened to be really good at football. But for many of us the loss of lifestyle, and the material benefits of being a footballer, are difficult to confront.

When you start your AFL career, everything is so tenuous that your focus is overwhelmingly on getting to play games. Then, maybe 50 games in, you broaden your horizon and begin thinking more about team success, because you understand that's what defines a successful footballer's career. That's definitely what it was like for me.

I'm extremely grateful I've been given those things, but there's a level beyond that too, where you recognise that even the most glittering career can't fill your soul – that there might be something more to be gained from a sporting career. That recognition requires more than just an understanding that your life has a greater purpose than playing football. It requires you to look at your football career itself with a broader perspective. Now I understand that it's not what

I accumulate through my career, but what I leave behind, that matters most.

There's a fascinating passage in the Qur'an that describes the moment God announces to the angels His decision to create human beings, and He chooses an intriguing phrase: 'I am making a *khalifah* on the Earth' (2:30). *Khalifah* is a rich and complex word with a huge range of meanings. At its most basic, though, it means 'successor', which immediately says something important about human life: that each of us succeeds those who came before us and inherits their legacy, only then to leave a legacy for those who succeed us. This idea is fleshed out when you consider a related word, *khalf*, which means 'behind', 'backwards' or 'back', or the verb *khullifu*, which means 'they are left behind'. There's something here telling us that one of the measures of the quality of our lives is what we leave in our wake. It might even be one of the reasons we were created in the first place.

At some level I've always had a sense of that. Even before I was drafted, as the buzz started to build that I might become the first practising Muslim to make it to the AFL, I could feel the weight of community hope and expectation, and I understood the symbol that I was for a lot of people who never thought they'd see someone like them make it. One of the reasons Mohamed Bakkar devoted so much of his time to helping me with my football all those years ago was that he knew I took my religion and my obligations to my community seriously – that I wanted to show other kids that it was possible for them to make it, no matter who they were. That expectation went to another level around the time of my draft camp.

In the lead-up to the draft itself, the curiosity of me being a practising Muslim meant I probably got more media attention than the players who were vying to be the number one draft pick. And once I got to Essendon, the impact I had was immediate. There were Lebanese guys banging on drums at my first game, almost like they were announcing the arrival of a new culture. And all the interviews about praying and fasting must have injected at least some awareness of these things into the culture of football, because I heard of clubs bringing them up with Muslim players who had played for them for years, but who never had the courage to raise it. Even Ali Fahour, who had spent a lot of time around VFL and AFL clubs, later told me that my arrival was the moment he felt brave enough to ask for a dedicated space in which he could pray. When I think back to the conversations I used to have with Ziggy about how football clubs were inherently hostile to leading an Islamic life, that change seems an incredibly significant thing.

My career exists at the meeting point between Muslim and non-Muslim Australians. I didn't necessarily ask for that – it's more a natural consequence of how things have played out – but it means I have responsibilities in both directions. It means coming face to face with tensions in society, with Muslims who might feel the rest of the country can be hostile to them, and with non-Muslims who might be fearful and suspicious of Islam, even if they don't know much about it. Sometimes those tensions come and find you. One such moment arrived on the opening night of Round 2, 2016.

'Hey, you jihadist!'

I still remember this voice emerging from the Collingwood

cheer squad clear as a bell, piercing the strange silence that had descended on the game as I went to gather the ball for a kick-in during the second quarter. *Did I just hear what I think I heard?* I thought. I had – and everyone else had heard it too.

I looked up immediately, and there was no mistaking who had said it, just as there was no mistaking that he was seriously drunk. I made eye contact with him, then looked away briefly before deciding to look back at him and shake my head. I didn't say a word.

I know this must be quite rare among Australian Muslims, but I'd never experienced this before. I grew up surrounded by Lebanese Muslims, and I went to an Islamic school, so there were probably relatively few chances for people to throw anti-Muslim abuse my way. And when I was outside that bubble, I probably looked much like anyone else. At the time I was drafted I had a spiky hairstyle and no beard – except for a 'flavour saver' under my bottom lip, as was fashionable in the 2000s. People who were paying attention to my story would have known I was a Muslim, but most others probably wouldn't have realised.

At the same time, I knew it was only a matter of time before something like this happened. By the time I got to Richmond, I had less hair on my head and considerably more on my face. The longer my beard grew, the more visibly marked out as a Muslim I became, and the more inevitable I thought it would be that someone in the crowd would call out something pretty awful.

About a year earlier, when we were playing against Melbourne, a 3AW radio presenter, John Burns, who was watching the game at the MCG, had apparently called me a 'terrorist', but I never heard it. It became a media story because a senior Richmond official made a complaint after overhearing it; Burns later said he couldn't remember making such a comment but apologised anyway. I had nothing to say about it publicly until the media were literally circling my car at training one day, because I'd never taken it on as my own experience. The Collingwood incident was different because it was said directly at me, and I'd heard it.

The early rounds of the 2016 season came at a particularly sensitive time. The previous season had ended with Adam Goodes, one of the legends of the game, being effectively booed into retirement. And it was around the time movements such as Reclaim Australia and the United Patriots Front were holding anti-Muslim protests; they were particularly targeting a mosque being planned for Bendigo. That might have seemed something that was only of interest to people in that country Victorian town, but there were people coming from as far away as Queensland to protest it. That very night we played Collingwood, someone held up a banner with the United Patriots Front's logo on it and the words 'Go Pies! Stop the Mosques'. The next week a similar banner appeared in Perth at the West Coast versus Fremantle game. This stuff was in the air.

To be perfectly frank, I didn't pay a lot of attention to the details of the Adam Goodes affair. As someone who takes in very little media, I didn't know every detail of who had said and done what, or how it became such a public controversy. But I knew enough to understand that these things could quickly get out of control. I had no criticism of the way Adam handled the crowd abuse he suffered, and I wouldn't even say I was trying to learn from his example, but the sheer scale of what he was going through made me realise that I had to figure out how I would handle something like that if it happened to me. I didn't want to react on instinct in the moment. I wanted to have thought it through beforehand.

I found my answer in a series of Islamic teachings. The first came from one of my favourite stories of the Prophet's life, concerning his next-door neighbour. She was apparently so hostile to him and his message that she would dump her garbage on the doorstep of his house every day. The Prophet never responded to it, until one day he noticed that she had stopped. He paid her a visit, saying that since he was no longer receiving her daily deliveries, he was worried she might be unwell. So touched was she by the Prophet's concern for her, even in the face of her long-term provocation, that she accepted Islam.

The story itself is probably apocryphal, but there are plenty of other examples that show the Prophet enduring similar treatment from his enemies. This one is particularly famous among Muslims because, whatever its historical reliability, it captures the way so many Muslims understand the Prophet's character. I wanted to respond to abuse in a way that was broadly in line with this approach.

I also knew that I was far more interested in education than in conflict, and that the best method of educating people is through your own example. If the chance arises for a conversation, it is right to speak gently. 'Invite to the way of your Lord with wisdom and beautiful exhortation, and argue with them in a way that is best,' says the Qur'an (16:125). Another passage describes the moment God sends Moses and Aaron to confront Pharaoh: 'Go, both of you, to Pharaoh. Indeed, he has transgressed. And speak to him with gentle speech that perhaps he may be reminded or fear [Allah]' (20:43–44). As Islamic scholars often comment, none of us is better than Moses or Aaron, and whoever you're talking to is not worse than Pharaoh, so if they can use gentle speech, so can you.

Of course, there are times for being firm and direct on these things – for taking a strong stand. But I didn't want that to be my first response. I'd decided that if I ever faced this moment, I'd look for the chance to have a conversation with whoever had abused me in as gentle a way as possible. I'd take it as an opportunity to educate, to talk to them about Islam, rather than to punish them. Then I'd see how they responded and take it from there.

Maybe that's why I wasn't particularly angry or shocked when it did occur that night against Collingwood. It was as though I'd already processed the abuse. It didn't even distract me for the rest of the match, because I ended up with 35 possessions that night and contributed really well. But that didn't mean it just washed off me, either. I was hurt, because apart from 'jihadist' being a horrible thing to be called, it was exactly the opposite of what I felt I'd stood for my whole life. I suppose the thing about stereotypes is that they have nothing to do with you as an individual – you just get lumped with them, and that's a special kind of offence. I spent the rest of the game thinking about it. All night I was rehearsing to myself what I'd say to this man if I could find him after the game. It would be brief and simple, but I felt I had to get it right.

Richmond fans will remember this as the night Brodie Grundy kicked a goal in the last ten seconds of the game for Collingwood to beat us by a point, after we'd somehow managed to throw away a three-goal lead with five minutes to play. Even with 90 seconds left, Collingwood was still two goals down and the game seemed over. Thousands of fans had already left to beat the traffic. Then a ruckman did the job of a rover, crumbed a marking contest in the goal square and kicked the ball just inches past my outstretched arms for a goal. It was the worst kind of chaos.

All of which probably meant the context wasn't ideal for me to have a conversation with someone in the Collingwood cheer squad who had abused me. But that was what I was about to do.

After the usual ritual of shaking hands with the opposition, I broke away from my teammates and jogged towards the Ponsford Stand. The moment I'd been preparing for had arrived. As I got closer to the cheer squad, I could sense their shock; I could almost hear them thinking, *Is he really coming over to us?* They all knew exactly what had happened during the second quarter, and exactly why I was heading their way.

I spotted the guy who had abused me: he was sitting more or less on his own, leaning against the fence, looking around, still drunk. When he saw me he looked rattled, like he knew what was coming. It probably didn't help that a security guard was close by too.

I began speaking to him quietly and calmly, but I'd barely got a word out before we'd attracted a crowd. His mate was the first to speak up, and he was surprisingly genuine and apologetic, if a little sweary.

'Bachar, what he did was completely f★★★ing wrong. He's a completely different f★★★ing person when he's drunk. He's a f★★★ing idiot. He just goes off!'

Soon, more of the cheer squad came over to join us. Again, they were surprisingly supportive, telling me that what this guy had said was unacceptable, and that they were going to report him. Maybe the fact they'd won the game had put them in a more generous mood. Whatever the reason, it was a lovely gesture of support, but it wasn't what I had in mind.

As the crowd got larger, the security guard began gesturing with his hands, as if to ask me whether I wanted him to get involved. I put my hand out, telling him to stop, then raised my voice to the crowd that had gathered.

'Stop, please, everyone. Just relax. Just settle down and let me talk here.' Soon enough, they did. I began addressing the one person whose insult had started it, but I knew I was really speaking to a whole group.

'You don't know who I am, so how can you abuse me like that?' I began. 'Seriously, if I was what you called me, would I have the ability to come over and have a decent chat with you? Someone else in my position would go and report this straightaway. Have a look at the security guard – he wants to intervene. I could have you ejected and make sure you never watch another Collingwood game again, because what you said isn't right. I'm not going to do that. I'm going to be a different person. I'm going to teach you something. Islam is not a religion of destruction. Islam's a religion of peace. It's not what you think it is, and I wish more people knew that.'

We spoke for two or three minutes. Much like the cheer squad members around him, the man was very apologetic. 'I'm so sorry,' he said. 'I totally understand. I'm so sorry. It will never ever happen again.'

You can never know with these things, but I hoped I'd reached him in some way – that he wouldn't do something like that again, and might even intervene if he saw others doing it. Or maybe he was too drunk to remember much of it. In any case, we parted ways and I felt it was done.

As I walked off the ground, Richmond's media manager asked me what had happened. I explained, but insisted: 'I don't want to make a big deal of this. I don't want it to go any further. I've already dealt with it.' Maybe if the Collingwood supporter at the centre of the incident hadn't been so remorseful, it might have been different. Maybe if the rest of the cheer squad had chosen to attack me rather than side with me, I might have felt it was worth escalating. I can't say for sure what I'd do in that situation, because I'm glad to say I've never faced it. But as it happened, my Plan A had worked. I felt like I'd dealt with it constructively.

Meanwhile, the broadcast cameras had spotted us chatting, leading the television commentators to wonder what was going on. Ali Fahour was watching at home, and called me to find out, partly as a friend, and partly in his role as the AFL's Multicultural Manager. I told him the story, explained that I'd done what I set out to do, and that as far as I was concerned it was over. But Ali had to tell the AFL's Integrity

Unit and the media team, because after everything the AFL had been through with the abuse Adam Goodes had suffered, it was taking a zero-tolerance approach to these sorts of incidents. The last thing they wanted was to be caught out if the incident broke in the media.

To their credit, everyone at the AFL was very supportive of me, making it clear that they would be happy to pursue the matter more aggressively. I could also sense that the story was growing, because Collingwood president Eddie McGuire texted me to offer his support, too. But the last thing I wanted was for the matter to become a big story. Aside from anything else, I'd given this guy my word that I would leave it there, and I didn't want to break my promise to him. Not only would that be unnecessary, it would be an un-Islamic thing to do. Ali made my position clear to the AFL: 'If anything changes come Monday once everything's calmed down, he'll let you know, but he doesn't want to make a big deal of it.' The story disappeared with barely a ripple.

When the media had me surrounded after the incident at the Melbourne game the previous year, I only gave them a few simple lines, but they captured the way I see these things. 'It's just sad to hear it, especially in this day and age with the way that we celebrate diversity and celebrate all different cultures,' I said. 'It's something that we shouldn't accept within our society. We've come a long way and it is definitely a minority – it's not the majority of Australians.'

That last point is an important one. These are sad events, but the tensions are generally caused by a minority. Most people tend to approach others with goodwill, and it's important to remember that before we regard each other with too much suspicion. I could easily have assumed the Collingwood cheer squad would handle the situation differently to the way they did, but my suspicions would have been misguided. And the only reason we knew about the Melbourne case at all was that a non-Muslim had found the comment unacceptable and stood up for me. He was the one who drove Richmond to lodge an official complaint, which led to John Burns saying that even though he had 'no recollection of making an offensive remark . . . the idea that something I have said has offended someone is mortifying to me'. Seeing my club take that stand and send the message that, as a society, we shouldn't tolerate that kind of behaviour made me proud. The truth was that I didn't need to play a role because the club was already leading on the issue, laying down a marker for what kind of society it thought we should be.

But I know that if I want to help build a more cohesive society, there's more to do than just deal with prejudice when it arises. I've always believed that it is just as important to empower the Muslim community too, so its members feel more confident in themselves, and more like they belong in this country.

In fact, this is the bit I understood clearly from the very start of my career. Straightaway I could see the effect I had on Muslim youth when I met them: how they'd listen attentively when I spoke, how I was an authority in their lives, rightly or wrongly. I was swamped with requests to give talks at Islamic schools, at community functions and at mosques. Ali Fahour used to handle the requests from multicultural community groups, and the AFL was keen for me to help them promote diversity. Ali shielded me from a lot of them, but even so he estimates that I ended up doing something like about 50 appearances in my first two years at Essendon. And because of the duty I felt, I'd stay there until every last person who wanted a photo with me got one.

One of the things that comes with being from a minority group and succeeding is that you're made into a role model well ahead of time. For most AFL players, such attention follows seniority and stardom. It's not common for someone in their first year, or who hasn't even been drafted yet. It was a lot for my 18-year-old shoulders to carry.

In fact, it was just about impossible to live up to this expectation. Most people don't understand how hard it is even to play a single AFL game, let alone to hold your place in such a ruthless industry. To be a role model when you're battling to establish yourself is a recipe for failure, because you'll almost inevitably end up letting people down. I felt that most keenly when I was struggling to get selected at Essendon. It's one thing to have family and friends asking why you aren't getting a game, but having an entire community that has pinned its hopes on you do the same adds another level of pressure. That was especially true in a community like mine, because I was always interacting with them at the mosque or at community festivals. Some even asked me if I had retired, which was probably the hardest thing to hear.

Then there was the negative talk. I wouldn't hear things directly from people, but it would get back to me one way or another that certain people in the community were saying

I was overrated, a mediocre player who wouldn't get far. I was left with this mix of huge community expectation coupled with community criticism – they wanted me to succeed but they didn't believe I was good enough.

And the fact that my career stalled after a year or two because I was injured left me feeling powerless to respond. At that point, I didn't feel much like a role model. I didn't even feel particularly supported. What I did feel was the pressure. Right from the beginning, my career wasn't my own. It came with responsibilities, and I felt like I was failing to meet them. That was an awful feeling.

So 2011 turned out to be a crucial year, for two main reasons. First, I started playing for Richmond, which marked the most profound turning point in my playing career. Second, it was the year Ali Fahour left Essendon to work for the AFL as its Multicultural Manager, which became a profound turning point in my life off the field.

It began straightaway, when he contacted me to tell me about his idea to appoint a series of players as Multicultural Ambassadors. He wanted me to be the first, and he told me he was also planning to contact Majak Daw and Nic Naitanui. Under the terms of the contract, I would go into the AFL headquarters one day each week to be involved in multicultural programs there, and I was to support the AFL's multicultural strategy in whatever way I could.

The offer came at a good time in my life, because I was struggling to figure out what I might do off the field after football. I'd already done bits and pieces for the AFL's multicultural programs, and because I trusted Ali I thought this could perhaps grow into something more significant, even the kind of thing I was looking to leave behind. When I was younger, I'd started studying education, thinking I might become a teacher, but it wasn't for me. I'd also started a building course and done some property development. But it wasn't enough. This was, and I jumped at the chance. We just didn't yet know exactly what the job looked like.

'What is it that you want to do?' asked Ali. 'Forget the multicultural program for a moment. What are you passionate about, what do you want to build, what do you want to get involved in?'

'Can it be something to do with our community?' I replied. 'I really want to give back to them.'

I knew the AFL had been working to promote multi-culturalism within the football industry and to its fans, but at this point there was nothing for the Muslim community itself, and I was in a unique position to fill that gap. It was obvious to me from my childhood that there were so many Muslims who loved footy to bits, but they seemed to be separated from the broader culture of the game. They might be playing in clubs like my brothers did, which are so dominated by their own ethnic group that they don't find a way beyond it. That could also mean they have talent that remains untapped, because they can't access the best coaching. I was fortunate to have played lots of great club and representative football as a kid, but I was also denied the opportunity so many other draftees had of playing school footy. While schools like Assumption College, Marcellin College, Carey Grammar and Caulfield Grammar were a virtual conveyer belt of AFL players, the Islamic school

I went to didn't play interschool football at all. I could see that there were so many ways Muslim kids could have a better experience with the game.

Around this time, I was growing in confidence as a person. I was playing regularly and feeling valued at Richmond, and had already developed a strong bond with Damien Hardwick and some of my teammates. Very quickly I felt I belonged at Punt Road more than I ever had at Essendon. And probably as a result, the negative chatter about me from the Muslim community had died down. I felt more like I had their backing and could be a leader without feeling self-conscious about it.

'What if we set up an academy?' asked Ali.

It sounds like something a university or one of those enormous European soccer clubs would do, not something two Leb footballers might throw together. But Ali was convinced it could work because he'd seen similar examples at the AFL, especially within the Indigenous program. There was the Kickstart Program, where the most talented Indigenous under-15s attended a high-performance camp that focused on both football and life skills. The best of those kids qualified for the Flying Boomerangs and did a three-day or five-day camp that gave them access to an elite training environment, but also involved sessions on cultural identity and leadership.

That sounded like something we could create for our community. It also combined the two things I wanted most for young Muslims: football, and strength and pride in their Islamic identity. I was in. We decided to set up the Bachar Houli Academy for Muslim kids in Victoria.

'But you have to go do the work,' Ali warned. 'I'm not going to do it for you. You have to develop the program, figure out what it looks like, as well as promote it.'

This was a time when I barely knew how to turn on a computer. Whatever the position that comes before 'scratch' is called, that's where I was starting from. But I was so passionate about the idea that I was prepared to learn whatever I needed to. And when the first camp took place in 2012, we had 50 kids participating, and I insisted on running the three days myself. I devised the schedule, led the education sessions and the prayers, and even set up the cones on the ground. I was determined. I was into this.

The remarkable thing was that doing this work actually helped my football. Sure, I was becoming older and more experienced as a player, but there's no doubt the sense of purpose the academy gave me was a big factor too.

'What else do you want to do?' asked Ali after that first program was a success. 'What's next?'

The camps would stay, but Ali was already looking to add more programs, to make the academy grow. I saw an opportunity to address one of the big regrets of my childhood.

'Bro, I went to an Islamic school and I never got to play interschool sport. How about we get all the Islamic schools together and run a football competition?'

The Bachar Houli Cup was born. The idea was to use interschool sport as a way of encouraging Muslim kids to join their local footy clubs. They'd get introduced to the game in a friendly environment where they had nothing to fear, they'd gain confidence in the game from the experience, and some might feel ready to go out into the broader football world. We'd also offer 30 or so kids a place in the academy program.

On it went. Year after year we added programs addressing a broader range of issues: sport, leadership, even employment, hence the name change from the Bachar Houli Academy to Bachar Houli Programs. It meant a lot to me, but I didn't really understand how much until my football career reached that fork in the road at the end of the 2016 season, when, as I discussed earlier, I seriously contemplated walking away from the game.

Looking back, I don't really know how close I got to leaving. It felt real at the time, and I remember all kinds of conflicting thoughts within me. I also remember thinking about all the standard reasons to keep going: football doesn't last long and I might regret retiring; I was unlikely to earn a similar amount of money in a different job – all that.

But the decisive thing for me was that, deep down, I knew I was a role model for Muslims, and I had a job to do. I recognised that I'd been given a unique opportunity to reach so many more people than I ever would in retirement. Bachar Houli Programs had been successful, but when I thought hard about it, I realised it could be so much more. In fact, I had a strong sense that it had to be, and that it would be impossible to achieve that unless I was still playing, even if I kept working on it as an employee of the AFL.

Football gives players a powerful platform, but that power erodes as soon as you no longer play. Only as a player was I able to help get the AFL to set aside space for prayer rooms at AFL venues, for example. When I asked the AFL to do this,

Andrew Demetriou, who was the CEO at the time, said he was surprised no one had thought of it before. But that was exactly the point: there had been no one there who would think of it.

Ultimately, I concluded that walking away from the game would have been a selfish act on my part. I represented a big community, and I would be letting them down. I would fail to leave a legacy, and I would have failed as a Muslim.

I'd rediscovered my purpose as a footballer, and it rapidly changed my attitude towards the game. I attacked everything – my football and my programs – with energy and enthusiasm because I felt like I was on a mission. And I knew from experience that when I fully embraced my academy work, my football improved too.

I could never have known that premierships and representative honours were ahead of me. I'm stunned when I think about what I'd have missed out on, had I retired, and how much greater my platform for building something long-lasting is now. Obviously, I don't expect everyone else to see it this way, but I truly believe this was the answer to the prayers I said on *hajj* in 2016. God knew what was best for me, and had plans that were better than mine.

Today, I can look happily at what I've used that platform to build. Having started with one academy camp, my team and I now run 13 programs worth around $1 million per year. There are now four football academies – for men and women, juniors and seniors – there's an employment program for ten unemployed young Muslims, and there's an institute specifically for Muslim girls, focusing on sport and leadership. There's also the elite performance camp, where I take the most talented footballers overseas to train at the best high-performance facilities I can get access to. And of course there's the annual AFL *iftar* in Ramadan, because you're not a serious Islamic organisation if you don't have an *iftar*! Something like 35,000 kids and 30 Islamic schools have been involved in all this.

We have five corporate partners, as well as partnerships with both the federal and Victorian governments. A lot of that is down to Ali's brilliance at getting a project to grow, but he also forced me to invest in relationships with people. Once, Ali used to bring me along to a meeting with government ministers with firm instructions: 'Tell them your story and then shut up!' These days he trusts me more, because I've built firm relationships with successive prime ministers and attorneys-general. I've needed to do likewise with the AFL and MCC executives. It's not my natural habitat, but now it's a major part of my world. Perhaps the most gratifying thing is that these people's support is a sign that they trust my character. I can be confident that I've represented Islam the best I could, and that my presence has made a difference to people's lives.

In January 2020 we established the Bachar Houli Foundation, which oversees all the programs we've developed. It might be the greatest thing I've ever done. After playing 200 games, winning two premierships and being selected as an All-Australian, I'm happy with my football career. Having set up the Bachar Houli Foundation, I'm happy to retire.

At about 8:00 am the morning after the 2019 Grand Final, I returned to the MCG with a team of young Muslims representing the Bachar Houli Academy. I was coaching them in a game against a team from Ajax, a famous Jewish football club in Melbourne that has been running for nearly 60 years. Some of my teammates were probably only just getting home from their first night of premiership celebrations, or perhaps they were still out. But for me there was no place I would rather have been than here, because creating something like this is the reason I play football.

To give these Muslim kids the opportunity to play in the greatest stadium in the world, fresh from having hosted the greatest event in the Australian sporting calendar, was to give them an experience they would remember for the rest of their lives, and which might even be a turning point for some of them. To see them play Ajax, and build a bridge between young men in the Muslim and Jewish communities over what have so often been troubled waters because of events overseas, was a source of genuine pride for me.

Maybe one of these kids is now a bit closer to believing he could one day play in the AFL. Maybe one of them will feel a bond with his Jewish countrymen he otherwise wouldn't have. And if things go well, maybe most of them will grow up as proud Australian Muslims who feel fully part of their society, who have the confidence to respond to whatever tests of discrimination they might face in their lives by being themselves and being open to others, and who are grateful for the many blessings they have in life. I'd love to see a Muslim AFL premiership captain. But if that doesn't happen, I'd settle for the rest.

All Muslims are ambassadors for Islam. Whether we want to be or not. Whether we've sought this out or not. Whether we're students, footballers, mechanics or accountants, we might be the only window other Australians have into Islam, a means of correcting its unfair portrayal in the media. Our role is always important, whether it's one that brings public attention or not. That doesn't mean we all have to be teachers, or even particularly knowledgeable. But we are obliged to show good character: to be honest, to have smiles on our faces, to be a source of warmth, love and generosity for others. If I could choose only one thing for which I was remembered, it would be my character. Whenever I find myself addressing a Muslim audience, and especially when talking to my academy kids, that's what I always end up saying. In my experience, a lot of young Muslims feel they have to stray from Islam to earn people's respect. My belief, and my message, is the opposite: that doing the right thing and being proud of your identity and beliefs will bring you real success – and even more than that, respect for yourself and your faith.

It's not always comfortable to be an ambassador, because we're all flawed human beings who sometimes need a chance to be our imperfect selves. But as difficult as it can be to know that you're always on show in your life for reasons that may have little to do with you personally, it's also an honour. The best way to take this is to understand that you've been placed in a particular time and place for a particular role. 'Allah does not burden a soul with more than it can bear,' says the Qur'an (2:286). The greater the task, the greater the compliment.

All I can hope is that, with whatever I leave behind with my football career, I will have shown myself worthy of having been gifted it.

ACKNOWLEDGEMENTS

THIS BOOK IS THE PRODUCT of a lifetime of work, love and play. It exists thanks to those who have helped me along the way, made me who I am, and inspired me in what I've done.

So I begin at the only place a Muslim should, with Allah, the Most Gracious, Most Merciful, to whom I owe any success I've enjoyed and to whom I dedicate my life, health, wealth and death, and who gave me the gift of sending the prophet Muhammad as the greatest example to follow.

Then the people who have made me: my family and friends.

My dad (Malek) and my mum (Yamama) are my heroes. Dad, it might have taken you a couple years to embrace my football, but once you did, your support was on another level. You taught me respect and patience at their best, which today is needed more than ever. And Mum, your love has been endless, even when you tried to convince me Middle Eastern food was the best pre-game meal!

My wife, Rouba, is the most unselfish human being I have ever met. Rouba, I've still never heard you raise your voice. My AFL journey and success has come from your patience, love, support and care. Allah has given me a wife who is perfect for me. And after three blessed children, you are the most beautiful woman in the world and bring coolness to my eyes and heart, *alhamdulillah*.

My siblings' contributions are so much bigger than a book can capture. You've all stuck with me through thick and thin, and jumped ship with me from team to team with total passion. I'll never forget the joy on all your faces as you shared in two premierships; you were a huge part of them. And I have to include Rash in this category, who was so much like an older brother to me, and who always believed I would make it to the top level even though he tried to get me into music back when he was a DJ. May Allah have mercy on Umm Rashid (who makes the best lasagne ever!).

To Wally, my fishing and hunting buddy who's always ready to drop everything instantly to lend a hand, and who encouraged me to 'go with what your heart tells you – you know what's best for you'; to Sheikh Abdullah, who has invested in me so much for the past decade and given me the greatest blessing of learning to recite the Qur'an correctly; and to Selim, who gave me invaluable spiritual advice when I had periods of doubt in my footy, and amazing home-cooked food on my long lunch breaks while at Essendon. You're a terrific mentor, strong community leader, and even a comedian! You have all changed my life.

And to my best mate, Maher. Well, well ... Maher, boy! I know you only get a single mention in this book, but I also know you're a person who hates his name being mentioned and who prefers to be rewarded by the greatest rewarder there is. Brother, it's a credit how much you have turned your life around from a young troublemaker to a successful builder running some huge projects, *masha Allah, tabarak Allah*. You're by far the most generous human being I have ever met; even when you only literally had two dollars in your pocket you managed to give five dollars to charity – the true definition of a giver whose left hand doesn't know what his right hand has given. You have taught me always to rely on Allah when it comes to sustenance: to give, and trust that the One from above will never, ever leave you unanswered. It's so true! *Jazak Allah khayr, habibi.*

On the football front, there are several people to whom I owe my AFL career. To my mentor, Mohamed Bakkar – mate, where do I start? No one wanted the AFL for me more than you, brother. No money can ever repay the invest-ment you made throughout my teenage years. You rode the bumps, the highs and lows, and always kept me going no matter what.

To Ziggy Kaddour: I will never forget how you put an arm around me and showed me the path to becoming an AFL player. You taught me maturity, and the dos and don'ts of life and footy, and, fair dinkum, who's who. I know you will know what I mean by this.

Thanks to my manager, Nigel Carmody, who has guided so many major decisions from the moment I entered the AFL right up to the writing of this book. 'Are you crazy? How is this possible? There's nothing to tell.' I said when you suggested it. 'Well, you're in for a surprise,' you replied. Nigel, like so often, you were right. Thank you dearly for all your service and friendship.

Kevin Sheedy had faith in me and allowed me to fulfil my dream. Your contribution to making the game diverse and inclusive will be remembered forever. And John Quinn made it possible for me to uphold my values as an Australian Muslim while playing at the highest level. Quinny, I felt lost in many ways when you left Essendon, but I'm glad I can still call you a close mate even after 14 years.

Blair Hartley and Damien Hardwick gave me a second chance at Richmond and believed I could play a part in taking our great club into a successful era. Your support has changed my life. And to my mates Trent Cotchin and Ivan Maric, with whom I share so much in common: you are amazing people, and I can count on you forever.

Then there are those to whom I owe my legacy. Ali Fahour, bro, you play a huge part in this book, and rightfully so. I thought at one stage we were writing the Ali Fahour story! You're a true brother who's driven my off-field development. I can't wait to continue the work with the Bachar Houli Foundation after football, *insha Allah*, as we have much more to offer.

To Andrew Dillon at the AFL, who gave me an opportunity nine years ago to take the first steps towards creating the

Foundation: whenever I have needed support, leadership or had reached my ceiling, you have been there to help, guide and support. I'm grateful for the opportunities you have provided and your personal commitment to see me grow as a person. Sorry you always had to get the phone calls for help!

And to the Bachar Houli Foundation team of Ali Faraj, Kashif Bouns, Emad Elkheir, Ahmed Saad and Adam Saad: your passion, vision and commitment make this work incredibly rewarding. It never feels like a job when I get to spend quality time on programs with such incredible people. Your friendship and guidance make this work possible.

To Waleed Aly, who helped me with this book: I've truly enjoyed the past 18 months catching up in person, long late-night phone interviews, and finally, Zoom meetings. I could only imagine trying to do this with a writer who didn't understand the terminology in Arabic. I admire the way you handle yourself and have watched you grow from the *Salam Cafe* days into a leading broadcaster on national television and radio. Where next? Maybe PM!

And finally, to my hundreds of passionate cousins, friends and extended community. I know I don't do this on my own, or for myself. A massive thank you, and may Allah bless you and your families.

INDEX

Discover a
new favourite

Visit **penguin.com.au/readmore**